Mission Viejo Library
25209 Marguerite Parkway
Mission Viejo, CA 9269
FEB 0 2 1999

3/16/02

D0406925

ALSO BY NEAL GABLER

Winchell: Gossip, Power and
the Culture of Celebrity
(1994)

An Empire of Their Own:
How the Jews Invented Hollywood
(1988)

Life the Movie

Life
the Movie

How Entertainment
Conquered Reality

NEAL GABLER

ALFRED A. KNOPF   New York

1998

This Is a Borzoi Book
Published by Alfred A. Knopf, Inc.

Copyright © 1998 by Neal Gabler

All rights reserved under International and
Pan-American Copyright Conventions. Published in
the United States by Alfred A. Knopf, Inc., New York,
and simultaneously in Canada by Random House of
Canada Limited, Toronto. Distributed by Random House,
Inc., New York.

www.randomhouse.com

Library of Congress Cataloging-in-Publication Data
Gabler, Neal.
Life the movie: how entertainment conquered reality /
by Neal Gabler.—1st ed.
p.   cm.
Includes bibliographical references and index.
ISBN 0-679-41752-4 (alk. paper)
1. Motion pictures—Social aspects—United States.
2. Motion pictures—United States—Influence.
3. Television broadcasting—Social aspects—United States.
4. Television broadcasting—United States—Influence.   I. Title.
PN1995.9.S6G23   1998
302.23'43'0973—dc21   98-36699
CIP

Manufactured in the United States of America
Published November 18, 1998
Second Printing, December 1998

Once again,
for my beloved daughters,
Laurel and Tanne,
And for all those
on the other side of the glass

What if the world is some kind of—of *show*! . . . What if we are all only talent assembled by the Great Talent Scout Up Above! The Great Show of Life! Starring Everybody! Suppose entertainment is the Purpose of Life!

—PHILIP ROTH
"On the Air" (1970)

Contents

Introduction   3

1. The Republic of Entertainment   11
2. The Two-Dimensional Society   53
3. The Secondary Effect   96
4. The Human Entertainment   143
5. The Mediated Self   192

Notes   245
A Select Bibliography   279
Acknowledgments   289
Index   291

Life the Movie

Introduction

THOUGH HE couldn't possibly have known it at the time, in 1960 the novelist Philip Roth posed what would become one of the central questions of our age: How could fiction possibly compete with the stories authored by real life? As anyone could see from browsing the daily newspapers, life had become so strange, its convolutions so mind-boggling that, Roth lamented, the "American writer in the middle of the twentieth century has his hands full in trying to understand, and then describe, and then make *credible* much of American reality. It stupefies, it sickens, it infuriates, and finally it is even a kind of embarrassment to one's own meager imagination. The actuality is continually outdoing our talents, and the culture tosses up figures almost daily that are the envy of every novelist."

At virtually the same time Roth was describing the challenge of reality to fiction, historian Daniel Boorstin, in his pathbreaking study *The Image: A Guide to Pseudo-Events in America*, was describing how everywhere the fabricated, the inauthentic and the theatrical were driving out the natural, the genuine and the spontaneous from life until reality itself had been converted into stagecraft. As Boorstin saw it, Americans increasingly lived in a "world where fantasy is more real than reality," and he warned, "We risk being the first people in history to have been able to make their illusions so vivid, so persuasive, so 'realistic' that they can live in them."

Roth was talking about real-life melodrama in America, and Boorstin about the deliberate manipulation of reality in America, but both were addressing what, in hindsight, was the same root phenomenon, one that may very well qualify as the single most important cultural transformation in this country in the twentieth century. What they recognized was that life itself was gradually becoming a medium all its own, like television, radio, print and film, and that all of us were becoming at once performance artists in and audiences for a grand, ongoing show—a show that was, as Roth noted, often far richer, more complex and more compelling than anything conceived for the more conventional media. In short, life was becoming a movie.

To compare life to a movie is not to say, as the cliché has it, that life imitates art, though surely there is truth to that. Nor is it to say that life has devised its own artistic methods and thus reversed the process—art imitates life—though that also is true, as one can see from the number of novels, movies and television programs that have been inspired by real-life events. Rather it is to say that after decades of public-relations contrivances and media hype, and after decades more of steady pounding by an array of social forces that have alerted each of us personally to the power of performance, life has *become* art, so that the two are now indistinguishable from each other. Or, to rework an aphorism of the poet Stéphane Mallarmé, the world doesn't exist to end in a book; when life is a medium, books and every other imaginative form exist to end in a world.

One need look no further than the daily news to realize how true this is now. It does not minimize the media excesses of the penny press, the yellow press and the original tabloids, to recognize that in the nearly forty years since Roth's essay the news has become a continuous stream of what one might call "lifies"— movies written in the medium of life, projected on the screen of life and exhibited in the multiplexes of the traditional media which are increasingly dependent upon the life medium. The murder trial of former football star O. J. Simpson, the life and death of Diana, Princess of Wales, the ongoing soap-operatic sagas of Elizabeth Taylor or television talk show hostess Oprah Winfrey, the shooting of Long Island housewife Mary Jo Buttafuoco by her husband's seventeen-year-old paramour, the bombing of the federal office building in Oklahoma City by right-wing dissidents, the repeated allegations of extramarital dalliances by President Bill Clinton, to name only a handful of literally thousands of episodes life generates—these are the new blockbusters that preoccupy the traditional media and dominate the national conversation for weeks, sometimes months or even years at a time, while ordinary entertainments quickly evanesce.

But however much we may be preoccupied with them, it is not just these "lifies" that make life a movie. As Boorstin observed, the deliberate application of the techniques of theater to politics, religion, education, literature, commerce, warfare, crime, *everything,* has converted them into branches of show business, where the overriding objective is getting and satisfying an audience. Acting like a cultural Ebola virus, entertainment has even invaded organisms no one would ever have imagined could provide amusement. Dr. Timothy Leary, onetime proponent of hallucinogens, turned his death into entertainment by using his computer Web page to chronicle his deterioration from prostate cancer, a show which ended with a video of him drinking a toxic cocktail in what he called a "visible, interactive suicide." A group of teenage thugs in Washington, D.C., videotaped their depredations, even posing for the camera after beating a victim while an "audience" of by-standers cheered. And one enterprising entrepreneur converted a former Nazi command post on the eastern front in Poland into a theme resort, while another planned an amusement park outside Berlin with the motif of East Germany under communism.

What traditional entertainment always promised was to transport us from our daily problems, to enable us to escape from the travails of life. Analyzing the mechanism through which this was achieved, literary scholar Michael Wood in his book *America in the Movies* described our films as a "rearrangement of our problems into shapes which tame them, which disperse them to the margins of our attention," where we can forget about them. This is what we really mean when we call entertainment "escapist": We escape from life by escaping into the neat narrative formulas in which most entertainments are packaged. Still, with movies there was always the assumption that the escape was temporary. At the end of the film one had to leave the theater and reenter the maelstrom of real life.

When life itself is an entertainment medium, however, this process is obviously altered. Lewis Carroll, commenting on a vogue among nineteenth-century cartographers for ever larger and more detailed maps, once cautioned that the maps might get so large they would interfere with agriculture, and waggishly suggested that the earth be used as a map of itself instead. Carroll's is an apt analogy for the new relationship between entertainment and life. By conflating the two and converting everything from the kidnapping of the Lindbergh baby to the marital misadventures of Elizabeth Taylor into entertainments that transport us from our problems, we need never leave the theater's comfort. We can remain constantly distracted. Or, put another way, we have finally learned how to escape from life into life.

While there are certainly those who will disapprove, one is almost compelled to admit that turning life into escapist entertainment is a perversely ingenious adaptation to the turbulence and tumult of modern existence. Why worry about the seemingly intractable problems of society when you can simply declare "It's morning in America," as President Reagan did in his 1984 reelection campaign, and have yourself a long-running Frank Capra movie right down to the aw-shucks hero? Why fret over the lack of national purpose during the doldrums of the post–Cold War era when you can convert a shooting war into a real-life war movie that reaffirms your destiny, as America did in 1991 with the Gulf War? Movies have always been a form of wish fulfillment. Why not life?

The conversion of life into an entertainment medium could never have succeeded, however, if those who attend the life movie hadn't discovered what the early movie producers had discovered years before: that audiences need some point of identification if the show is really to engross them. For the movies the solution was stars. For the life movie it is celebrity. Though stardom in any form automatically confers celebrity, it is just as likely now to be granted to diet gurus, fashion designers and their so-called supermodels, lawyers, political pundits, hairdressers, intellectuals, businessmen, journalists, criminals—anyone who happens to appear, however fleetingly, on the radar of the traditional media and is thus sprung from the anonymous mass. The only prerequisite is publicity.

Celebrity is by now old news, but it says a great deal about modern America that no society has ever had as many celebrities as ours or has revered them as intensely. Not only are celebrities the protagonists of our news, the subjects of our daily discourse and the repositories of our values, but they have also embedded themselves so deeply in our consciousness that many individuals profess feeling closer to, and more passionate about, them than about their own primary relationships: Witness the torrents of grief unleashed by the sudden death of Princess Diana in 1997, or the mourners who told television interviewers that her funeral was the saddest day of their lives. As Diana confirmed, celebrity is the modern state of grace—the condition in the life movie to which nearly everyone aspires. Once we sat in movie theaters dreaming of stardom. Now we live in a movie dreaming of celebrity.

Yet this is not nearly as passive as it may sound. While the general public is an audience for the life movie, it is also an active participant in it. An ever-growing segment of the American economy is now devoted to designing, building and then dressing the sets in which we live, work, shop and play; to creating our costumes; to making our hair shine and our faces glow; to slenderizing our bodies; to supplying our props—all so that we can appropriate the trappings of celebrity, if not the actuality of it, for the life movie. We even have celebrities—for example, lifestyle adviser Martha Stewart—who are essentially drama coaches in the life movie, instructing us in how to make our own lives more closely approximate the movie in our mind's eye.

Of course, not everyone is mesmerized. Many have deplored the effects of entertainment and celebrity on America, and there is certainly much to deplore. While an entertainment-driven, celebrity-oriented society is not necessarily one that destroys all moral value, as some would have it, it *is* one in which the standard of value is whether or not something can grab and then hold the public's attention. It is a society in which those things that do not conform—for example, serious literature, serious political debate, serious ideas, serious anything—are more likely to be compromised or marginalized than ever before. It is a society in which celebrities become paragons because they are the ones who have learned how to steal the spotlight, no matter what they have done to steal it. And at the most personal level, it is a society in which individuals have learned to prize social skills that permit them, like actors, to assume whatever role the occasion demands and to "perform" their lives rather than just live them. The result is that *Homo sapiens* is rapidly becoming *Homo scaenicus*—man the entertainer.

As the culture submits to the tyranny of entertainment, as life becomes a movie, critics complain that America has devolved into a "carnival culture" or "trash culture," where everything is coarsened, vulgarized and trivialized, where the meretricious is more likely to be rewarded than the truly deserving and where bonds of community that were once forged by shared moral values and traditions are now forged by tabloid headlines, gossip and media. "We had fed the heart on fantasies," wrote William Butler Yeats. "The heart's grown brutal from the fare."

No doubt Americans who hold this view of modern culture will want a program of action that will help us "disenchant" ourselves and restore our reality and our values. One can certainly sympathize with them. But to pretend that one can provide a remedy would be not only naive but duplicitous, since it would necessarily indulge the same sort of fantasy that got us here in the first place: that problems, like crises in movies, are susceptible to simple narrative solutions. You simply present a monster in the first reel and then have the hero vanquish it in the last.

Anyone looking for heroes, solutions or even high dudgeon will not find them here. While this book is not without an attitude, particularly toward some of the absurdities to which entertainment has driven us, readers are here forewarned that it is diagnostic rather than prescriptive, an investigation rather than a screed. Its object is to provide a new context for something so gargantuan that it has slid beyond the borders of context and frequently beyond our powers of analysis. That context is entertainment.

There is obviously no such thing as a unified field theory of American culture, but if there were, one could do worse than to lay much of what has happened in late-twentieth-century America to the corrosive effects of entertainment rather than to the effects of politics or economics, the usual suspects. Indeed, Karl Marx and Joseph Schumpeter both seem to have been wrong. It is not any ism but entertainment that is arguably the most pervasive, powerful and ineluctable force of our time—a force so overwhelming that it has finally metastasized into life.

As a tool of analysis, entertainment may just be what under-girds and unites ideas as disparate as Boorstin's theory of manu-factured reality, Marshall McLuhan's doctrine of media deter-minism, the deconstructionist notion that culture is actually a collectively scripted text, and so much of the general perspective we call postmodernism. If so, understanding how and why enter-tainment permeates life as it does may enable us to comprehend the brave and strange new world in which we live—the world of postreality.

What Daniel Boorstin said of *The Image* may also be true of this volume: "This is a large subject for a small book. Yet it is too large for a big book." It is a vast territory we tread, nothing less than life itself, and no one could possibly chart it all. Every day the life medium generates new episodes. Every day someone finds more inventive applications for its use. The profusion is so bewil-dering that the Italian semiotician Umberto Eco, acknowledging the voraciousness of the mass media to devour everything, be-lieved we could ease our minds around the issue only by taking a whole new cognitive approach to our reality. "We have to start again from the beginning," Eco wrote, "asking one another what's going on."

This book is an attempt to start again and ask what's going on: to understand why entertainment became the primary value of American life, to examine what the implications have been for our public culture and to analyze how it has changed and continues to change our lives.

Chapter One

The Republic of Entertainment

I

WHAT *Is* ENTERTAINMENT?

ALMOST FROM the beginning, something was wrong with America. When Mrs. Frances Trollope, a very proper Englishwoman and the mother of the future novelist Anthony Trollope, toured the United States in 1828, she was revolted by the casual boorishness she found. "One man in the pit was seized with a violent fit of vomiting, which appeared not in the least to annoy or surprise his neighbors," she wrote of a visit to a theater in the nation's capital. "The spitting was incessant; and not one in ten of the male part of the illustrious legislative audience sat according to the usual custom of human beings; the legs were thrown sometimes over the front of the box, sometimes over the side of it. . . ." Other European visitors made similar observations. Americans were ill-mannered, disrespectful, rowdy, unkempt, illiterate, malodorous. After his own visit, Matthew Arnold concluded that "in what concerns the higher civilization they [Americans] live in a fool's paradise."

In truth, most Americans didn't seem to know or care much about higher civilization. Whatever else one said about them—and visitors did praise their pragmatism, their industriousness, their democratic brio—the overwhelming majority were certainly not terribly cultured by European standards, and there was real doubt whether art, which one critic has described as "a kind of divine service to truth and beauty," could survive in a country where the cacophony of the masses drowned out the sweet music of more genteel souls. What especially worried America's own cultural elite was that their fellow Americans not only had little affinity for art but seemed to have an active antipathy to it.

Of course, the same thing could probably have been said at the time of the general population of any country, even France, Britain or Germany, the places from which many of America's critics came. There, as here, what was popular was seldom called art and what was called art was seldom popular. Nevertheless, there were differences between European culture and American culture besides the obvious one that European culture was hundreds of years old and American culture in the nineteenth century had scarcely been born.

For one thing, already by the mid-nineteenth century the popular culture here was much vaster than that in Europe and had permeated society much more deeply. Nostalgists may like to think of America in that time before movies and television as the land of Abraham Lincoln, Ralph Waldo Emerson, Frederic Church and Emily Dickinson, though saying so is like saying that the America of the late twentieth century was the land of Martin Luther King, Jr., John Updike, Richard Diebenkorn and Robert Lowell. It is true, but only so far as it goes. In the nineteenth century, as in the twentieth, there was another America, a much larger, more polymorphous America, one which has been expunged from most cultural histories partly because its products were not meant to endure and partly, one assumes, because many cultural historians would just as soon forget about it. This America was not genteel or high-minded. This America loved what even then scolds labeled "trash."

Trash was everywhere. The same period that saw the rise of Nathaniel Hawthorne, Herman Melville, Henry David Thoreau and Walt Whitman and would come to be called the American Renaissance for the quality of its writing, also saw the rise of vapidly sentimental but enormously popular novels like Susan Warner's *The Wide, Wide World* (1850), a logy, lachrymose tale of a young woman whose parents decamp to Europe, leaving her at the mercy of a series of mentors and tormentors; of bawdy humor almanacs that took delight in skewering polite society and celebrating impertinence; of titillating crime pamphlets that recounted the gory deeds of miscreants like Major John Mitchell, who castrated a young boy with a jagged piece of tin, or the Knapp brothers, who masterminded the murder of Captain Joseph White in hopes of gaining his inheritance and then joked about it afterwards; of a large erotic and pornographic literature; of salacious novels, like George Lippard's *The Quaker City* (1845), that ripped bodices in the service of ripping the façade off genteel hypocrisy, and of dime novels that purveyed the exploits of heroes like Buffalo Bill Cody in simple, light-footed prose that any schoolboy could understand.

Nor was the situation very different in the nonliterary precincts of the culture. While some historians have made much of the popularity of Shakespeare on the nineteenth-century American stage, it was not the sanctified Shakespeare of college English classes that those audiences enjoyed. The plays were reconceptualized, compromised, bowdlerized. Lines were cut and others freely changed, characters were consolidated, whole scenes were excised and, above all, melodramatic elements were heightened, so that only Shakespeare's basic plots survived, not his language or the depth and complexity of his themes. In addition to this dumbing down, the plays usually had to share the evening with a farce or comic opera, not to mention the variety acts that were interpolated throughout the performance: singers, dancers, acrobats, magicians, comedians. For a time there was a rage for the physically deformed.

Similarly, though opera was performed even in the American backwaters, singers seldom escaped demands for a popular song or patriotic ditty along with, and often right in the middle of, their arias. Classical music was limited to the wealthy. Most Americans seemed to prefer music that was functional, something they could dance to or sing with or tell a story through. As the century wore on, American tastes ran to earsplitting band music, which concertmaster John Philip Sousa extolled over classical music because "entertainment is of more real value to the world than technical education in music appreciation." In the visual arts, the monumental canvases of Church, Thomas Cole and Albert Bierstadt, which were exhibited in great halls as if they were widescreen movie epics, yielded to lithographs and eventually to postcards and photographs—an increase in the quantity of images that arguably led to a diminution in their quality.

Though there were clearly major differences between, say, the conventional novels of Susan Warner and the radical novels of George Lippard, nevertheless, by the lights of refined society both contributed to an effulgence of junk, the amount of which and popularity of which could not be underestimated. *The Wide, Wide World* had thirteen printings in two years, thirty-seven by century's end, and sold an estimated five hundred thousand copies—by some reckonings second in sales only to *Uncle Tom's Cabin* among books published in the nineteenth century. "I should have no chance of success while public taste is occupied with their trash," Hawthorne complained of Warner's success, "and I should be ashamed of myself if I did succeed." *The Quaker City* sold nearly as many copies. As for the juvenile dime novels that emerged in the late 1850s, individual titles sold as many as eighty thousand copies, and one publisher alone produced four million volumes in just five years, this at a time when the entire population of the country was less than twenty-five million, making the dimes, according to an 1879 *Atlantic Monthly* survey, the "greatest literary movement, in bulk, of the age. . . ."

But what almost no one seemed to have recognized then was that this flood of trash was the beginning of a cultural revolution, one that would permanently transform America's taste and change its tastemakers. Prior to the arrival of mass-produced entertainment, American culture, like European culture, had been the special preserve of the wealthy, the educated, the refined—this country's own aristocrats, virtually all of them landholders. They assumed the responsibility for determining what qualified as good because they felt they alone were capable of enjoying what one critic has called the "highest pleasure, the pleasure of complexity," which "must be learned." Not to have governed the culture would have been an abdication. "The great cultures of the past have all been elite affairs," observed the critic Dwight Macdonald, himself an elitist, "centering in small upper-class communities which had certain standards in common and which both encouraged creativity by (informed) enthusiasm and disciplined it by (informed) criticism." And so it was here.

As in Europe, the American elite's idea of culture was a rather narrowly defined notion of art. Whatever these other things were that now overwhelmed the nation—these fat sentimental tomes and slender dime novels, these crime pamphlets and rude almanacs, these stage melodramas, these coarse musicales and this loud band noise—art they certainly were not. For the custodians of culture, art was sublime. It redirected one's vision from the sensual to the intellectual, from the temporal to the eternal, from the corporeal to the spiritual, all of which made art a matter not only of aesthetics but of morality as well because its effect was to encourage one's better self. Consequently, artists were expected, as cultural historian Henry Nash Smith observed of nineteenth-century American writers, "to present images of beauty and nobility in order to inspire emulation," and "to offer readers opportunities to identify themselves with virtuous and attractive characters."

In contrast, cultural aristocrats sneered, the new popular entertainment was primarily about fun. It was about gratification rather than edification, indulgence rather than transcendence, reaction rather than contemplation, escape from moral instruction rather than submission to it. As one elitist has put it, the difference between entertainment and art is the difference between "spurious gratification and a genuine experience as a step to greater individual fulfillment." Of course entertainment could, and often did, make concessions to morality by propounding some simple homiletic lesson, if only to fend off enemies, but no one could possibly have attributed the power of entertainment to this. Rather, as critics recognized, its appeal seemed to be that it deliberately shirked the obligations of art.

Moreover, while it was a tenet of culture that art demanded effort to appreciate it, specifically intellectual effort, entertainment seemed to make no demands whatsoever, intellectual or otherwise. Art enlisted the senses, but it enlisted them in the service of the mind or soul; it was hard work rewarded by divine experience. By contrast, to the extent entertainment enlisted the mind at all, it was only in the service of the senses and emotions; it was passive response rewarded by fun. Operating on the emotions and the viscera, on the seats of irrationality and irresponsibility, entertainment was beyond the reach of intellect. As Goethe expressed it in a letter to Schiller as early as 1797, "Nonsense placed before the eyes / Has a magical right. Because it fetters the senses / The mind remains a vassal." Before the word became synonymous with "lurid," this is what critics meant when they called entertainment sensational, one of the nineteenth century's most pejorative adjectives. They meant that entertainment induced reactions by exciting the nervous system in much the same way drugs did. In fact, it was entertainment, and not, as Marx declared, religion, that was the real opiate of the masses.

Thus, dime novels were a "stimulus or opiate," fumed the Rev. Jonathan Baxter Harrison. Lyrical ballads filled man's need for "gross and violent stimulants" that also "blunt the discriminating powers of the mind," wrote William Wordsworth, obviously distinguishing his own *Lyrical Ballads* from more vulgar ones. Popular music, according to the German-born conductor Theodore Thomas, was "the sensual side of the art and has more or less the devil in it." Tocqueville was slightly more charitable in drawing the same conclusion about theater. "Most of those who frequent the amusements of the stage do not go there to seek the pleasures of the mind," he wrote, "but the keen emotions of the heart." And in what may be the most poetic description of entertainment's mindlessness, the critic Edwin Percy Whipple lacerated George Lippard's sensational novels as "the body of history without the soul, events without ideas, effects without causes,—the very atheism of narrative"—a denunciation that has been echoed in contemporary criticism of big-budget special effects films that are said to offer "increasingly jangled and incoherent narratives that also yield instantly to pleasure."

Already in the nineteenth century, the entertainment aesthetic was bigger, faster, louder, as if the desire for sensory overload were, like sex, almost a raw biological urge that one was at pains to resist. Even then audiences seemed to prefer graphic entertainments like the theater over more cerebral ones like novels. But the most convincing proof of the nexus between entertainment and sensation would not come until much later, with the arrival of the movies and television. These most popular of pastimes were also the ones that attacked the viscera most directly and stimulated the senses most actively, though entertainment would never give up its endless quest to find new ways of upping the sensory ante. Hence MTV, which testified to the fact that music alone was no longer a sufficient stimulus, high-definition and wide-screen tele-

vision, virtual-reality games and new and improved sound reproduction systems at the movies that could blast you out of your
seat.*

The sensational component of entertainment was so central to
the operation of entertainment that it was impregnated into the
word itself. The etymology of "entertainment" is in all likelihood
from the Latin *inter* (among) and *tenere* (to hold), and in its English evolution it had come to mean variously a form of servitude,
the provision of support or sustenance, the manner in which one
treated others, a discussion, receiving, holding (as in the entertainment of an idea) and hosting (as in entertaining guests), as
well as the more familiar definitions: "that which affords interest
or amusement" and a "public performance or exhibition intended
to interest or amuse."

None of these definitions had really shaken the word's Latin
origins. In one way or another, each incorporated the idea of
"holding among," including the now most common use of the
word. Entertainment—movies, rock music, pulp novels, comic
books, television, computer games—sinks its talons into us and
pulls us in, holding us captive, taking us both deeper into the work
itself and deeper into ourselves, or at least into our own emotions
and senses, before releasing us. All one has to do is watch people
filing silently out of a movie theater, their eyes vacant, their faces
slack, to see how one must *re*emerge after being *sub*merged this
way in a film. Art was said to provide *ekstasis,* which in Greek
means "letting us stand outside ourselves," presumably to lend
us perspective. But everyone knows from personal experience
that entertainment usually provides just the opposite: *inter tenere,*
pulling us into ourselves to deny us perspective.

Finally, to all these other differences was added the difference

---

* This is also why critics in the 1990s routinely used amusement park metaphors to
describe the new blockbuster films—"fun machine," "thrill ride," "joyride," "wildest movie
ride," "roller-coaster ride"—until these terms became clichés. The reviewers were only
expressing what the nineteenth-century critics of mass culture understood: that entertainment is basically a pleasurable form of sensory experience.

between the ways in which art and entertainment regarded the audience. According to the elitists, art treated each viewer, listener or reader as an individual, eliciting a unique personal response to a work. Entertainment, on the other hand, dealt with its audience as a mass, a set of statistics, a "non-man," in Dwight Macdonald's word. It denied personal taste or sensitivity or intelligence—anything that might pry the individual away from the undifferentiated lump and thus narrow the appeal of a movie or book or TV show. In other words, art was directed at *a* person; entertainment was directed at the largest possible number of *people*.

It followed as a kind of corollary that if artists seemed to create their work assuming that different spectators would have different experiences of it, entertainers created theirs by deploying familiar words, images, symbols, techniques or stories in an attempt to manipulate a spectator not only into having a particular experience but in ensuring that every member of the audience would have the same experience. That is why art is thought of as *inventional and entertainment as *conventional or formulaic; entertainment is constantly searching for a combination of elements that has predictably aroused a given response in the past, on the assumption that the same combination will more than likely arouse the same response again. As the art critic Clement Greenberg, comparing a high artist, Picasso, to a representational artist of kitsch, the Russian Repin, wrote, "Where Picasso paints *cause*, Repin paints *effect*," adding that the latter "predigests art for the spectator" and "provides him a short cut to the pleasure of art." *

---

* Formulas also help explain one of the seeming contradictions of entertainment—to wit, if it is reliant on the senses, then why is so little of it abstract, or what might be called pure stimulation? One answer is that shrewd entertainers have discovered reliable ways of eliciting responses from an audience through formulas, which is what makes them formulas in the first place. Emotions and sensations are the ends, but they are not necessarily the means. As Edgar Allan Poe, who elevated effect above all other aesthetic values, described the effectiveness of "The Raven," it is not "referrible either to accident or intuition—that the work proceeded, step by step, to its completion with the precision and rigid consequences of a mathematical problem" (*Poe: Essays and Reviews* [New York: Library of America, 1984], pp. 14–15).

In drawing comparisons between art and entertainment, the cultural aristocrats were obviously demonstrating the superiority of the former and issuing a ringing indictment of the latter without ever really defining exactly what the latter was. But despite their rhetorical overkill, and despite the fact that in the twentieth century distinctions between art and entertainment have become more artificial than ever before, if they were ever really valid, the bill of particulars against entertainment also amounted to a surprisingly accurate description of its blandishments. One does not necessarily have to cluck in disapproval to admit that entertainment is all the things its detractors say it is: fun, effortless, sensational, mindless, formulaic, predictable and subversive. In fact, one might argue that those are the very reasons so many people love it.

At the same time, it is not hard to see why cultural aristocrats in the nineteenth century and intellectuals in the twentieth hated entertainment and why they predicted, as one typical nineteenth-century critic railed, that its eventual effect would be "to overturn all morality, to poison the springs of domestic happiness, to dissolve the ties of our social order, and to involve our country in ruin."

In part their hostility sprang from their disdain for anything that had been designed primarily for fun. Fun was not something much esteemed among intellectuals. The Dutch philosopher-historian Johan Huizinga, in his epochal book *Homo Ludens: A Study of the Play-Element in Culture,* discovered that the word "fun" was of recent origin and that no other language had an exact equivalent to the English meaning, leading him to speculate that fun was neither readily understood nor fully accepted until the twentieth century. At the highest levels of culture it was taken for granted that good things were serious things. "[S]how business is amusement, faintly culpable," Umberto Eco once explained, "whereas a lecture, a Beethoven symphony, a philosophical discussion are boring experiences (and therefore 'serious'). The son who gets a bad grade at school is strictly forbidden by his parent to go to a rock concert, but may attend a cultural event (which, on the contrary, will supposedly be good for him)."

Another reason intellectuals felt such antipathy toward entertainment was their distrust of the popular sensibility. In their view, the great majority of people were lazy, stupid and infantile, distracted by fun and captivated by sensation, and thus incapable of appreciating art, much less of setting the nation's cultural agenda. Yet that was exactly what the general public seemed emboldened to do with its mass culture. *"The characteristic note of our time,"* José Ortega y Gasset urgently wrote in the 1920s, *"is the dire truth that the mediocre soul, the commonplace mind, knowing itself to be mediocre, has the gall to assert its right to mediocrity, and goes on to impose itself where it can."*

But perhaps the biggest reason why intellectuals excoriated entertainment was that they understood all too well their own precariousness in a world dominated by it. For whatever the overt content of any particular work, entertainment as a whole promulgated an unmistakable theme, one that took dead aim at the intellectuals' most cherished values. That theme was the triumph of the senses over the mind, of emotion over reason, of chaos over order, of the id over the superego, of Dionysian abandon over Apollonian harmony. Entertainment was Plato's worst nightmare. It deposed the rational and enthroned the sensational and in so doing deposed the intellectual minority and enthroned the unrefined majority.

Therein, for the intellectuals, lay utmost danger and deepest despair. They knew that in the end, after all the imprecations had rung down around it, entertainment was less about morality or even aesthetics than about power—the power to replace the old cultural order with a new one, the power to replace the sublime with fun.

II
THE AMERICAN QUESTION

STILL, THERE WAS the American question. If entertainment was fun, if it was accessible to everyone, if it provided a release from order and authority, if its sensuous appeal was so primal as to be practically biological in origin, why didn't ordinary Europeans in the nineteenth century succumb as readily as ordinary Americans did? Why was America the Republic of Entertainment, and not France or Britain or some other country? Why, even at the end of the twentieth century, was the great export of America its popular culture, the way Switzerland exported chocolates or Holland tulips?

The answers seemed to come both from distinctive characteristics of Europe that impeded entertainment and from distinctive characteristics of America that encouraged it. The role of religion was a central factor in both places. Throughout Europe, organized religion raised vigorous opposition to amusements, in explicit recognition that the values of entertainment frequently vied with those of the church. As ministers commonly expressed it, so long as man was possessed by his senses, he could not look to his spirit; so long as he was distracted, he could not focus on God. While the upper classes were still permitted to indulge in theatrical entertainments, presumably because they were not as likely to be led astray as were the less high-born, this pervasive religious disapprobation effectively restricted entertainments for the masses. At its most extreme, in Geneva, the seat of Calvinism, all theater was prohibited on the principle that leisure activity invariably corrupted.

But religion did not act alone. Its censure was reinforced by the secular cultural establishment. Every European nation had a solidly entrenched cultural aristocracy that not only dictated its society's cultural agenda, as America's own elite did, but was authoritative enough to marginalize anything it did not sanction.

As early as the Renaissance, the nobility in much of Europe had begun devising a learned high culture for itself that was separate from the popular culture of bards, itinerant players, festivals and carnivals. By the eighteenth century a middle class was emerging in Europe that slowly began easing art away from its dependence on noble patronage and making it reliant on the marketplace instead, but this was largely a matter of power and economics rather than aesthetics, since the middle class's idea of what constituted art was not terribly different from the aristocrats'. In any case, in attempting to demonstrate their own cultural sophistication, they had very little interest in lowering the barrier between high culture and low. In fact, they had a much greater stake in raising it, because doing so further distinguished them from the hordes.

Neither of these obstacles—religion or aristocratic control—impeded popular culture for very long in America. In the first place, despite Tocqueville's observation that he had found no country in which "the Christian religion retains a greater influence over the souls of men than in America," America was not a deeply religious nation, at least as far as organized religion was concerned. By one estimate, only one out of seven Americans belonged to a church in 1850, up from one out of fifteen a half century earlier. Nor did religion have the power to enforce its strictures here as it did in Europe, where it was typically supported by state authority. America had no state religion. Rather it had dozens of denominations from which one was free to choose, and even within a denomination Americans' own very active sense of democracy made church authority far less dictatorial and far more tolerant than elsewhere, if only because a dissatisfied worshipper could always leave one denomination for another.

None of this is to say that organized religion did not try to restrict amusements here just as it did in Europe. One thinks immediately of the Puritans, though they were hardly alone. As in Europe, ministers fulminated against the theater as Satan's instrument and warned congregants against submitting to its lures. (One of the most fervent crusades of the century was the campaign for Sunday laws that would have prohibited amusements on the Christian Sabbath.) But in America the condemnation had less force not only because religion here had less force generally but also because religious practice in this country was itself often so highly entertaining that it seriously undermined the obligatory expressions of contempt against entertainment.

By the mid-nineteenth century the most popular religious movement in America was evangelical Protestantism, a form of worship that would have been unrecognizable to most Europeans. Compared with religious practice in Europe, where authority was centralized, where worship was formalized and where prayer itself was mediated through church officials, evangelical Protestantism was a democratic religion—highly personal rather than hierarchical, vernacular, expressive and enthusiastic. Eschewing doctrine and restraint, evangelicals preferred emotion to theology. They believed in experiential religion, one in which, as a religious historian has described it, the "sinner had to *feel* in his very bones the smoldering of guilt, abasement, hope and assurance."

Other religious practices may have been devoted to controlling one's passion and subordinating it to reason. The evangelicals believed in releasing it. Nothing in their worship was decorous. At large, communal revival meetings that functioned as religious services, congregants were overcome by catalepsy, jerks, visions, uncontrollable fits of laughter, sudden explosions of song and even barking jags in which celebrants yapped like dogs—the depth of the feeling a testament to the depth of one's faith, the degree of irrationality a testament to the degree to which one had abandoned himself to God.

In rejecting a sedate, rational religion for an intemperate, emotional one, however, the evangelicals courted the disapproval of the better classes. Just as the mass audience was ridiculed by elitists for allowing sensation to trample reason in the cultural sphere, so evangelicals were scorned by religious traditionalists, virtually the same group as the elitists, for allowing emotion to supersede mind in the spiritual sphere. And once again the elitists were not far off the mark. They realized that America's largest religious movement was arrayed along the same battle line as entertainment—two sensationalist cannon firing at the rationalist princes of privilege.

Whether or not the leaders of evangelical Protestantism recognized the similarities and affinities between evangelicalism and entertainment, the worshippers themselves seemed to. Walt Whitman, observing that workingmen attending revival meetings in the 1830s behaved as if they were at the theater, called the revivals "our amusements." Frances Trollope made a similar observation of young women attending a church service and remarked that a "stranger from the continent of Europe would be inclined, on first reconnoitering the city, to suppose that the places of worship were the theatres and cafés of the place." A Unitarian minister in Cincinnati commented: "We have seen it out here in the West, where beside our rivers and lakes the town expands; the first petal it puts forth is the Church—the second is the theatre."

Others noted how theatricality had begun insinuating itself into the religious services of even nonevangelical sects. Where once sermons had been marked by their stern theological rigor, one was now more likely to hear stories, humorous anecdotes and colloquial asides. "Execution sermons," in which ministers recounted horrifying murders, were especially popular at midcentury. What was true of content was also true of delivery. Performance was the key. "Nothing gives me more pain and distress," complained a religious newspaper in 1837, "than to see a minister standing almost motionless, coldly plodding on as a mathematician would calculate the distance of the Moon from the Earth. . . ." A great preacher, like Henry Ward Beecher, Dwight Lyman Moody, Knowles Shaw or Samuel Porter Jones, was one who could hold an audience rapt. Those who did became stars. (According to the historian Richard Hofstadter, "The 'star' system prevailed in religion before it reached the theater.") As a result of these evangelical endowments, religion in America not only failed to inhibit entertainment but fed the appetite for it even as its ministers issued futile pronouncements against it.

The role of America's cultural elites in obstructing popular culture was somewhat more complex. Visitors to this country liked to say that it had no aristocratic class, so powerful was the solvent of democracy. "[I]f at the present day it is not actually destroyed," Tocqueville wrote of the aristocratic element, "it is at any rate so completely disabled that we can scarcely assign to it any degree of influence on the course of affairs." Though this was actually far from the truth, democratic effusions certainly must have made it seem so. America, alone among nations in the nineteenth century, had been an idea for a country even before it became a country, and the nation had been stamped in the image of that idea. No nation was more self-consciously democratic in its values. No nation was more assertive in the display of those values.

And this was not just platitudinous rhetoric. In Europe, where there was no tradition of democracy, the common citizenry accepted the social order and their place within it, the French Revolution notwithstanding. When social agitation did occur in Europe, it was more likely to originate in the middle class than the working class—a case of an ascendant group demanding recognition. Here in America, where the common citizenry sought to level the social order and where the working class was at least as vocal as the middle class, there was vigorous opposition to the very idea of an aristocratic class, let alone aristocrats themselves. Aristocracy was European, and Europe was everything America was not and should not be: effete where America was earthy, refined where America was natural, intellectual where America was practical, decadent where America was moral, oppressed where America was free. "Of all the countries on the face of the earth or that ever existed on the face of the earth," raged William Leggett, onetime editor of the *New York Evening Post,* in a standard sentiment of the time, "this is the one where the class of wealth and aristocracy are the most unfounded, absurd, and ridiculous." Still, Leggett continued, Americans were menaced by "our old enemies," only this time they were not a "steel-clad feudal baron or a minor despot" as in Europe, but a "mighty civil gentleman who comes mincing and bowing to the people with a quill behind his ear. . . ."

These aristocrats, aping the manners and parroting the ideas of their European counterparts, were thought by ordinary citizens to constitute a fifth column here that undermined the country's democratic institutions, and as such no group was more reviled. Radical and working-class literature repeatedly scorched aristocrats as duplicitous and degenerate in a tone that was, as one critic described it, "indescribably bitter, and expressive of intense hostility against the possessors of property and culture." Contemporary theater made aristocrats the butts of gibes while the commonsensical Yankee, the backwoodsman and the Negro became theater's dominant figures. Even in daily conversation, to call someone an aristocrat was as cutting an insult as one could issue. When Daniel Webster of Massachusetts was so labeled in the 1840 presidential election, he retorted that his siblings had been reared in a log cabin and boiled that anyone who labeled him an aristocrat was "not only a LIAR but a COWARD."

But the antipathy toward aristocrats was not just verbal. In New York in the 1820s, a group of New Year's merrymakers who called themselves the Callithumpians would march down Broadway past the mansions of the well-to-do, banging drums and blowing horns and whistles, before marching back uptown to the City Hotel, where a celebration of the rich was just concluding, so that the democratic revelers could hoot and harass the departing partygoers. Frequently this sort of tomfoolery escalated into violence. Other times young louts actively sought physical confrontations with members of the upper classes. Over the years 1830 to 1860 there were by one count thirty-five major riots all told in Baltimore, Philadelphia, New York and Boston, and though not all of them were class-based, many were.

One did not have to go any further than the 1828 presidential election campaign, pitting General Andrew Jackson against incumbent John Quincy Adams, to see how intensely the issue of class antagonism inflamed America. A friend of Jackson's accurately framed the election as a "great contest between the *aristocracy* and democracy of America." Adams, the well-traveled ex–Harvard professor, Massachusetts Brahmin and son of former President John Adams, was a representative of the sort of European intellectualism that ordinary Americans increasingly repudiated, while Jackson, the crusty military hero from Tennessee who had won the Battle of New Orleans in the War of 1812, was the very embodiment of the natural American man uncontaminated by civilization. "John Quincy Adams who can write / And Andrew Jackson who can fight," went a campaign couplet crisply delineating the difference between the two.

When the fighter beat the writer, the symbolism was clear that a new order was aborning not only politically but, perhaps even more important, culturally. If, prior to Jackson's election, there had been a cultural aristocracy that governed the nation's artistic life, his victory emboldened the forces of anti-intellectualism to take action against it, and helped discredit high culture, which had always been suspect anyway. As Ralph Waldo Emerson happily saw it, "this rank rabble party, the Jacksonism of the country, heedless of English and of all literature—a stone cut out of the ground without hands;—they may root out the hollow dilettantism of our cultivation in the coarsest way. . . ."

"The coarsest way" was right. In the event, the surge of trash followed close on the heels of Jackson's election with the scandalmongering penny press, the scathing cheap novel and the pretension-puncturing almanacs, among other things, all arising over the next decade. To the old beleaguered aristocrats this was just further evidence of the intellectual limitations of the common

man. Give him a choice, and he will invariably choose sensationalism over art.

The problem with this analysis was that the majority of nineteenth-century Americans were not the primitives and dolts their
detractors made them out to be. Literacy among ordinary Americans was relatively high then, and nearly everyone seemed to love
to read. Not only did the number of published books skyrocket in
this period, thanks in part to less costly printing techniques, but
between 1828 and 1860 the number of newspapers in the country
rose from 852 to 4,051 with a combined annual circulation of
nearly one billion. (The circulation of newspapers was to increase
another 400 percent between 1870 and 1900 while the population
increased only 95 percent.) Most ordinary citizens were also familiar with opera and Shakespeare. These same folks would sit for
hours listening to political debate and wait patiently in line to see
the monumental paintings of Thomas Cole and Frederic Church.
If they were fools, they were at least fairly knowledgeable ones.

Of course there was another way to explain the rise of popular
culture in the wake of Jackson's victory than to chalk it up to
philistinism, but it would have been much harder for the elitists to
accept. By this analysis, sensationalist trash was not the default
culture for the intellectually impaired but rather, like the election
itself, a deliberate, self-conscious expression of cultural hostility—a willful attempt to raze the elitists' high culture and destroy
their authority by creating a culture the elitists would detest. In
this view, trash was a choice, a choice made precisely *because* it
seemed so antithetical to Culture and *because* promoting it would
infuriate the aristocrats, so that there was actually a cause and
effect between how much the elitists decried entertainment and
how much entertainment flourished. Or, put another way, whatever else it was, mass entertainment may have begun as the
democrats' revenge against the elites they despised.

In effect, this made entertainment the cultural equivalent of
Jackson's political egalitarianism, though, as it turned out, cultural

democracy may have been much more substantial than political
democracy. Politically speaking, the awful truth was that for all
its symbolic significance Jackson's election only underscored the
inability of the system to redress inequality even when there was
a sympathetic figure in the White House. According to one
study, during the so-called Era of the Common Man, the wealthi-
est 1 percent of the citizenry in the large cities held roughly 25 percent of the wealth in 1820; by 1850 it held 50 percent. The
much-vaunted social mobility that Tocqueville celebrated was
equally hollow. Roughly 90 percent of the wealthy were descended
from families of affluence and social position; only 2 percent had
been born poor. To make matters worse, these same individuals
were also the ones most likely to hold public office. All of which
led one historian of the period to conclude that "the common man
appears to have gotten very little of whatever it was that counted
for much."

Yet that was not entirely true. Though he may have been
deprived of wealth, social mobility and political power, the common man quickly learned to compensate for his impotence in
those arenas by channeling his energies instead into the one arena
in which he did seem paramount, culture, and into the one form
of culture that was truly his own, entertainment. Nothing could
have been more democratic than entertainment. Everyone had
access to it, the majority ruled in it, and no one's aesthetic judg-
ment of it was deemed better than anyone else's. This is what
Dwight Macdonald meant when he complained that popular culture was a "dynamic, revolutionary force, breaking down the old
barriers of class, tradition, and taste, dissolving all cultural distinctions. . . ." And that is what nineteenth-century Americans understood when they raised entertainment's banner.*

---

* This same process has occurred in modern China, where liberalization in the 1980s
unleashed a tide of popular entertainments from television situation comedies to soap
operas to trashy novels. Given the opportunity and the opening, the Chinese giddily

In Europe, the antiestablishment impulse was exercised sparingly, either at carnivals where, for the brief period from January to Lent, mock celebrations inverted the social order and the peasantry were allowed to insult their social betters with impunity, or at festivals where carnivalesque behavior was permitted. In America, thanks to entertainment, the carnival never ended. Here it seemed the cultural order was always inverted; high art was always under siege. And it was the sheer rebellious exhilaration of that siege against Culture that gave entertainment its charge. As the critic Pauline Kael has said of movies, though her observation applies equally to most products of popular culture, "Perhaps the single most intense pleasure of movie-going is this non-aesthetic one of escaping from the responsibilities of having the proper responses required of us in our official (school) culture. . . . It's the feeling of freedom from respectability we have always enjoyed at the movies. . . . [T]hey are stripped of cultural values."

This was where the central theme of entertainment conjoined with one of the central themes of America, the two reinforcing each other as they could in no other, less democratically inclined society. Entertainment was first and foremost about the triumph of sensation over reason. Nineteenth-century America was largely about the triumph of democracy over oppression. The fit between the aesthetic and the social could not have been more perfect. When these linked, they posed a formidable force that not only swelled the amount of entertainment but supported it against elitist attack. Because of this alliance, popular culture would become the nation's dominant culture. Because of this alliance, America would henceforth be a Republic of Entertainment.

---

seized popular culture as the democratic alternative to their own oppressive elite: the Communist Party. Totalitarian regimes may encourage kitsch, which is their idea of art without the content of art, but they prohibit true popular culture, presumably because they realize its democratizing potential. (See Zha Jianying, *China Pop: How Soap Operas, Tabloids, and Bestsellers Are Transforming a Culture* [New York: New Press, 1995].)

III

WARFARE

TO SAY THAT POPULAR CULTURE was swept along on the tide of Jacksonian democracy, however, begs the question of what this really meant in the cultural trenches. In the trenches, the citizenry fought a long war of attrition that may have begun in the 1820s but has yet really to end. The battle plans called for fusillades of disdain from newspapers and pulpits mixed with occasional attempts at uplift by the high-culturists and all manner of guerrilla deviltry by the low.

One form of warfare was the way audiences behaved at theatrical performances, the behavior that so chagrined Mrs. Trollope. Though she regarded theater rowdyism—the incessant spitting, the shouting, the bombardment of the richer patrons by the poorer and even of the performers themselves with fruit and vegetables, the "music of cracking peanuts," as the *New York Mirror* described it, and the stamping of feet—as a sign of the audience's ignorance, others found it a deliberate demonstration of cultural independence by the general citizenry and a way to exhibit "their entire contempt for the 'polite company' in the boxes," as one periodical at the time put it. Walt Whitman exulted at the "whole crowded auditorium, and what seeth'd in it, and flash'd from its faces and eyes, to me as much a part of the show as any— bursting forth in one of those long-kept-up tempests of handclapping peculiar to the Bowery—no dainty kid-glove business, but electric force and muscle from perhaps two thousand ful-sinew'd men. . . ."

These impolite, often riotous displays may have confirmed the power of ordinary people and the ascendance of their entertainment culture, but the elitists were not about to suffer such indignities. Instead, they left. At one time the masses and aristocrats had shared the same theaters and the same amusements—the "better" classes in the orchestra and boxes, the lower ones exiled to the gallery, while the newly emerging middle class occupied the pit. By the 1830s this intratheater segregation was beginning to give way to intertheater segregation, with each class safely sequestered within a house of its own. In New York, the higher classes retreated to posh uptown theaters, the lower classes to downtown establishments where they could carouse as they pleased, and the middle class to places in between where they could comport themselves like aristocrats without having to pay the aristocrats' high tariff.

Within the general process of this cultural segregation, the opening of the Astor Place Opera House in New York City on November 22, 1847, was a signal event, largely because of the theater's unprecedented opulence and unabashed appeal to the rich. A "generally diffused air of good breeding pervaded the entire atmosphere," reported one newspaper of the opening night, which featured Verdi's opera *Ernani*. Even curiosity-seekers among the audience of eighteen hundred who paid one dollar for the boxes and fifty cents for the gallery arrived with the women in their finery, the men with their whiskers shaved and hair pomaded. The Astor Place Opera House seemed to demand that kind of deference.

But its grandiosity was also what would make it the site of one of the defining moments of American culture—one that would both crystallize and energize the war between art and entertainment. The occasion was a scheduled engagement there by the celebrated British Shakespearean actor William Charles Macready in a production of *Macbeth* in the first two weeks of May 1849. The fifty-six-year-old Macready was an intellectual actor: precise and restrained and, to his detractors, rather cold. In his style and in his Britishness he clearly appealed to the reserved cultural aristocrats who frequented the Astor.

But it so happened that at the very same time Macready's company would be performing at the Astor, the American Shakespearean actor Edwin Forrest was to appear as the rebel Spartacus in a production of *The Gladiator* at the Broadway Theatre. Though in more temperate times there would have been no reason for conflict between these simultaneous performances, now, once the shill began for each, the issue was joined. In contrast with Macready, Forrest not only was an American but had adopted what his adherents called an "American" style of acting that was expressive, extravagant and outsized. Macready himself had once praised Forrest for his "vehemence and rude force" but thought that his talent had been overtaken by a kind of theatrical demagoguery. "The injudicious and ignorant flattery," he would write after their confrontation, "and the facetious applause of his supporters, the 'Bowery lads' as they were termed, in low-priced theatres, would fill his purse, would blind him to his deficiency in taste and judgement, and satisfy his vanity, confirming his self-opinion of attained perfection."

By the time the performances began, the two actors had been inflated into symbols of two nations and two cultural stations. Being that Macready's station was in the minority, it put him in a distinctly disadvantageous position. On May 8 shiftless young louts—"b'hoys," they were called—infiltrated the audience at the Astor and began hooting until Macready was forced to discontinue the performance. "A more wanton, tyrannous and scoundrelly outrage than this we could not well conceive," spluttered the *New York Tribune* the next day. "And yet every one of the miscreants who practice this atrocious and impudent tyranny will boast of his readiness to fight for Liberty. . . . They can't imagine any better Democrat than they, unless it be Forrest."

Meanwhile, the penny press, cheap newspapers that appealed to the lower and middle classes, began stoking the actors' feud with daily stories in a conspicuous campaign to gain circulation and sales. Most of these papers took the personal approach: Forrest was accused of having hissed Macready during a performance on a trip to England several years back, while Macready was quoted unflatteringly on Forrest's talent. Others preferred a cultural/nationalistic approach. One provocateur named E. Z. C. Judson, who wrote dime novels under the pen name of Ned Buntline and who headed a nativist group calling itself the American Committee, harangued crowds milling outside the Astor Place Opera House that week and papered New York with broadsides asking, "Shall Americans or English Rule in This City?"

By the night of May 10, both sides were braced for a conflagration. "B'hoys" had bought seats in the Opera House. Policemen stood at the ready in the back of the theater. Macready took the stage as Macbeth and was immediately greeted by boos and hisses from the intruders. By the fourth scene, as Macready vainly tried to continue above the din, one of the police officers gave a signal. "[T]he police rushed in at the two sides of the parquet," Macready later wrote, "closed in upon the scoundrels occupying the center seats, furiously vociferating and gesticulating, and seemed to lift or bundle them in a body out of the centre of the house, amid the cheers of the audience."

But no sooner had these ruffians been bodily removed than a group outside estimated at ten thousand b'hoys, alerted to what had happened within, began shouting and pelting the theater with bricks. Still, by racing through the scenes, Macready managed to finish his performance to the cheers of the aristocratic audience, before dressing himself as Malcolm and sneaking out with the theatergoers to return to his hotel. Meanwhile, the ruckus escalated when the b'hoys fortified themselves with stones from a building site across the way and began heaving them. By this time the police had called in the local militia for assistance. Standing its ground around the theater, the militia fired one volley over the crowd. When this failed to disperse the rioters, they fired another volley into the crowd, and when the b'hoys retreated only to surge forward again, the militiamen fired once more. At the end of the scuffle twenty-two people had been killed and more than one hundred wounded—all because, as the *New York Tribune* assessed it, "two actors had quarreled!"

Of course, it was not for an actors' quarrel that these unfortu-
nates had given their lives. What they had really sacrificed themselves for was entertainment—for the right to assert their own
cultural authority. That was the sentiment when, at a rally outside
City Hall the night after the riot, one speaker read a resolution
which cast the tragedy as a kind of cultural Boston Massacre.
"[O]ur citizens have a perfect and indisputable right to express
their approbation or disapprobation in all places of public amusement," went the declaration, "and we regard the arrest and impris-
onment of persons last night, for merely expressing their opinion
in the Opera House as only surpassed in atrocity by the outrage
perpetrated outside amongst the people." Another speaker at the
rally asked rhetorically in reference to the massacre, "Was it done
for the sake of justice?," and answered that it was done to "please
the aristocracy of the city at the expense of the lives of inoffending
citizens."

But if the riots were seen as a blow struck for cultural independence, what they demonstrated was just how deeply riven American culture was. "[T]he 'White and the Red Roses of York and
Lancaster' were never more distinctly divided into antagonistic
parties, than the 'B'hoys' of New York and the 'Upper Ten,' " editorialized the *Home Journal* two days after the eruption.

> The white handkerchiefs that waved all over the boxes and
> parterre diffused an atmosphere that made the house as fragrant
> as a perfumer's shop; while the rotten eggs, potatoes, pennies and
> coarse placards equally betrayed the domestic habits of the oppo-
> sition. . . . Macready's real offence in the eyes of those who drove
> him from the stage, is in being rather rancidly superfine in his
> personal manners, and in being dined out continually by the
> uptowners.

To this, the *Philadelphia Public Ledger* added in its own postmortem of the Astor Place Riot: "It leaves behind a feeling to
which this community had hitherto been a stranger . . . a feeling

that there is now in our country, in New York City, what every good patriot had hitherto considered it his duty to deny—a high and a low class."*

THE ASTOR PLACE RIOT only reinforced and further expedited that division. The old heterogeneous audience was gone. More and more the upper classes sought to differentiate themselves from the so-called rabble by building even fancier theaters with even higher ticket prices that effectively excluded ordinary citizens from attending. At the same time, behavior within the theaters began to change. Under pressure from the emerging middle class, which was as eager as its European counterpart to demonstrate its own propriety, the hissing and shouting, the eating, the hurling of fruit and vegetables at disfavored performers, the hum of small talk during the show, all began to disappear, and in their stead came the polite, passive spectator who no longer commanded the show but was in thrall to it. (The same bourgeois transformation occurred in Europe, where once spectators had frequently sat upon the stage itself, getting up and accosting friends right in the middle of the performance as the spirit moved them.)

As the riots helped further segregate audiences, so did they further segregate the forms of entertainment these audiences preferred. Gradually the variety fare that had long shared the stage with tragedy and farce and that had helped unify the audience was consigned to its own venues in vaudeville and minstrel shows, saloons and beer gardens, the circus and burlesque. According to one study of New York City in 1880, there were twenty-five play-

---

* The riots did not hurt Edwin Forrest's career. He became America's leading actor, touring widely and taking in a record $11,600 for a five-night stand in Chicago in 1866. He was also known for the vicissitudes of his personal life. A bitter divorce—he had found his wife with her head nestled in the lap of a fellow thespian—made national headlines. When a court ordered Forrest to pay $3,000 a year in alimony, he took to pleading his case onstage, thus turning even his status as a cuckold into an entertainment.

houses seating between one thousand and two thousand patrons, with half of these situated in affluent neighborhoods and all charging a one-dollar admission, which was four times more than that of other theaters. A second, larger group of theaters catered to the Protestant middle class. A third, still larger group presented vaudeville, minstrel shows and cheap melodrama for the lower-middle and working classes and charged roughly a quarter. Next were seven thousand saloons and beer gardens. Finally, at the bottom of the cultural pyramid, came the vice districts.

This kind of separation had become both the central fact and the main theme of America's cultural life. At the 1893 Columbian Exposition in Chicago celebrating the quadricentennial of Columbus's voyage to America, the fairgrounds were divided between the exhibition halls, which were the embodiment of high culture, and the Midway, a carnivalesque environment with fan dancers and freaks and games of chance that was the embodiment of mass culture. And as this imaginative city was divided, so increasingly were America's real urban centers divided between the new institutions of symphony halls, art museums and opera houses, on one side, and vaudeville theaters, burlesque houses, dime museums and amusement parks, on the other. As if to finalize the divorce between high culture and low, by the turn of the twentieth century the legitimate theater had finally emerged as a distinct entity after nearly two centuries as a hybrid.

Clearly the old elites had a vested interest in this segregation. However much they might berate the rabble, they had come to enjoy their independence from them and their assumed superiority to them. More, the rabble's cultural debasement only served to justify the inequality of American society from which the elites so amply benefited. Attempting to ensure that the masses would be excluded from high culture forever, the elites in the late nineteenth century began a process that the cultural historian Lawrence W. Levine has called "sacralization." Through sacralization, art, which had always been said to have a spark of the divine, was now lifted into the realm of holiness, a pathway to perfection. As such, it had to maintain its purity. It could have no truck with anything that might compromise its sacredness, which is to say, anything that contained popular, demotic elements. This was the rationalization for why forms that had previously commingled, like Shakespeare and variety divertissements, now suddenly had to be quarantined from one another.

While one can easily see the benefits for the elites in this situation, what is less obvious is that the masses also had a vested interest in cultural segregation and that the sacralization of high culture and the commodification of low culture were in a symbiotic relationship, each one defining the other. The result was a kind of uneasy cultural gerrymander. The elites retained control of high culture without having to fend off the heathens or concern themselves with their betterment, and the heathens were permitted to promote and control mass entertainment even as the elites made their scornful rebukes.

The proponents of entertainment took this opportunity and ran with it by further desacralizing popular culture in almost direct proportion to how much the elites were sacralizing high culture. Ordinary playgoers now sought, in the words of the theater critic George Jean Nathan, "horse-play, belly laughter, pretty girls, ingenious scenery, imported ladies of joy and eminent home talent, insane melodramas, lovely limbs, lively tunes, gaudy colors, loud humors, farce, flippancy, fol-de-rol." Working-class youths formed social groups that they called "pleasure clubs." And wild dance crazes became the vogue among the common folk, converting the willingness to be vulgar into a sign of naturalness that the elites could not essay. "The trouble is that these high people don't know how to dance," theorized one young woman concerning the elites' scorn for such popular recreations. "I have to laugh when I see them at their balls and parties."

Though contemporary remarks like these make the division seem somewhat cleaner than it actually was, what really complicated the separation was a third factor in the cultural equation: the middle class. By the time of Jackson's presidency this new group was already expanding and making demands of its own. It was composed primarily of merchants, lawyers, doctors and other professionals as well as of master craftsmen who had entered the ranks of entrepreneurship—people who had earned their money and, they thought, their status. These individuals found their interests diverging from those of their workers and of manual laborers generally, but they also had little community of interest with the elites whom they threatened to supplant. Unlike the elites, they subscribed to a meritocracy, believed devoutly in material rewards for their hard work and identified their own advancement with the progress of both democracy and America.

As a political force the middle class, again like its European counterpart, became a catalyst for change, a change one social historian has described as the transformation of the country in the first half of the nineteenth century from a "mercantilist republic, still cradled in aristocratic values, family, and deference, to an egalitarian market democracy, where money had new power, the individual new standing, and the pursuit of self-interest new honor." In helping to effect this transformation, it was the middle class, as well as the working class, that vented anger at the old elite and challenged its power, and it was the middle class that would, by century's end, displace the elite as the custodians of culture.

As a cultural force, however, the middle class found itself in a much more vexing situation. On the one hand, it had the same disdain for effete, Europeanized, aristocratic culture as the lower classes did. It found the whole lot of it un-American, in part because it was so removed from the practicalities of daily life. (This was what the critic Van Wyck Brooks meant when he said that American culture was divided not between art and entertainment but between "highbrow" and "lowbrow," which he defined nonjudgmentally as "on the one hand a quite unclouded, quite unhypocritical assumption of transcendent theory ['high ideals']; on the other a simultaneous acceptance of catchpenny realities.") At the same time, the middle class had no desire to identify itself with the entertainment culture of the lower classes and thus sully itself. Having assumed the role of custodian of official culture, it aspired to gentility.

This dilemma of the middle class was no less vexing for the cultures on either side of it. For the rapidly shrinking cohort of elitists comfortably sniping at low culture from their aerie, the middle class represented a cultural threat every bit as terrifying as the political danger they posed. Popular culture may have overwhelmed high culture, but no one took popular culture seriously, and in any case, the proponents of popular culture had absolutely no designs on high culture. On the contrary, they were happy to have it continue to demonstrate its irrelevance. The elitists could not be as sure of the middle class, which, after all, had its own cultural pretensions. At the same time, the partisans of entertainment fretted that moralistic middle-class reformers might try to do what high-culturists had never shown much inclination to do: either enlist government agencies or create institutions of their own to regulate amusements.

Amid these concerns the middle class itself was groping its way toward a culture of its own. While in Europe the bourgeoisie gradually wrested power from the aristocrats by co-opting aristocratic culture, here it found a middle way between high and low culture, snobby art and trashy entertainment. Dwight Macdonald would call this solution "Midcult," from "Middle Culture," and describe it as trying to have things both ways: ". . . it pretends to respect the standards of High Culture while in fact it waters them down and vulgarizes them." Midcult was the form of art without its content, the affectation of art without the struggle art allegedly entailed. It was grandiose paintings, light opera, genteel novels, purple poetry, sentimental melodrama—all of it in extremely good taste, completely inoffensive, highly moral and "dull and unsensual," in the sociologist Richard Sennett's words, though the aristocrats likely would have found it a bit too blunt and unsubtle themselves.

Most critics would come to think of Midcult this way—as a method of dumbing down high culture. But what Macdonald failed to see is that Midcult need not operate only on high culture. It could also work its wiles on low, obviously not dumbing it down but spiffing it up. Through this process entertainment could be domesticated, its most vulgar elements purged, its democratic danger removed, the enjoyment it provided made safe. This way the middle class would not have to resist the gravitational pull of entertainment and its glorious dumb fun as the aristocrats did. It could have its pleasures and its respectability too.

Of course, this meant that the middle class frequently took its lead from the lower classes, setting in motion a dynamic process that may by now be the iron law of American popular culture: Popular entertainment forms originated by the lower classes (and later by youth and minorities, who would come to fill the inventive functions of the lower classes) invariably get adopted, and then co-opted, by the middle class, which reconfigures them to remove their subversive elements. Thus in the nineteenth century the sensational dime novel was transmuted by the middle class into the sensational but moralistic novel that used the format of the dimes but to purportedly more wholesome effect. Similarly, music saloons and beer halls where laborers could enjoy a drink and a show were transmuted into vaudeville theaters that were much cleaner and presented fare more tasteful than the saloons and that appealed to patrons who, as one observer put it, were "not likely to be distinguished from audiences that uphold grand opera." The burlesque show was transmuted into the cabaret. In the early twentieth century, so-called "nigger dances" like the turkey trot, the bunny hug and the grizzly bear were transmuted into the refined dances of Vernon and Irene Castle, while black ragtime music was transmuted by composer Irving Berlin into "Alexander's

Ragtime Band." And in the late twentieth century, to cite one of the most dramatic of dozens of examples, the threat of black blues was transmuted into Elvis Presley's white rock and roll, and white rock and roll eventually into Presley's middle-aged, middle-class Las Vegas act.

Looking at the way Midcult enlisted middle-class Americans into entertainment's cause, one might well have concluded that public amusements at the end of the nineteenth century had effected a reconvergence of sorts in American culture; in an increasingly diverse nation it had united Americans of different classes, incomes, sexes, religions, ages and geographical sections, all but those who were black and those who still insisted on holding themselves intellectually and culturally superior. Through the dizzying rush of entertainment, Americans had, it seemed, practically all become one.

IV

THE ULTIMATE WEAPON

BUT THE APPARENT UNITY was deceptive. While Americans did congregate together at baseball games, dime museums, amusement parks, dance halls and arcades, tensions still roiled. The middle class may not have been as supercilious as the elites it replaced, but middle-class reformers were every bit as strident as those elites in condemning unsanitized working-class entertainments, and for the same reason: These entertainments constituted a challenge to the class's social control. Where the middle class differed from the elites was in its belief that entertainment was not entirely beyond redemption. The middle class saw itself as industrious, righteous, honest, rational and forward-thinking, and thought it could and should impose these values on American society. But it did not see why entertainment, in the right hands, could not be a vehicle to bring these values to the lower classes.

At the same time, entertainment culture, having seen the old elites vanquished, was not about to surrender its independence to another group of cultural overlords. Because the middle class kept co-opting entertainment through Midcult, the entrepreneurs of mass culture kept having to stake out new ground where they could continue to provide disenfranchised Americans with something that was adversarial, something that pushed against the limits of good taste. Otherwise Midcult would have sapped entertainment of its raw contrarian energy. As a result of these competing agendas, American culture in the late nineteenth and early twentieth centuries found itself in a state of turbulence, with the middle class promoting its values by modifying the popular, the lower classes trying to undermine the middle class by reenergizing the popular, and what remained of the elites declaring a pox on both their houses.

Yet it was a battle the outcome of which was not seriously in doubt for very long. The middle class may have finally taken over the role of cultural arbiters from the elites, but lowborn entertainment had all the advantages. In the first place, entertainment had the force of numbers. It gained a tremendous infusion of new troops with the arrival of more than eleven million immigrants between 1870 and 1900, so many that by 1900, 60 percent of the residents in America's twelve largest cities were either foreign-born or first-generation American. These were people who had come with no idea of what mass culture was but were drawn to entertainment's sensational spell. Not incidentally, the commanders of the entertainment industry would increasingly come from their ranks.

Entertainment also had the assistance of technologies like electrification, which lit the cities and ran the streetcars that would take poor patrons to their shows, and of printing advances that allowed for illustration and later photographic reproduction in books, newspapers and magazines which, one contemporary observer noted, were now "aimed at entertainment alone, and achieved it, in typical cases, by liberal extravagance with photographs accompanying casually improvised articles about actresses or queens, or persons deemed socially important."

More, it had the advantage of a change in labor conditions in which wages rose and hours declined, leaving ordinary citizens more money and more leisure time. Real nonfarm wages increased 50 percent between 1870 and 1900, while the average manufacturing worker toiled three and a half fewer hours per week in 1910 than in 1890. But it was not just a matter of dollars and time. There was also a new attitude among laborers that accompanied these changes—a "spiritual reaction," as one historian called it, against the numbing conditions of the machine age. At the end of the workday, workers left their factories wanting to have a good time and wishing to declare their independence off-hours in ways they were prohibited from doing when on the clock. Entertainment helped satisfy those desires.

Even within the labor force there arose a new contingent that would contribute mightily to the growing dominance of popular culture. These were young, unmarried women, many of whom moved from employment as domestics to jobs as saleswomen and secretaries in which they were no longer forever lashed to the workplace. "The shorter work day brought me my first idea of there being such a thing as pleasure," a young woman at the time told an interviewer. "It was quite wonderful to get home before it was pitch dark at night. . . . Before this time it was just sleep and eat and hurry off to work." Disenfranchised not only from official American culture but from male working-class entertainments like saloon shows and burlesque, these women began searching for leisure activities of their own and found them in dance halls, amusement parks and later movie theaters, all of which brought still more new recruits to popular culture.

Clearly all these factors strengthened popular entertainment's hand against both high culture and Midcult. But what would finally make popular culture America's dominant culture was the way these all converged to provide entertainment with what would prove to be the ultimate cultural weapon—a force at once so appealing and so influential that it would change the entire cultural calculus of the country. If popular culture had seemed disparate, with no central focus, the new weapon would provide one. If popular culture had seemed to skulk about, constantly reminding one of its disreputability, the new weapon would put it squarely at the center of public awareness. And if popular culture had seemed to belong only to the lower classes, the new weapon would eventually humble everyone, even as it threatened to remake America in its image. As the poet Vachel Lindsay rhapsodized about it: "It has come then, this new weapon of men, and the face of the whole earth changes. In after centuries its beginning will be indeed remembered."

The new weapon was the movies.

By now the story of the movies is a familiar one: how they arrived late in the nineteenth century as a novelty; how they were presented first in vaudeville houses, where they were frequently used at the end of shows as "chasers" to roust the middle-class audience, and then in the back rooms of penny arcades; how they began moving in 1905 to storefront nickelodeon theaters named after the cost of the show. What is less familiar is how quickly the movies were embraced by their patrons as the latest and most powerful avatar of the old Jacksonian fervor that Midcult had been rinsing from entertainment, and how self-consciously they were wielded as an instrument of empowerment.

The movies' cultural power resided in the fact that they had not just appeared as a result of technology; they had arrived as a kind of fulfillment of American dreams and longings. Almost from the country's inception, American men of letters had been calling for a sinewy native art shorn of "any ultramarine, full-dress formulas of culture, polish, caste, &c.," as Whitman put it. Whitman had expected this new art to come from literature, particularly poetry, and while his own work certainly qualified, it would not be poetry but the movies that would be America's own native form.

Here was a medium free of any traditions whatsoever, much less the taint of European culture. Here was a medium that would sound the barbaric yawp as no American form before it ever had or could. Here at last was a medium to beat back the commissars of culture.

So while in Europe the movies catered immediately to the middle class as a technological marvel, here they catered to the working class as a cultural weapon. Seventy-two percent of the audience came from the laboring class, according to one study of New York City moviegoers in 1911, which also showed that those individuals working the longest hours were the ones who attended the movies most frequently. The same study estimated that only 3 percent of the audience could be considered members of the leisure class. By comparison the legitimate theater audience was only 2 percent working-class and 51 percent leisure-class, with the remainder from what the study called the "clerical" or middle class. Another survey indicated that 60 percent of the working class regularly attended films. All of this led the *Atlantic Monthly* to state the obvious: "that in the larger towns, where the higher-priced drama coexists with the motion-picture plays, the line of cleavage is sharply drawn in the character of the audience, and this line is the same line which marks the proletariat from the bourgeoisie and capitalist class."

At the movies this sense of democracy was palpable. The movie house "emancipated the gallery" and created a "great audience" which was "none other than the people without distinction of class," opined *Motion Picture World*. Another observer watched the workingman at the movies and concluded, "He will sit on the ground floor, with his own kind, feeling as it were a kind of proprietorship in the playhouse. Here he is apart from his daytime distinctions of class; he is in an atmosphere of independence." The same observer predicted that the "movies will become ever more powerfully a factor in the growth of class-consciousness."

But it was not just that the lower classes attended these first movies and the upper and middle classes did not that made film the "democratic art," as it was often called. It was how the lower classes purposefully shaped the moviegoing experience to make it anticultural. As in the theater, before the audiences began segregating themselves and before the middle class began enforcing its protocols of passivity, working-class patrons made a display of their lack of breeding. Crammed into small and often steaming nickelodeons, members of the audience would neck during performances, munch peanuts or eat fruit, talk, wander, shout at the screen. Even today the fact that one eats popcorn at the movies and would not think of doing so at the ballet, opera or symphony is a demarcation between low and high culture as well as a vestige of Jacksonian populism. The crunch of popcorn and the slurp of soda are the Whitmanian sounds of cultural democracy.

On the screen, as in the audience, movie after movie ridiculed elites and punctured pomposity. "I especially liked the reduction of authority to absurdity, the notion that sex could be funny, and the bold insults hurled at pretension," filmmaker Mack Sennett said of his comic shorts in what could also have served as a description of three of the movies' early preoccupations. Not for nothing were people in these films continually being chased, kicked, sprayed, smacked, thwacked and poked. And not for nothing was the biggest star of the movies' second decade Charlie Chaplin, whose ribald antics as a tramp provocateur drew denunciations from middle-class critics. (LOW GRADE PERSONS ONLY LIKE CHARLIE CHAPLIN AND MARY PICKFORD, PASTOR SAYS, screamed a headline in the *Detroit News*.) These early films, so distinctly urban, immigrant and working-class, reified the concerns of their audience, chiefly what one film historian described as "the change from Victorian to modern life that was at once so hopeful, so problematical, and so fearful." In the movies the old was forever yielding to the new, the hypocrites of the past to the forthright new Americans of the future.

Naturally, given the working-class character of the movie audience, the democratic nature of the moviegoing experience and the seditious subtext of the movies themselves, films were bound to raise howls of protest from the rump cultural elite and from the larger middle class which saw their values being mocked. The elites looked at the movies and saw the anarchy they had always feared from entertainment: the vapidity, the silliness, the escape from reason. Progressive reformers, largely drawn from the professional classes, looked at the movies and saw moral peril. The reformers found a link between the darkness of the theater and illicit sex, between the depiction of crimes in movies and juvenile delinquency, between the amount of attention one devoted to the screen and the inattention one devoted to education. In most major cities they campaigned to regulate films, to censor them, to seize them and even, as happened briefly in New York City during Christmas week of 1908, to shutter movie theaters altogether—in that particular case on the pretext that they posed a potential health hazard to patrons.

Yet nothing could derail the movie locomotive. The Motion Picture Patents Company, a film-production monopoly formed by inventor Thomas Alva Edison, reported in 1911 that 11,500 theaters were devoted exclusively to movies, up from roughly 5,000 in 1907. By 1914 there were 18,000 theaters in America, with an estimated seven million daily admissions. By one report, New York City alone had 400 movie theaters in 1911, compared with 40 low-priced vaudeville theaters, 10 burlesque houses, 16 low-priced stage theaters and 31 high-priced legitimate theaters. A similar survey of Boston in 1909 found the weekly seating capacity of the city's movie theaters to be 402,428, over 30,000 more than that of all other amusements combined.

Astonished by the movies' sudden and unprecedented popularity, analysts searched for reasons why, besides the obvious ones that film was cheap and that it satisfied the hankerings of the masses for fun. But the answers were all there in the film experience. No other entertainment could provide the same immediacy, the same vast scale, the same phenomenological impact as the movies. In a society that loved sensationalism, they were sensationalism's apotheosis. The Harvard psychology professor Hugo Munsterberg, writing of this almost mesmerizing effect, cited reports that "sensory hallucinations and illusions have crept in; neurasthenic persons are especially inclined to experience touch or temperature or smell or sound impressions from what they see on the screen. The associations become so vivid as realities, because the mind is so completely given up to the moving pictures."

What Munsterberg was describing made the movies not just more of; it made them different from. They had interpenetrated reality in a way no other art or entertainment had, in part because as a photographic medium they were fashioned from the materials of reality. Early audiences reportedly would shrink as a train onscreen pulled into a station, fearing that it would burst through and run them over. They had to be constantly reminded that what they were seeing was only an illusion. "Should you ever seek the source of the moving pictures of the vaudeville theater," *Moving Picture World* felt compelled to warn its readers in 1907, "you will learn that the comic, the tragic, the fantastic, the mystic scenes so swiftly enacted in photographic pantomime are not real but feigned."

What made the movies seem even more real, and what made them even more powerful in their effect, was how the audience mentally processed them. As Munsterberg noted, the movies played in our heads and seemed to replicate our own consciousness. Conspiring with the dark, they cast a spell that lulled one from his own reality into theirs until the two merged. This was precisely what concerned some of its more astute critics. They realized that the movies seemed to cross the line that separated reality from imagination. To Jane Addams, the social reformer and director of Chicago's Hull House community center, the movie theater was a "veritable house of dreams," which was "infinitely more real than the noisy streets and crowded factories." And

Addams worried that the movies, having displaced reality for the young, would now be "forming the ground pattern of their social life."

Addams was right to be concerned. The America of the late nineteenth and early twentieth centuries, which was the America of rapid industrialization, urbanization and immigration, was suffused with a new sense of possibility that made its citizens especially susceptible to the movies' fantasies. Old values and the old social order that sustained them were being challenged. In their place had come a feeling, fed by democratic wellsprings and encouraged by these brisk social changes, that one could do anything, be anything, dream anything—including anything one saw on-screen.

Addams understood that in this kind of environment, where fantasy counted for so much, the movies were more than another subversive entertainment thumbing its nose at polite culture. They were a whole new way of thinking about life. If the central theme of the nineteenth century was, as Richard Sennett has said, "appearances as signs of personal character, of private feeling, and of individuality," then the movies, which were a primer for appearance, were a principal agent in advancing that theme. And if, as the late historian Warren I. Susman has said of America at the beginning of the twentieth century, that "[t]ransformation seemed to be what the new culture was all about," including the ability to transform oneself into one's dreams, then the movies, which lent themselves especially well to transformations of all sorts, were a principal agent in reinforcing that preoccupation too. At the movies, and under the affect of the movies, reality for the first time seemed to be truly malleable.

Because the movies were both so entertaining and so useful, they would in time grow in popularity, rapidly extending their power over the middle class, ultimately leaving behind the working-class storefronts for capacious uptown theaters as opulent as the Astor Place Opera House had been—cathedrals for the new faith of movies. In time the movies would exert their power psychologically as well, insinuating themselves so deeply into our consciousness that they would become the die from which the country would be cast. And in time, after nearly a century of combat, the movies, the ultimate weapon, would seal not just the triumph of entertainment over high culture and Midcult; they would seal a much greater and more profound victory: the triumph of entertainment over life itself.

Chapter Two

The Two-Dimensional Society

I

THE NEW COSMOLOGY

DURING THE LAST HALF of the nineteenth century and the first decades of the twentieth, the period during which the idea of the movies became a reality, something momentous happened in America, and it happened not only to American culture but to the American consciousness. Historian Daniel Boorstin would find its source in what he called the "Graphic Revolution," by which he meant the remarkable rise in the quantity of visual material that had become available to the public. Images began to flood the market. Publications that had been limited to text were now, thanks to new print technologies, cluttered with illustrations, so much so that some critics even began complaining about "over-illustration." Photography only added to the deluge. In 1851 there were already one hundred daguerreotype studios in New York City alone, with people queuing up to have their portraits taken.

Scarcely thirty years later halftone technology would bring the same photographic obsession to newspapers and magazines.

Nor was it just a matter of graphic reproduction. Everywhere in America there seemed to be a new emphasis on seeing, whether it was the sudden dressing of department store windows which were carefully arranged to provide maximum visual stimulation, or the vogue for box cameras. As if in testimony to the ascendance of the eye, Shakespeare had, by the end of the nineteenth century, fallen out of favor because, surmised the *New York Times*, he was an aural anachronism in a society that opted for the visual. All of which led the editor and critic E. L. Godkin to conclude ruefully that America had become a "chromo-civilization," one where visual reproductions had driven out authentic culture.

But what made the Graphic Revolution revolutionary was less the quantity of images than their effect on the American mind. Already at the turn of the twentieth century one analyst fretted in the *Atlantic Monthly* that images would eventually replace words and that visual symbols would become the primary form of discourse. Boorstin's own concern was that the Graphic Revolution encouraged what he called image-thinking—thinking in terms of an "artificial imitation or representation of the external form of any object, especially of a person." This came at the expense of what he called ideal-thinking—thinking in terms of some idea or value toward which one could strive. The glut of images directed us to the here and now, to something immediately useful; the ideal directs us to something above and beyond, to something the utility of which is not readily apparent. In Boorstin's view, then, the Graphic Revolution was a moral revolution too because it replaced aspiration with gratification.

But Boorstin was still basically talking at the level of culture, not of consciousness. Neil Postman, one of the most brilliant and articulate critics of popular culture, saw the Graphic Revolution inaugurating a whole new way of appropriating information that would ultimately change the nature of information itself. In

Postman's view, each medium is a "unique mode of discourse" that enforces its own form of mental processing and its own ideas of intelligence. Print demanded ratiocination. "To engage the written word means to follow a line of thought which requires considerable powers of classifying, inference-making and reasoning," Postman wrote in *Amusing Ourselves to Death*. It followed that a predominantly print-based society, as America's was until the late nineteenth century, while not necessarily one coruscating with intellectual brilliance, nevertheless was one in which logic, order and context prevailed. An image-based society, on the other hand, dispensed with all these because images did not demand them. How much logical discipline did one need to recognize a picture?

To Postman, however, the Graphic Revolution was only the beginning of a long march toward antiratiocination that would finally culminate in television. No medium generated images like television. Abhorring dead air, compelled to keep us stimulated lest we switch channels or switch off the set altogether, television took everything on its screen and converted it into entertainment, which was *its* natural form of discourse. "No matter what is depicted or from what point of view," Postman wrote of TV, "the overarching presumption is that it is there for our amusement and pleasure." But because television had become the primary means through which people appropriated the world, it promulgated an epistemology in which all information, whatever the source, was forced to become entertainment, the age of typography giving way to the age of television and transforming our way of thinking in the process.

Boorstin, Postman and most other critics would lay the blame for chromo-civilization and its discontents at the foot of the technology that made mass-produced images possible. As Marshall McLuhan theorized, " [A]ny technology gradually creates a totally new human environment," and that certainly seemed to be true for the changes wrought by the technologies of image creation, especially television. But it was also and equally possible that

McLuhan had gotten it wrong and that the converse of his theo-
rem was in fact true: Totally new human environments create new
technologies. By this view, it was not the Graphic Revolution that
had triggered a change in the American consciousness; it was
a change in the American consciousness that had triggered the
Graphic Revolution. Indeed, the Graphic Revolution, including
television, could just as easily be seen as part of a much larger,
more significant movement in American life. That movement was
the Entertainment Revolution.

The desire for entertainment—as an instinct, as a rebellion, as
a form of empowerment, as a way of filling increased leisure time
or simply as a means of enjoying pure pleasure—was already so
insatiable in the nineteenth century that Americans rapidly began
devising new methods to satisfy it. Naturally, they gravitated to
those forms most congenial to providing mindless fun: forms that
were outside the control of the elites as images generally were,
forms that appealed to the senses, forms that challenged the hege-
mony of typography and with it the typographic modes of thinking
that Postman had celebrated. Television may very well have
become, as Postman has said, the "command center of the new
epistemology" that had begun with illustration, telegraphy and
photography. But if television was the latest epistemology, entertainment itself was the cosmology that had governed American life
with increasing vigor since at least the turn of the century. That
meant the new consciousness was a function not of television or
even of images but of entertainment.

In fact, the various forms of entertainment, including television, were only shadows on the wall of the cave. What made
entertainment a cosmology was the constellation of expectations
that these shadows created, expectations that would weigh heavily
on the American consciousness and change our mental architecture. Though it was hardly the only factor, entertainment of all
sorts had helped inspire—and would benefit from—what *Vanity
Fair* editor Frank Crowninshield approvingly described in 1914 in

his magazine's inaugural issue as an "increased devotion to pleasure, to happiness, to dancing, to sport, to the delights of the country, to laughter, and to all forms of cheerfulness." Because pleasure was so pleasurable, this attitude had led in turn to an expectation that everything should provide pleasure if only because anything that did not would very likely be shoved aside by something that did. That power of expectation had led in turn to a power of conversion in which more and more of American life would come to resemble entertainment in order to survive.

Yet all this was inchoate until the movies arrived to galvanize it. As the most powerful form of entertainment, the movies were also the most powerful agents of its cosmology, and long before television they had become the central metaphor for American life. What the movies provided, early critics like Jane Addams realized, was a tangible model to which one could conform life and a standard against which one could measure it, both in seemingly trivial ways, like fashion or behavior, and in more serious ways, like the movie-induced expectations one had about the course of one's own life or the value of one's own deeds. Why can't life be more like the movies? viewers asked, and then answered that it could.

Even more important than providing a model, however, the movies provided a new set of shared experiences for the entire nation, naturalizing every viewer as a citizen of a country of the imagination that would eventually supersede and devour the country of the material. "Everybody could go into the same dark room—no matter where it happened to be located—and zero in on precisely the same dream," was how the critic Geoffrey O'Brien described the bonds of this new citizenship. For many Americans the dream was as vivid as their own lives and even inextricable from them. "An analyst tells me that when his patients are not talking about their personal hangups and their immediate problems," film critic Pauline Kael commented, "they talk about the situations and characters in movies. . . . They don't see the movie as a movie but as part of the soap opera of their lives." The result of this vast fund of movie experience was that the movies became, like Immanuel Kant's categories, a scrim through which to view reality. As O'Brien put it, "Movies were not 'out there.' They had long since been internalized by most humans on the planet. . . ."

If the movies had begun supplanting reality, they were certainly well suited for this task. The French film critic André Bazin wrote that one of the functions of art is to cheat death by creating immortality, and to that end he posited what he called the "myth of total cinema," a theory of aesthetic predestination in which the movies would attempt to accomplish what no other medium had ever done: to replicate reality completely. That was the engine, Bazin believed, driving the movies' evolution from silence to sound to color to three-dimensionality to wide screens to smell-o-vision to anything that might bring film closer to the very texture of life itself—a form of "felt life" beyond Henry James's wildest dreams. This was film's destiny, said Bazin, its very reason for being.

As it turns out, Bazin was right—or almost right. The movies would come to approximate reality more closely than any previous medium, but the process would not be impelled by our desire for immortality, it would not be the result of any aesthetic or technological advances and it would not be what we now call "virtual reality," some simulacrum of real life. Rather, total cinema would be the result of the entertainment cosmology leaping tracks from screen to life.

What Bazin could not possibly have foreseen is that the medium of total cinema would not be film. It would be life itself. Life would be the biggest, most entertaining, most realistic movie of all, one that played twenty-four hours a day, 365 days a year, and featured a cast of billions. Life would be the new fountainhead of images, narratives, stars, themes. And the life movie would be the new nation of our common citizenship, only this nation would now exist outside our imaginations too, in the corporeal world. The total cinema would exist in, and consist of, reality.

II
The First Invasion

THE FIRST PORTAL through which entertainment slithered into life and then conquered it was journalism. As the sociologist Robert E. Park described the process in 1927, "[T]he reason we have newspapers at all in the modern sense of the term, is because about one hundred years ago, in 1835 to be exact, a few newspaper publishers in New York City and in London discovered (1) that most human beings, if they could read at all, found it easier to read news than editorial opinion and (2) that the common man would rather be entertained than edified."

Though news as entertainment was not entirely unheard of before the 1830s—one paper named *Hawk & Buzzard* subsisted in New York from 1826 through 1833 largely on gossip—Park was essentially correct. Prior to the 1830s most American newspapers weren't newspapers at all. They were party broadsheets largely devoted to advertisements and partisan editorializing so rabid that Tocqueville attacked the American journalist as an uneducated vulgarian who makes "an open and coarse appeal to the passions of his readers; he abandons principles to assail the characters of individuals, to track them into private life and disclose all their weaknesses and vices."

When Benjamin Day founded the *New York Sun* in 1833, in the flush of Jacksonian egalitarianism, he was breaking that journalistic mold. Before the *Sun,* the target audience for most papers was the wealthy and the professional classes. Day explicitly appealed to "mechanics and the masses generally." Before the *Sun,* most papers cost six cents. The *Sun* cost a penny; hence the name "penny press" that attached to it and its imitators. Before the *Sun,* a typical daily newspaper in New York City could expect to sell roughly 1,200 copies, with the total circulation of all eleven daily papers in the city in 1833 reaching only 26,500. After the appearance of the penny press, readership skyrocketed. In June 1835, by one report, the combined circulation of the penny papers alone was 44,000.

But the real difference between these new papers and the traditional press—and the real reason for their swelling circulation—was their content. If the six-penny papers were primarily opinion sheets, the penny papers were news organs, the very first daily news organs in the country. In the penny papers one could at long last read about life in the city, the nation, even the world, and discover not what an editor thought but what people had done, or at least what they were purported to have done. Nor was it only a matter of news; it was also a matter of purview. According to the press historian Michael Schudson, the penny papers were the first to acknowledge the importance of everyday life and the first to promote the "human interest story," which would soon become a journalistic staple.

Still, the success of the penny press raised an inevitable question: Why did news rather than opinion appeal to the mass reader? One could certainly attribute the allure of the news to the need among atomized citizens in burgeoning urban areas for some sense of common experience such as news provided. Or one could attribute it to the ability of the news to reinforce the suspicion on the part of many citizens that depravity lurked just beneath the city's surface, a suspicion that undermined the moral authority of the local elites. Still another factor may have been an intensifying sense in people that they had to know what was happening because as technology shrank the community and the nation, events that once seemed distant might now impact on their lives.

No doubt all these factors, as well as others, played some role. But the single most important attraction of the penny press may have been the most obvious one—namely, that for a constituency being conditioned by trashy crime pamphlets, gory novels and overwrought melodramas, news was simply the most exciting, most entertaining content a paper could offer, especially when it was skewed, as it invariably was in the penny press, to the most sensational stories. In fact, one might even say that the masters of the penny press *invented* the concept of news because it was the best way to sell their papers in an entertainment environment, and it was certainly no small matter that while the six-penny papers were sold primarily through subscription, the penny papers were hawked on the streets, meaning that the content had to be interesting enough to entice readers into buying a paper.

The publishers of the penny press didn't necessarily protest the idea that they were in the entertainment rather than the information business. From its inception the penny press began specializing in crime, with an emphasis on murder, to distinguish it from what the *New York Herald* called the "dull business air of the large morning papers." In its first two weeks of publication in May 1835, the *Herald* itself featured three suicides, three murders, the death of five persons in a fire, a man accidentally blowing off his head, an execution in France by guillotine and a riot in Philadelphia.

But the *Herald*'s real breakthrough as an entertainment medium came a year later, when it pounced on the case of a murdered nineteen-year-old prostitute named Helen Jewett to build its circulation. The Jewett case had all the hallmarks of the stories that would dominate the tabloid press a hundred years later, and the tabloid television news shows fifty years after that. On the night of her death, April 9, 1836, which also happened to be her birthday, the victim had entertained a prosperous young clerk named Richard P. Robinson, who had recently become affianced to a woman of good pedigree and who had visited Jewett, said her madam, Rosina Townsend, to retrieve some items he had given her. Townsend had seen them together in Jewett's room at eleven o'clock that evening. When Townsend found the young woman's battered and bloody body in a smoldering bed early the next morning, Robinson was the obvious suspect.

On the evidence, Robinson certainly seemed guilty. A cloak found in the yard behind the brothel was traced to him. The ax that had struck the killing blows was identified as one the defendant had used to chop wood. Whitewash from the back fence was discovered on his trousers. A pharmacist testified that Robinson had purchased arsenic a week earlier. The accused's roommate confessed that Robinson had been out late the night of the murder. Nevertheless, at his trial that June it took the jury only ten minutes to deliver a verdict of not guilty.

The significance of the Jewett case, however, had little to do with jurisprudence or justice. Its significance lay rather in what it mainlined into the bloodstream of the American press: the incalculable entertainment value of a lurid or prurient tale. Not only did the story demonstrate how the press might contour news to the hoariest conventions of melodrama, it showed as well just how quickly the press came to appreciate the appeal of these conventions in a realistic context and how quickly it learned to exploit them, thus setting the terms for the American press forevermore.

The keenest of these new press barons was James Gordon Bennett, Scottish-born steward of the *Herald* who would later gain notoriety for his scurrilous methods and crude behavior. (He once urinated in his fiancée's piano during a soiree.) Bennett realized he was on to something good with the Jewett story and did everything he could to milk it. There was a long, scandalous profile of the victim, as overwrought as anything in the sentimental novels of Susan Warner, portraying Jewett as a poor good girl seduced by a rogue and then abandoned, a ruination that set the course for her wayward life. There was what purported to be a firsthand description by Bennett of the victim's room while the body still lay in it. There was an interview conducted by Bennett with Rosina Townsend (though Townsend denied having given it). And there was story after story assessing Robinson's guilt or innocence, first listing this way and then that before finally settling on Townsend as the real murderer, abetted by the police and, of all people, Bennett's chief penny press rival, Benjamin Day of the *Sun*.

Unsurprisingly, critics decried what the Jewett case had

unleashed. Charles Dickens, after a visit to America in 1842, wrote that no matter what Americans did, "while the newspaper press of America is in, or near, its present abject state, high moral improvement in that country is hopeless." Within a few years of the Jewett case, a coalition of clergymen, financiers, rival editors and Van Buren Democrats, all of whom had been offended by Bennett, launched what came to be called a "Moral War" against the *Herald*, pressuring readers, advertisers and distributors not to read, advertise in or distribute the paper—in effect, to place it in Coventry. One warrior accused Bennett of "moral leprosy."

But, as with the criticism of conventional entertainments, the issue really had less to do with morality than with cultural control. The *Herald*, as an engine of trashy entertainment, challenged the genteel social order and did so in a new arena outside the boundaries of traditional entertainment, which seemed to make it even more invidious. In attacking the paper, then, the genteel elites were once again trying to destroy an institution that clearly threatened their authority. And once again, they were right to be alarmed. Though he occasionally affected a concern for moral values himself, Bennett, drawing as had other entertainers on the power of Jacksonian democracy, was a born agitator. He intended, said his official biographer, to rescue his readers from "affected prudery" and "mawkish refinement," and took pride in claiming that he had "entered the hearts of the people," "shown them their own sentiments" and "put down their own living feelings on paper. . . ."

In the end, the elites were no more successful in suppressing the penny press than they had been or would be in suppressing other entertainments, especially since their condemnation was itself part of the appeal of the penny papers. Bennett's *Herald* boasted a daily circulation of 20,000 during the Robinson trial and 51,000 by the time of the Moral War—larger than the total circulation of the papers run by what he sneeringly called the "Holy Allies." To his critics' everlasting regret, he knew that his readers, as he would later say, "were more ready to seek six columns of the details of a brutal murder, or the testimony of a divorce case, or the trial of a divine for improprieties of conduct, than the same amount of words poured forth by the genius of the noblest author of the times."

Even the Civil War, the nation's bloodiest tragedy, could not escape exploitation by the sensationalist impulse. Newspaper sales soared during the peaks of conflict—Bennett sold 135,000 copies of the *Herald* with the attack on Fort Sumter and published three daily editions thereafter—then dropped when the action seemed to flag, and some seemed to see a correlation not between information and circulation but between entertainment and circulation. "A week passed without reports of a battle with thousands killed and wounded," complained Colonel Charles S. Wainwright sarcastically, "is very dull, rendering the papers hardly worth reading." Another observer worried that the public's taste for sensation might actually prolong the war just so they could get more of it. "When it was feared and believed that General Lee might take Washington, Philadelphia, and even New York," he wrote, "there was no panic in those cities, nothing beyond a new sensation, which I believe they enjoyed as much as the spectators of Blondid and Leotard [two daredevils] did their feats of daring and danger."

Critics generally assumed that the curse of sensationalism was the legacy bequeathed by Bennett's *Herald* to the American press. "He made the newspaper powerful, but he made it odious," was how rival editor Horace Greeley of the *New York Tribune* put it. What was a less obvious but arguably a far more important legacy, is that Bennett breached the walls that divided imagination from reality and separated clearly defined entertainments like the theatrical drama, the dime novel and the musicale from a kind of entertainment for which there is still no name, perhaps because people are still loath to acknowledge that it *is* entertainment—an entertainment in life. In short, by inventing the news, Bennett confused realms so thoroughly that no one would ever be able to resolve the confusion. Thus did he confirm Edgar Allan Poe's prescient observation: that the penny press affected "the interests of the country at large" in ways "probably beyond all calculation."

WHAT JAMES GORDON BENNETT had brought together, no man could tear asunder. By 1883 Joseph Pulitzer, a spiritual heir of Bennett's, had assumed command of the *New York World* and taken up where Bennett had left off. Like Bennett, Pulitzer purported to be a populist making his appeal to the working class and immigrants of the city by attacking the establishment and campaigning to tax luxuries, inheritances, large incomes and corporations. But as with Bennett, this was largely a cover for Pulitzer's real agenda, which was selling papers. The dilemma for a publisher, wrote the sociologist Robert E. Park, was designing a newspaper for a "public whose only literature was the family story paper or the cheap novel." The solution, he said, was to "write the news in such a way that it would appeal to the fundamental passions." Pulitzer was so successful at doing so that the *World's* daily circulation rose from 15,000 when he assumed control to 350,000 just four years later. It was the largest readership at the time of any paper in the United States.

The formula Park described was of course just an adaptation of the old penny press's sensationalist recipe. Pulitzer's first issue featured a report of an attack by Haitian rebels that resulted in four hundred deaths, a man struck by lightning, a jailhouse wedding and a condemned murderer who refused the solicitations of a priest. His headlines read like the titles of Gothic novels. BAPTIZED IN BLOOD announced the *World* when a dozen pedestrians were trampled to death on the newly opened Brooklyn Bridge. A FIEND IN HUMAN FORM screamed another to describe a child molester. A condemned murderer was described as going to the gallows SCREAMING FOR MERCY, and an infanticide as A MOTHER'S AWFUL CRIME.

But if the essentials were Bennett's, Pulitzer did add better showmanship. Bennett had been stuck with the written word and with the content of his stories to stir his readers. Pulitzer had packaging. He introduced the right-hand lead—placing the day's major story in the far-right column—which gave greater prominence to a single article, and then unveiled the multicolumn headline, which even he compared to a department store window beckoning customers. He pioneered the use of illustrations, cartoons and comic strips. He employed color lavishly and frequently even printed the headlines in red ink to intensify their effect. The sum of Pulitzer's contributions was to make the newspaper not only an entertainment medium but a *visual* entertainment medium, one in which even the typography was meant to be seen more than read. "In the final stages of the process," observed cultural historian Gunther Barth, "words almost seemed superfluous and at times were superfluous, as audiences became increasingly wearied by logically arranged words as a vehicle of opinion."*

William Randolph Hearst, Pulitzer's incorrigible competitor who bought the *New York Journal* in 1895 to take dead aim at the *World,* also took aim at journalism's pretension that it was a form of public service instructing readers about their world. "The public is even more fond of entertainment than it is of information," averred an early *Journal* editorial, and Hearst was not about to deny the public what it wanted. His *Journal* was more sensational than the *World,* more given to wild effusions of sex and scandal without the patina of respectability that Pulitzer still attempted to preserve. (When reporter Alan Dale met actress Anna Held, the *Journal* head ran: MLLE. ANNA HELD RECEIVES ALAN DALE, ATTIRED IN A

---

* It should be noted that while the penny press was named for its price, the yellow press was named for a character in an R. F. Outcault comic strip drawn first for the *World* and then for the *Journal,* a wisecracking street urchin who wore a yellow gown and was called The Yellow Kid. The difference may have reflected a growing sophistication among critics. The critics of the penny press latched onto price as a way of discrediting the papers and their uncouth readers, while the critics of the yellow press latched onto its sensationalist devices. The first was snobbism, the second a recognition that papers like the *World* were purveying entertainment.

NIGHTIE.) As a mark of its disreputability it sold for a penny, half of the *World*'s price, until Pulitzer was forced to cut it to compete.

In journalism history Hearst would often be credited—or blamed—with having shifted the newspaper decisively from its information function to its story function. His real achievement may have been more novel. Where Bennett was constrained by the written word and Pulitzer by actual events, Hearst treated the news the way an artist might treat a model: as raw material for his imagination. As W. A. Swanberg, one of Hearst's biographers, put it, "The news that actually happened was too dull for him, and besides it was available to other papers." So Hearst decided to make some improvements.

It was both the degree and the shamelessness of the improvements that separated Hearst from his penny press forebears. Sometimes he would create stories whole. Though the *Journal* once described its human interest features as "News Novelettes from Real Life: Stories Gathered from the Live Wires of the Day and Written in Dramatic Form," another Hearst biographer saw this as a euphemism for fabrication. Other times Hearst, who had organized a "murder squad" to patrol the morgue for possible leads, would inject the *Journal* into the story to fan its flames. Thus, when a dismembered corpse was discovered in June 1897, the *Journal* launched an investigation which led to identification of the deceased as Willie Guldensuppe and to the arrest of Mrs. Augusta Nack, a fellow boarder of Guldensuppe's, as she was being chased from the premises by a *Journal* goon squad. Declared Hearst: "The *Journal,* as Usual, ACTS While the Representatives of Ancient Journalism Sit Idly By and Wait for Something to Turn Up."

On a somewhat grander scale, when Evangelina Cosio y Cisneros, the seventeen-year-old grandniece of the president of the insurrectionist Cuban government, was imprisoned for allegedly having lured the military governor Colonel Berriz to her father's home to be abducted, Hearst dispatched a reporter to rescue her by removing the bars on her cell window and then dressing her as a boy to smuggle her out of the country on a steamer headed for the United States. (The guards had actually been bribed to allow the prison break.) The *Journal*, calling her the "Cuban Joan of Arc," filled 375 columns with tales of her New York visit before suddenly dropping her for the next story. It was not long after the "Cisneros affair," however, that Hearst began running jingoistic editorials and inflammatory headlines agitating for an American declaration of war against Spain. "You furnish the pictures and I will furnish the war," went a famous, if apocryphal, cable to the artist Frederic Remington after Remington, on assignment to cover Cuban civil unrest for the *Journal*, had wired Hearst that the country was quiet.

The Spanish-American War in 1898 that Hearst provided was his epic—an entertainment so big that Pulitzer couldn't hope to match it. Having forced President McKinley's hand even before the explosion of the *Maine* in Havana's harbor would rouse America's patriotic fervor, Hearst took an almost proprietary pride in the conflict. HOW DO YOU LIKE THE JOURNAL'S WAR? ran a banner across the paper's front page for several days until he was convinced to remove it. He sent legions of reporters to Cuba to cover the war, and made a foray there himself aboard his yacht. The *Journal* even introduced a promotional contest called the Game of War with Spain. Meanwhile, Pulitzer capitulated and joined the fray. He was later reported to have said, "I rather like the idea of war—not a big one—but one that will arouse interest and give me a chance to gauge the reflex in our circulation figures."

There was as yet one more element for Hearst to add to the life show he was providing his readers. In stage-managing dramatic events with appealing heroes and heroines like Cosio y Cisneros, he had essentially discovered one of the secrets of the movies even before there were movies: Famous Players in Famous Plays, as Paramount Pictures head Adolph Zukor later described his own formula for success. Hearst had great stories and likable leads.

But while he may have been able to orchestrate the action, he was still at the mercy of the events' own protagonists. Taking a page from the old newspaper exposés, which thrust a reporter into the starring role by sending him or her undercover into an insane asylum or a slum or a house of ill repute, Hearst postulated that a dashing reporter would be the protagonist of *any* story he covered, thus shifting the emphasis from the event itself and its characters to the person who wrote about it. In a way, when Hearst assigned the handsome playwright, novelist and quondam journalist Richard Harding Davis to Cuba to cover the insurrection there, he was providing the final link between the news and the nascent motion picture: the star who could be featured against any backdrop and who would bring his own aura to the scene.

As with the penny press, there was no lack of critics of this kind of journalism. They saw it as creating an insatiable appetite for trash that would, despaired one journal, soon make it necessary "to provide fresh new abattoirs in which they [readers] may daily revel." In the same vein, E. L. Godkin groused in the *Nation*, "The condition of excitement into which the press has been thrown during the past fortnight by the marriage of one rich woman and the divorce of another, in fact, seems hardly distinguishable from a form of dementia." He concluded that "by the time the young journalist reaches his place he is apt, in good truth, to look on the world as a stage, and the men and women on it as bad actors, and humanity itself, with all its hopes and fears, as simple 'copy.' "

Partly in reaction, the *New York Times*, rehabilitated and reinvigorated under the ownership of Adolph Ochs, was snapped up by the wealthy and by aspiring middle-class readers who felt that in buying it they could demonstrate their superiority over the presumably moronic readers of the *Journal* and *World*. ("All the World's News, but Not a School for Scandal" was the winning entry in a *Times* contest to find a new slogan.) So important was respectability to certain segments of the middle class that when the *Times* cut its price to a penny to build circulation, many of these same readers were outraged that it, and they, might be thought to be losing status.

Sacralizing itself, the respectable press liked to think that what distinguished it from the yellows was not only tone but function. The journalistic standards of a paper like the *Times* dictated that reporters cover stories of public import on the premise that the chief obligation of the press was to help create an informed citizenry. By the same token, the yellows, like the penny papers before them, believed their chief obligation was satisfying public interest. Traditional journalists saw their work as service. Supposedly less reputable ones saw their work as solicitation.

But in rebuking the yellow press for appealing to man's basest instincts and extolling the respectable press for appealing to man's best ones, the critics were really reiterating yet again the old argument against entertainment and for art. Information about world affairs arrayed in neat, orderly columns was grist for reason, so the argument went. Stories like those in the *Journal,* slathered across the page and proclaimed with deafening headlines, were fuel for passion. "Information is a genre of self-denial," the press historian Michael Schudson has written, succinctly delineating the difference, "the story one of self-indulgence."

Promoting the genre of self-indulgence, the newspaper may have been the single most popular form of entertainment prior to the movies. From 1880 to 1890 newspaper circulation increased more than 135 percent. And whereas in 1880 only four cities had a ratio of less than two readers per paper, by 1890 fifteen cities had such a ratio, and by 1900 nineteen, which meant that more and more people were buying their own newspapers to read. Why the popularity? Short of some sudden surge in civic consciousness, the reasonable explanation is that newspapers, at least the most popular of them, were fun to read. By one study, one-third of the papers in the twenty-one largest metropolitan centers were yellow, but in nearly every major city the circulation leader was a yellow paper while, according to one journalism historian, "Papers of highest news and literary quality had the lowest circulations and made the least money." Moreover, readers themselves now explicitly thought of their newspapers, especially the hefty Sunday papers loaded with features, as an entertainment medium, dashing the hope of poet and publisher William Cullen Bryant that "there is too much moral sense in our community to allow such a speculation proving profitable." Clearly, there wasn't.

EVEN SO, the success of the yellows turned out to be short-lived. The conventional wisdom has it that they perished from their own excesses. The constant blood, sex and scandalmongering finally reached a critical mass that impelled offended bourgeois Americans to pressure the papers and, more important, their advertisers to reform. The lightning rod may have been Hearst's vilification of President William McKinley and what seemed to be the publisher's veiled invitation for someone to assassinate him. "If bad institutions and bad men can be got rid of only by killing," editorialized the *Journal* just months before McKinley was killed in 1901 by a self-proclaimed anarchist at the Pan-American Exposition in Buffalo, New York, "then the killing must be done."

Certainly the president's assassination chastened readers and newspapers alike, though even before it, Pulitzer, in a sudden change of heart, expressed regret at the *World*'s "excess of zeal" and instructed his subordinates to transform it into a "normal newspaper" in the hope of attracting a more affluent readership and classier advertisers. But there was another possible explanation for the demise of the yellow press. The yellows had arrived at virtually the same time as the movies and soon found themselves in competition with them. While Hearst waged the Spanish-American War in the pages of the *Journal,* the movies could actually show the action each night. Crowds wound up packing vaudeville theaters, the venues where the war movies were being screened, to see rather than read about the events of the day.

The movies were also competitors in a deeper sense. Even before they had become a national phenomenon, they upped the ante for the yellow press, forcing newspapers to become even more extreme, more sensationalist to vie with the genetic sensationalism of film. In fact, it wasn't the *New York Times* or the *Tribune* or the reconstituted and newly upscale *Herald* that provided real competition for the *Journal* and *World;* those papers had a completely different audience. It was the movies, which had the same immigrant and working-class audience as the yellows. Given their superiority in providing sensationalist pleasure, it was only a matter of time before movie sensationalism would displace press sensationalism, one entertainment medium shouldering aside another, just as images had shouldered aside print.

Still, it overstates the case to say that newspaper sensationalism suddenly subsided; more accurately, it stagnated once Hearst and Pulitzer were no longer engaged in their ongoing circulation wars and after Pulitzer had decided to move upscale, only to be reenergized in the 1920s with the tabloids. This time, however, there was a difference. When the tabloids arrived to make another sensationalist assault on journalism, they no longer anticipated the movies, as Hearst's *Journal* had; they arrived having already absorbed the lessons of the movies, particularly the lesson that pictures packed more wallop than words.

Appropriately, the first modern American tabloid was named the *Illustrated Daily News,* and it was launched in New York by the *Chicago Tribune* publisher Joseph Medill Patterson on June 26, 1919, with a simple principle: "The story that is told by a picture can be grasped instantly. . . ." Tabloids feasted on pictures, usually a large photo nearly filling the front page and dozens of others scattered about inside, everything from world leaders at a conference to a portrait of a wronged wife to sunbathers at Coney Island. A story that couldn't be illustrated was virtually useless. Pictures are the "very essence of tabloidism," editor Philip Payne declared in 1924 when, under Hearst's auspices, he launched the *New York*

Daily Mirror, a rival tabloid to the *News.* Putting his paper where his philosophy was, Payne devoted two-thirds of the *Mirror's* non-advertising space to photographs in its first year.

To those who saw the tabloid as yet another stage in the degradation of American journalism, this reliance on illustration spoke to the stupidity and even illiteracy of the tabloids' readers, many of them immigrants who had rejected traditional newspapers because, presumably, they couldn't read them. (Though this characterization was more cultural high-hat, it was in fact true that while newspaper circulation in New York soared with the advent of the tabloids, and the *Daily News* alone hit one million readers scarcely five years after its debut, all the growth apparently came from new readers since the circulation at other papers did not dip.) But once again, lost amid the moral outrage and insult, was the deeper effect of tabloid visuals on the culture. By turning the newspaper into a picture book, the tabloids had not only edged closer to the movies but managed to extirpate what may have been the last vestige of traditional journalism: context.

In the tabloids, pictures functioned as symbols, a kind of self-contained shorthand that frequently didn't even require accompanying text, other than a caption. As the critic Richard Schickel would write of this "emblematic" journalism, "Everything it reports exists outside history entirely, is made to live on the page only for the reader's instant gratification." This meant that as entertainment the tabloids were providing a purer form of sensationalism than had previous papers. It also meant that they had disassembled life into a series of pictures that no longer even needed any news value to crack the newspaper. Through the tabloids America was becoming a two-dimensional society in which the news, like the movies, was now measured in images.*

---

* Even photographs were not sacrosanct. The *New York Daily Graphic,* perhaps the most notorious of the tabloids, invented what it called composographs: fabricated photos, using models, of incidents for which there were no actual photographs. The upshot was that the photo, like the text, was a product of the imagination.

At the same time, the tabloid had learned something else from the movies. It had learned that photos could be used as publicity stills for sustained narratives—serials really. Tabloids told stories and told them in such a hyperdramatized manner that already in the late 1920s Robert Park could say that the "news story" and the "fiction story" are "now so much alike that it is sometimes difficult to distinguish them" and adding that the "daily press writes fiction in the form of news." Serial fiction had long been a staple of newspapers. The tabloids now provided serial nonfiction, sagas that kept on unspooling and that ended only when a new narrative arrived to take the place of the old one. (As meteorologists would speak of a storm "organizing," then making landfall and finally dissipating, so a lifie would organize in the media, hit the landfall of headlines and then dissipate while a new lifie gathered strength.) The result was that the tabloid newspaper was almost exactly analogous to a movie theater. It was the place where the lifies played.

Not surprisingly in an entertainment medium, most of these lifies concerned sex and murder. According to one study of New York morning papers, 58 percent more column space was devoted to crime in 1923 than in 1899, which was the heyday of the yellow press. Another survey, from 1929, found that crime news had increased exponentially from an average of one-tenth of a column inch in the *World* in 1881 (before Pulitzer's takeover) to 6 inches in 1893 to 165 inches in 1926.

The best and longest-running of these stories had all the elements of a good movie melodrama, with the enormous advantage that no one could possibly know how the story would end. In the Hall-Mills murder case, which fixated the country for much of the 1920s, a prominent minister named Edward Wheeler Hall was found murdered on DeRussey's Lane on the border of Middlesex and Somerset counties in New Jersey on September 16, 1922. Next to his body was that of one of his parishioners, Mrs. Edward Mills, who had been shot three times in the head, which had then been nearly severed from her body. Around them were scattered scraps of love letters between the two. Newspapermen immediately descended on New Brunswick. Suspicion centered on Mrs. Hall's eccentric, possibly retarded brother Willie Stevens. But when a grand jury refused to issue indictments for lack of evidence, the case seemed to dribble off into oblivion. Mrs. Mills's daughter, Charlotte, told reporters that she was turning to spiritualism to contact her mother and learn the identity of the real killers.

Nearly three years had passed—with the tabloids running other crimes—when Arthur S. Riehl, who had married the Halls' upstairs maid, petitioned to have the marriage annulled on the ground that his wife had withheld information from him about the murders—namely, said Riehl, that on the night of the murders she had accompanied Mrs. Hall, Willie Stevens and the Halls' chauffeur to Phillips Farm, where Stevens shot Mr. Hall and Mrs. Mills. This was precisely the opportunity the tabloids needed. On July 14, 1926, the *Mirror* ran the story on its front page and then launched a daily series daring the authorities to reopen their investigation and charge Mrs. Hall. (It even ran a comic strip on the case.) Two weeks later, murder warrants were issued for Mrs. Hall, her brothers Willie and Henry and their cousin, Henry D. Carpender.

Previous trials, including Richard Robinson's, had certainly attracted media attention. But no trial heretofore had been as dramatically staged or as heavily exploited as Mrs. Hall's. Her trial preparation even included having photo portraits taken of herself to correct what she said was the "injustice done to me through snapshots showing me as a terrible ugly scheming woman. They will have pictures of me at any cost, and I decided that I might as well submit and have a picture taken to show me as I know I am."

When the trial opened in Somerville, New Jersey, that November, refreshment stands were erected along Main Street, one hundred camp chairs were set up in the courtroom to increase capacity, the switchboard from the Dempsey-Tunney heavyweight-championship fight was shipped to handle the calls and a

New York radio station "broadcast" the trial by having a reporter shuttle between the courtroom and an anteroom where he described testimony. The *News* assigned sixteen photographers and reporters, the *Mirror* thirteen. Charlotte Mills covered the proceedings for the Hearst syndicate, even though she had herself testified as a witness, and her father sold his late wife's diaries to Hearst's *American* for five hundred dollars. As for why the respectable *Times* had also assigned sixteen reporters to the trial, Adolph Ochs said, "The yellows see such stories only as opportunities for sensationalism. When the *Times* gives a great amount of space to such stories, it turns out authentic sociological documents."

After one month, 157 witnesses and great manic headlines, the proceedings ended with the acquittal of the defendants. Three months later they filed a libel suit against the *Mirror* for having jiggered the trial in the first place. (Hearst wound up settling.) But like the Helen Jewett case, the real importance of the Hall-Mills case had nothing whatsoever to do with legalities. It had to do with the media. Though the press had embellished other trials and heightened their drama, this time it had actively collaborated with the prosecution to create an event that would heighten itself. Since there was no credible evidence against the defendants, it almost seemed as if the trial had been staged by and for the media, which is exactly what Mrs. Hall said upon her acquittal.

Even the witnesses seemed to realize that they were actors in a media show—especially an overweight, slovenly and somewhat addled farm woman named Jane Gibson who testified for the prosecution. Gibson, labeled the "Pig Woman" by the press because she kept swine, had been riding her donkey the night of the murders and claimed she had seen the assailants—Mrs. Hall and Willie Stevens. The press, knowing a good story when it saw one, embraced the Pig Woman the way a later generation of reporters covering the murder trial of former football star O. J. Simpson embraced his pixilated houseguest Kato Kaelin. When Gibson arrived at the courthouse—ever the self-dramatist, she was suffering from an undefined illness and had to be carried into the courtroom on a stretcher—she was followed by six carloads of reporters and photographers. "Never," opined the *World,* "had a more theatrical day in court been staged."

Now that the show had closed, however, a new drama was required. Early in 1927, just months after the Hall-Mills verdict, media attention shifted to the prosecution of housewife Ruth Snyder and corset salesman Judd Gray for the bludgeon murder of Snyder's husband, and when a photo of Snyder being electrocuted was sneaked out of the Sing Sing Prison death house and run on the front page of the *Daily News,* the paper sold 250,000 additional copies. According to one press historian, "[V]irtually every sizable paper had its largest average circulation during intensive murder trial coverage; its single best days were when verdicts were announced or when executions were carried out." By the end of 1927 one observer, writing in *Harper's Magazine,* was calling the "nationally famous trial for homicide" an "institution, as periodic in its public appearances and reappearances as the cycle of the seasons."

But if Hall-Mills muddled the lines between entertainment and life yet again, the tabloids still hadn't finished the process. At roughly the same time as Hall-Mills, the *New York Graphic* editor Emile Gauvreau, with an insight not unlike Hearst's when he decided star reporters could make stories, realized that the papers could create characters from real people and then "star" them in adventures that could be featured on the front page—a kind of news repertory company. Once they were created, anything these individuals did would be news simply by dint of their recognizability.

His first candidate was a clownish middle-aged real estate magnate named Edward West Browning. Browning had already made the tabloids when his wife ran off to France with her dentist and the bereft realtor placed a newspaper ad for a girl to adopt to keep him company. When that scheme erupted into a tabloid serial—his allegedly innocent teenage adoptee turned out to be a worldly twenty-one-year-old who demanded she be returned to her parents—Browning, now called "Daddy," announced plans to marry a sixteen-year-old girl named Frances Heenan, whom he had met at a high school sorority dance he had organized. Gauvreau, appreciating the appeal of these characters, nicknamed Miss Heenan "Peaches" and promptly put her under contract to provide a running account of her life.

Though no one at the time seemed to recognize it, this was a bizarre new wrinkle in the news: personalities contracted to play out their lives for the amusement of the readers. Those readers evidently loved it. The wedding day issue of the *Graphic* sold 300,000 copies, and Peaches's ongoing "Honeymoon Diary" fueled a daily circulation of 600,000, well over the *Graphic*'s average circulation before Browning and Peaches. When circulation declined, Peaches boosted it again by providing her own sequel. She filed for a separation from "Daddy" and then gave the *Graphic* a series of exclusive interviews on her peculiar marriage, including hints about Browning's unusual sexual practices, which the paper illustrated with its composographs.

"The philosophy which inspires the whole process," Walter Lippmann wrote of the various tabloid excesses,

> is based on the theory, which is no doubt correct, that a great population under modern conditions is not held by sustained convictions and traditions, but that it wants and must have one thrill after another. Perhaps the appetite was always there. But the new publicity engine is peculiarly adapted to feeding it. We have yet to find out what will be the effect on morals and religions and popular government when the generation is in control, which has had its main public experiences in the intermittent blare of these sensations.

He concluded: "There is something new in the world of which we can but dimly appreciate the meaning." The meaning, we would soon discover, was entertainment.

III

THE NEXT EVOLUTIONARY PHASE

FIFTY YEARS AFTER the inauguration of the tabloids, whatever barriers had separated the traditional press from the scandalous press seemed largely to have fallen, and it was generally accepted, if not always openly expressed, that the news media were a branch of entertainment and readers an audience to be entertained or else. "There was a time," Daniel Boorstin wrote in *The Image*, "when the reader of an unexciting newspaper would remark, 'How dull is the world today!' Nowadays he says, 'What a dull newspaper!'" The change could be gauged by how the media presented themselves to the public. The *New York Times* once launched an advertising campaign promising that reading the paper would help one "be more interesting." By 1991 another *Times* ad campaign was asking readers to "share your commute with a well-known entertainer"—namely, the *Times* itself.

In truth, newspapers were no longer adequate to the task of entertaining, though it certainly wasn't for want of trying. Like painters who had devised techniques to approximate three-dimensionality or movement on the canvas, the tabloid kept trying to approximate the movies, but it was finally a lost cause. For all its pictures and garish graphics and for all its emphasis on sustained narrative melodrama, it simply was no longer the most entertaining news medium when there were other media that could generate sensation through sound and movement as well as through text and pictures.

For a time radio seemed poised to overtake the newspaper as a news/entertainment medium, but what it gained in one area, sound, it lacked in another, visuals. (Still, newspapers were so terrified of being usurped that in the early 1930s they successfully prohibited wire services from providing news to radio stations.) The film newsreel seemed an even better candidate to advance the cause of real-life entertainment. But even though newsreels did have sound *and* movement, they lacked the immediacy and the portability of the newspaper, not to mention the newspaper's ability to penetrate wherever its reporters could, and in any case, as preludes to feature films, newsreels were always subordinate to them. As a result, the newsreel never had the transformative effect on the news that its successor was to have.

That successor of course was television, which, like the movies, was a visual medium with an affinity for sensational entertainment. But because in its early days it was live and because it had so many hours to fill, it also had an affinity for news. These affinities quickly meshed; a form of entertainment discovered the best medium for its expression. Television not only had all the advantages of the newsreel, which were the advantages of the plasticity of film, but had the additional benefit of being able when necessary to broadcast events as they happened. This made television the ideal vehicle for the realization of the old dream of the tabloid press to find a way to make the news entertaining enough to rival the movies. In a sense, television news was the tabloid come to life.

There may be no subject in media studies more exhaustively dissected than the influence of television on American culture. As far as the news was concerned, though, its primary effect was simple. With rare exceptions, like *The NewsHour* on the Public Broadcasting System, television turned every report into entertainment—new, improved lifies. Partly this was a function of selection. Like film, and tabloids for that matter, television loved action and suspense, and it didn't matter whether these were provided by conventional entertainment or by reality. By the 1990s scarcely a week passed without a video of a high-speed car chase or an air show accident or a gruesome assault like a trainer's being mauled by a lion or a hostage standoff with reporters anxiously hovering for the denouement or a sky diver whose parachute failed to open. ("You should be warned that what we're about to show you is graphic footage," the anchorperson solemnly intones.) And while everyone knows that the informational value of a car chase or skydiving accident is nil, everyone also knows that the entertainment value is enormous—which is to say, we'll watch.

But if television made news out of anything that had the rudiments of entertainment, it also made entertainment out of anything that had the rudiments of news. Indeed, to television, as to the tabloid, the world was viewed as an endless source of raw material that the medium could process into programming. Film director Billy Wilder had it just about right in his 1951 drama *Ace in the Hole*. An embittered down-on-his-luck newspaper reporter, played by Kirk Douglas, has been furloughed to a geographically and dramatically arid New Mexican desert where a laborer has been trapped while exploring an archaeological ruin. Rescue seems a relatively simple operation; one has only to enlarge the entrance and pull him out. But Douglas, sensing a much bigger story, conspires with the man's estranged wife to have rescuers instead drill another long tunnel perpendicular to the one in which the man is trapped. Proposed as a safer method, it also happens to be a much more protracted one, which gives Douglas a chance to prolong the suspense. Will they reach the laborer in time? How long can he survive? Will the operation even work? Meanwhile, spectators descend on the site in a carnival atmosphere with vendors barking, picnickers lunching and loudspeakers blaring a running commentary on the rescue. (*The Big Carnival* was in fact the film's alternate title.) In the end the reporter gets his story, the readers get their thrills, the media their audience. That the worker dies is almost incidental—a weak, anticlimactic payoff for a great story.

Wilder had obviously intended the film as an indictment of media amorality, but what it described rapidly became standard operating procedure and not only in the low-rent tabloid press but in the news media generally, especially television. For television, it was no longer sufficient to provide news; the news had to be large enough, exciting enough, suspenseful enough or titillating enough to satisfy an audience whose expectations had been steadily and systematically ratcheted up since the 1830s. If an event didn't measure up, one could rest assured that television in its frenzy would make it measure up.

Seen as a television series, which is precisely how television regarded it, the trial of former football star O. J. Simpson for the murder of his wife and a young friend of hers was certainly the most watched and arguably the most entertaining show of the 1990s as well as the most expensively mounted. "In Los Angeles, we've got a movie in which the lead speaks no lines, a blonde bombshell turns out to be a man and the $5-a-day extras in the jury box keep walking off the set," wrote television producer Don Hewitt during the trial, which he accurately called "TV's longest running entertainment special." When the verdict was announced, nine national television networks, including the cable sports channels ESPN and ESPN2, covered it live. ABC revised its prime-time schedule for a two-hour special. NBC and CBS offered continuous coverage from 7:00 A.M. to 5:00 P.M., and all three major broadcast networks had their anchormen hosting the reports. All this, again, not because the trial was an intrinsically important event in American life but because it was an astonishingly entertaining one: part thriller, part murder mystery, part pornography, part courtroom drama.

The Gulf War of 1991 may have been even more bizarre a series. Apparently thinking of the war as it thought of its conventional entertainment programming, each of the television networks introduced its coverage with a title card: ABC's and CNN's was "Crisis in the Gulf"; CBS's was "Showdown in the Gulf" before the war and "War in the Gulf" during; NBC's, the more dramatic "America at War." Each network also had a logo and a musical signature, undoubtedly making this the first war introduced by a theme song. As if that weren't enough, on-site reporters like CNN's Peter Arnett and NBC's Arthur Kent were instantly transformed into stars. The handsome, youthful Kent, flinching and wincing at the detonations of the Russian Scud missiles Iraq fired at Israel, even won the moniker "Scud stud." As the *Nation* quipped, "General Sherman had it all wrong. War ain't hell—it's entertainment."

Nor was television's power to convert events into entertainment confined to America. When the rebel commander Shamil Basayev of Chechnya, a former Soviet republic, took two thousand hostages in southern Russia, the Russian prime minister, Viktor S. Chernomyrdin, negotiated their release over national television. With seemingly the entire country watching raptly, the prime minister, in performance mode, shouted encouragement to Basayev over the screen. The episode prompted one reporter to write bemusedly that "[w]hat happened on television almost overshadowed what happened in Budyonnovsk," where the hostages were first captured.

All this may seem absurd, but none of it is surprising. It has become such a commonplace that the news is just another entertainment in television's endless skein of entertainment, that as early as 1975, when screenwriter Paddy Chayefsky parodied television news' lust for show business in the film *Network*, the satire already seemed tepid. Chayefsky's was the story of anchorman Howard Beale (Peter Finch), a "mandarin of television," whose fortunes and ratings have steadily declined until he is finally fired. But when he delivers a scathing on-the-air valedictory denouncing his own broadcasts as "bullshit," a young programming VP (Faye Dunaway) sees his potential entertainment value. His news broadcast is immediately reconceived with a soothsayer named Sybil, a gossip named Mata Hari, a *vox populi* segment and Beale's own lunatic rants. "Television is not the truth," Beale yells on one of his broadcasts. "Television is a goddamn amusement park. . . .

We're in the boredom-killing business." When his ratings flag once again, the programming VP arranges to have a terrorist group assassinate him on the air, thus providing a ratings boost for both the news hour and the *Mao Tse Tung Hour,* the network's docudrama series of real-life terrorist activities.

In the years since *Network,* television has proved that the film hadn't overstated its case by much, a fact that may have been most obvious in the medium's obsession with its news anchors. When Connie Chung was dismissed from her coanchor position on the *CBS Evening News,* CBS executives cited her "lack of chemistry" with fellow anchor Dan Rather the way a movie producer might cite the lack of chemistry between stars. Moreover, these executives defended the move by saying they had sent Ms. Chung to Oklahoma City to cover the bombing of the federal building there that resulted in 168 deaths in an attempt to rehabilitate her reputation as a journalist. They failed to mention that it had to be rehabilitated from CBS's having had her interview Faye Resnick, a friend of O. J. Simpson's murdered wife and the author of a quickie book on Mrs. Simpson's wanton lifestyle, and for having sent her to Europe with figure skater Tonya Harding, who had been implicated in a scheme to disable rival skater Nancy Kerrigan. Ms. Chung countered that her image had suffered on behalf of ratings, though it had really suffered on behalf of entertainment.

Yet one can't fault the networks. The reason they are anchor-crazy is that anchors and star reporters do for television news what Richard Harding Davis once did for the yellow press and what actors do for movies: They carry their star power wherever they happen to appear. That is what makes them such valuable commodities. As *New York Times* television critic Walter Goodman once described the symbiosis between the networks and their anchors, "[T]he anchors win a degree of fame and fortune far beyond the lot of mere reporters and the networks have stars to promote." Thus, placing an anchor in front of a backdrop—the cratered Berlin Wall during the fall of communism, the Iraqi desert during the Gulf War, Princess Di's funeral cortege—turns every news event into a photo opportunity that signals its gravity and importance by virtue of the fact that the star is there bearing witness. "It's show business," Marvin Zindler, the most popular news anchorman in Houston, Texas, told a reporter after recounting his numerous plastic surgeries. "And if this isn't show business, then I'm a fairy godmother." *

It has turned out to be pretty good show business too. Over the years television has so successfully heightened reality and increased its entertainment value that life, at least life as it is captured by a television camera, has become every bit as entertaining as most of the conventional programs that surround it. Back in 1953, in his cautionary novel *Fahrenheit 451*, Ray Bradbury outlined a harrowing future in which people lolled about most of the day watching giant television screens that featured lengthy broadcasts of police chases and criminal apprehensions. Aside from the prescience of this prophecy in a culture where television programs like *Cops* do exactly what Bradbury's screens did, Bradbury here anticipated the power of reality to fascinate us. He foresaw that life, with its built-in suspense and automatic plausibility, would become the very best show on television. In the words of a promotional campaign for Court-TV, a cable network specializing in the broadcast of actual courtroom trials: "Great Drama. No Scripts."

Picking up where Bradbury left off, the 1998 film *The Truman Show* suggested that real-life entertainments don't have to be harvested from reality; reality can be coextensive with entertainment, without any news peg whatsoever to justify broadcasting it. Television executives label this "reality programming," although

* Network news surely isn't the worst of it. Because local television news generates so much of the revenue for its stations and because that revenue is predicated on good ratings, it is far more beholden to entertainment than the network news organizations. In fact, local news is really the tail that wags the news dog, reporting on stories that the network news seems loath to report but that it must finally present once the local news has done so. It is a matter of keeping up with the entertainment competition, only in this case the competition happens to be what's playing on the local screens.

"voyeurism programming" might be more accurate. In the film, Truman Burbank (Jim Carrey) is adopted at birth by a media conglomerate and placed with two actors assigned to play his parents; the whole "family" is then set down within a cheery seaside elysium named Seahaven, which, unbeknownst to Truman, is actually a giant enclosed set in which every resident, including his own wife and his best friend, is an actor taking cues from on high. Thus settled, Truman unwittingly lives his entire life under the scrutiny of thousands of hidden television cameras for an ongoing show— a show that, in the words of its creator, provides "hope and joy and inspiration to millions." And why? Because, says the creator, "We've become bored with watching actors do phony emotions." Raw reality—even the appearance of raw, undramatized reality— is better entertainment.

AS IT POLISHED, processed and packaged reality into news, television wound up integrating life and entertainment more thoroughly and inextricably than any previous news vendor ever had or could. Even though the newspaper in its entirety was an entertainment medium, newspapers nevertheless were divided into spaces which clearly demarcated one department from another: hard news from columns from features from editorial from sports from humor from whatever. Television, on the other hand, was divided by time, which proved a much more fluid and porous boundary. On television one thing flowed into another until the divisions gradually began to disappear entirely and only entertainment remained.

Nowhere was this more evident than in what may have been the medium's most ingenious fusion of life and show: the television newsmagazine. The art critic Robert Hughes, who was one of the original cohosts of the ABC newsmagazine 20/20 before being dismissed after a single program, acidly enumerated the hybrid's characteristics:

There was the voyeuristic interest in confession of sins. There was the fixation on celebrity. There was the almost total absence of any serious news—by which I mean narratives and explanations which enable viewers to get a handle on the world in a rational way. There was the phony sentimentality, the mock humanism. Above all, there was the belief that reality must always take the back seat to entertainment, so that the audience must not be overtaxed, so that they will come back for more of the same Twinkle.

What Hughes didn't say is that television newsmagazines, unlike news broadcasts or news specials, were competing against entertainment programming and were explicitly judged by television's ultimate standard of entertainment value: ratings. Like any other program, be it a situation comedy or a drama, they were compelled to attract an audience. "If you're running a magazine show and your mandate is to keep that show on the air," admitted Thomas Lennon, a former producer at *20/20*, "you know what you have to do. And if you don't do it, you will be replaced by someone who does."

What you have to do is give the audience a good show since presumably it is entertainment that people want. That is why television newsmagazines are so enamored of crowd-pleasing aesthetic stratagems that even the network news programs wouldn't dare deploy: musical overlays on scenes of tragedy or poignance, ambush interviews, hidden cameras, the implacable lingering on an interviewee's emotional breakdown. That is also why television newsmagazines jockey for star interviews or for an interview with the latest newsmaker: a prostitute who has compromised a public official, a domestic dishing the dirt on his or her famous employer, a disgraced celebrity, the latest hot criminal. Acknowledging the difference between this expansive television newsmagazine idea of news and even traditional television news, *Rolling Stone* magazine labeled the former the "new news," which commentator Bill Moyers defined as a "heady concoction, part Hollywood film and

TV, part pop music and pop art, mixed with popular culture and celebrity magazines, tabloid telecasts and home video." In short, a grab bag of sensation.

Television journalists have usually been quick to disassociate themselves from the idea of the "new news" even as many of them have necessarily served it. "[W]e should all be ashamed of what we have and have not done," CBS news anchor Dan Rather once lectured a group of news directors. "They've got us putting more and more fuzz and wuzz on the air, cop-shop stuff, so as to compete not with other news programs but with entertainment programs, including those posing as news programs, for dead bodies, mayhem and lurid tales. 'Action Jackson' is the cry. Hire lookers, not writers. Do powder puff, not probing interviews."

Most observers would have found Rather's description all too accurate, but once again television was only a symptom and not the cause. The cause was the public's hunger for entertainment; fiction or reality-based, it made no difference. And though television had clearly expedited and expanded news-as-entertainment, the print media were racing to keep pace for fear of being thought obsolete or irrelevant.

The creation of the national newspaper *USA Today* was a case in point. If television was the tabloid come to life, *USA Today,* with its lively colors, its bold layout, its brief stories, its numerous graphs and maps, was television come to print. Here, indeed, was a paper to watch, not to read. Yet it wasn't just sensation that *USA Today* provided; like a typical nonreality-based television show or feature film, it provided escapism too. With its chatty tone and chirpy outlook, *USA Today* had what journalist David Remnick called "an overwhelming desire to please and unite the citizenry, such an obdurate unwillingness to face the sorrows and complexities of the modern world," which is precisely how one might have described the most popular television situation comedies and the most popular motion pictures.

Yet even traditional papers, faced with the competition of television news, felt the pull of interest over import. Some simply added more color and graphics like *USA Today*'s. Some increased celebrity coverage. And some resorted to their own form of docudrama. When figure skater Nancy Kerrigan and her rival and accused attacker, Tonya Harding, arrived at the Olympic venue in Lillehammer, Norway, to compete in the 1994 Winter Games, the Pulitzer Prize–winning *Newsday* ran a "composograph" of Kerrigan and Harding practicing side by side under the headline FIRE ON ICE, though the two had not actually skated together. It was, to put it charitably, a speculation.

A more subtle effect of television on the print media was the way newspapers began to apply the methods of fiction to news stories, so that more and more news reports opened the way novels did: by setting the scene or establishing characters. On one typical day the *New York Times* ran six stories on its front page. One, a periodic report on Vietnam, began: "Their streets are blocked by peddlers, beggars and parked motorbikes, their houses are overflowing with young children and visiting relatives. . . ." Another, on an unlicensed driver who ran a red light and killed three members of one family, opened: "He found equanimity poking through the entrails of a car." A third, on heroin use among the wealthy, began: "The rising young fashion photographer was acting jumpy. He scratched the label off a beer bottle and skittered his fingers over the buttons of a cellular phone without ever dialing." Two other stories began less novelistically, but only one began with what might be called straight reporting. "I want the traditional, first-paragraph lead, which when well done is infinitely better prose than this feeble imitation of story openings in the *Saturday Evening Post*," Jacques Barzun wrote of this phenomenon, and added, "It is no excuse that the fake fictional style ushers in feature stories rather than news, for what has happened at the same time is that much more news than before is now given in the feature form."

Still other times the print media, while not necessarily fabricating events as Hearst did, added narrative contours that made them more dramatic. This was particularly true of confusing and essentially nonnarrative situations, such as the U.S. savings-and-loan scandals of the 1980s or the revolutions rippling through Communist Eastern Europe in the late 1980s and early 1990s. So desperate were foreign journalists to give majestic sweep to the fall of the Czech Communist Party, for example, that they portrayed its defeat as a sudden capitulation to democratic demands when it had in fact been the result of long, protracted negotiations between the party and dissidents, negotiations that were anything but dramatic.

As analyzed by Janos Horvat, an Hungarian journalist, even the toppling of the Berlin Wall seems actually to have been the result of similar efforts by the foreign press to provide a single gesture large enough and dramatic enough to symbolize the fall of communism. In Horvat's chronology, on November 8, 1989, it was reported that the East German Politburo had resigned in the face of mounting political tensions after East Germans began fleeing to the West via Hungary. The next day Günter Schabowski, a member of the new Politburo, announced at a televised news conference that the government might consider permitting free travel. Asked when, Schabowski replied, *"Ab sofort* [immediately]," meaning that *deliberations* to permit travel would begin immediately. When the press failed to report the distinction, preferring instead to interpret Schabowski as having surrendered to the public will, East Germans understandably began storming the wall. On November 10 the *New York Times,* the *Los Angeles Times* and the *Washington Post* all reported that East Germany had at long last removed all restrictions on travel. The *Post's* headline read: EAST GERMANY OPENS BERLIN WALL AND BORDERS.

This, Horvat claims, was simply not true. But the press seemed, in his words, to have a "desire to portray the event both as an unbridled manifestation of collective sentiment and popular will, and as a clear victory for liberalism and democracy in the theater of global politics." It wanted a definitive "tearing down of the wall" rather than the bureaucratic chipping at it that was a much more likely eventuality had the press not provided its own script. Having provided it, the actors performed it.

Some of the best and most sensitive journalists recognized this new impulse to reshape the news to make it more entertaining, and agonized over their own complicity and culpability. "I realized that the time had come to pull out of Bosnia," wrote Peter Maass, who covered the civil war in that country for the *Washington Post.* "You were on the lookout for these stories, not because anybody back home was going to do anything about it, but because it was good copy. The agony of Bosnia was being turned into a snuff film. I couldn't see any wisdom in risking my life to help produce the final reel."

Finally, the influence of television was evident in the kind of story that even the most respectable newspapers now felt obliged to report lest they be co-opted. In May 1987 virtually every paper in the country carried accounts of Democratic presidential candidate and U.S. senator Gary Hart's spending the night with an attractive young woman who was not his wife, most of them on the somewhat strained pretext that this was relevant information in judging his fitness for the presidency and not just an appeal to our prurient interest. Similarly, the *New York Times,* the benchmark of journalistic respectability, not only covered the Palm Beach rape trial of William Kennedy Smith, a nephew of the late President John F. Kennedy, but also broke journalistic tradition by naming his accuser and detailing her allegedly unsavory past, though the only apparent purpose served by doing so was to provide some lubricious entertainment for jaded readers.

But the real watershed moment in the convergence of the respectable press and the tabloid and of information and entertainment may have been the Gennifer Flowers story in 1992. Flowers was a onetime Little Rock, Arkansas, television reporter who claimed to have had a long-term affair with then–presidential candidate and Arkansas governor Bill Clinton. Seizing her moment in the spotlight, she had sold her story to the *Star,* a supermarket tabloid, and then appeared at a press conference to promote the paper.

In the past no mainstream newspaper would have touched a story from so tainted a source as a supermarket tabloid. (Hart's apartment had at least been staked out by a reporter from the *Miami Herald* who had taken the candidate at his word when, declaring he had nothing to hide, he dared journalists to trail him.) Rather, rightly or not, respectable papers would have quarantined the story by disdaining it, claiming that it wasn't "fit to print," that it had neither credibility nor relevance, and they would have done so in a pique of pride intended to demonstrate how much they favored the information function of the news over the salacious interest function—all apropos of what one writer noted about *New York Times* publisher Adolph Ochs on the paper's seventy-fifth anniversary: "He in the end taught them [competitors] that decency meant dollars."

Now, however, Flowers's disclosure was reported everywhere: in the nonsupermarket tabloids, on tabloid television shows, on most local news broadcasts, on television network news broadcasts and finally, if somewhat tentatively, in the respectable press. (The scandalous press would suffer from these incursions on its turf; by one report the three leading supermarket tabloids—the *National Enquirer,* the *Star* and the *Globe*—each lost 30 percent in circulation from 1991 to 1996.) Why had the respectable press accepted the terms not even of the tabloid press but of the *supermarket* tabloid press? What had happened was the old iron law of popular culture at work, the law that decreed that any entertainment originating at the margins of the culture would eventually be co-opted by and domesticated for the middle class.

The tabloid had been a working-class organ scorned by the middle class. But television news arrived without the stigma of the tabloids, and as a result it was able to present the same scandalous stories as the tabloids while absolving its middle-class audience of any guilt for watching them. This made television not only the fullest realization of sensational tabloid entertainment but its Trojan horse as well, sneaking news/entertainment right into the middle-class living room from which it had always been banned. Once television had done so, once it began airing tabloid stories that had little traditional claim to importance but that could attract more viewers—and here the local television news was more avid than the network news—the respectable press was no longer bound by its old obligations. To hold the line when everyone, including its own middle-class reader, was already familiar with a story, when everyone seemed to think it was the biggest story around, would have been foolish and self-defeating. The Flowers disclosure was only the final station on this long road to conflation.

But leveling the barriers had another, deeper effect than that of making the respectable press resemble its old nemesis. It also leveled once and for all the old standard of journalistic value and raised a new one in its place: entertainment. By the old standard of public importance, one took it on faith that a president's State of the Union address was more newsworthy than, say, the verdict in a civil trial. By the new standard of entertainment, this was no longer necessarily true. When President Clinton's 1997 State of the Union message happened to coincide with the announcement of the verdict in the wrongful-death action against O. J. Simpson, television networks were faced with a textbook dilemma of hallowed journalistic tradition versus terrific entertainment. In the event, it turned out that President Clinton finished his speech just in the nick of time for the jurors to announce their decision, sparing the network news organizations from having to choose between these stories. Still, the public hand-wringing by the media as they deliberated which story to headline only underscored how much things had changed since the days when the respectable press and the tabloid press seemed to inhabit different worlds.

In fact, it may have marked the last time that the media, television or print, would ever waver in the face of an entertaining story. In January 1998, when reports began circulating on the Internet, an even less accountable source than a supermarket tabloid, that *Newsweek* magazine had held a story about independent prosecutor Kenneth Starr's investigating an alleged affair between President Clinton and a twenty-four-year-old former White House intern named Monica S. Lewinsky, the media, including the respectable press, revved themselves into a state of high excitement, even though *Newsweek* itself, in a rare bout of journalistic conscience, had chosen not to print the story initially because the magazine's editor had doubts about Lewinsky's credibility.

In running with a story that at the time was all allegations and no hard evidence, it was possible the other media had passed through their own hypocrisy in the Gennifer Flowers incident and now actually believed that reporting the details of the president's supposed sexual affair was a public service, especially with the convenient pretext that his real offense was not the affair itself but his having lied about it during a legal deposition. It is more likely, though, that the media, so often accused of liberal favoritism, were simply revealing—and reveling in—their true bias, the bias toward any story that had entertainment value. What Lewinsky gave them was a great new lifie to exploit: "Crisis in the White House," as ABC immediately labeled the series.*

Whatever this said about the mores of the media—and in fairness the superiority of information over entertainment was never as self-evident as critics of the press contended—the triumph of tabloidism did reveal something new and profoundly important

---

* The news journalists themselves obviously couldn't admit this. They spent the first weeks of the Lewinsky story desperately trying to justify their coverage of it by insisting that it was a matter of grave national concern. But the public knew better. With President Clinton's approval ratings high and with his alleged behavior having demonstrably had no effect on his ability to govern, the public, in television ratings and polls, made two things clear: (1) They loved hearing about the Lewinsky affair, but (2) they believed the affair had no relevance to anything beyond itself. It was, in short, entertainment.

about American culture. Because the news was entertainment and because the news provided a common window on public reality, the window through which most of us apprehended those parts of life with which we didn't have direct contact, entertainment had stealthily become the standard of value for reality itself. In a society in which even news events were prioritized by sensationalism, it was as difficult for the public as for the media to resist the notion that what was most entertaining—the O. J. Simpson trials, Tonya Harding's attack on Nancy Kerrigan, any juicy crime, a sex scandal—deserved our attention and that what wasn't entertaining didn't and should be pushed to the periphery of our consciousness, even if the public felt no need to invoke the journalistic pretense of some higher purpose. Through the wiles of television news, everything in the public sphere was now to be measured by entertainment. Or to put it another way, through television, entertainment had finally escaped the news and seized life.

Chapter Three

The Secondary Effect

I

THE MÖBIUS WORLD

IF THE PRIMARY EFFECT of the media in the late twentieth century was to turn nearly everything that passed across their screens into entertainment, the secondary and ultimately more significant effect was to force nearly everything to turn itself into entertainment in order to attract media attention. In *The Image*, Daniel Boorstin had coined the term "pseudo-event" to describe events that had been concocted by public relations practitioners to get attention from the press. Movie premieres, publishing parties, press conferences, balloon crossings, sponsored sporting contests, award ceremonies, demonstrations and hunger strikes, to name just a few examples, all were synthetic, manufactured pseudo-events that wouldn't have existed if someone hadn't been seeking publicity and if the media hadn't been seeking something to fill their pages and airwaves, preferably something entertaining.

But the idea of pseudo-events almost seemed quaint by the late twentieth century. Most people realized that the object of virtually everyone in public life of any sort was to attract the media and that everyone from the top movie stars to the parents of septuplets now had to have a press agent to promote them. What most people were also coming to realize, if only by virtue of how much the media had grown, was that pseudo-events had proliferated to such an extent that one could hardly call them events anymore because there were no longer any seams between them and the rest of life, no way of separating the pseudo from the so-called authentic. Almost everything in life had appropriated the techniques of public relations to gain access to the media, so that it wasn't the pseudo-event one was talking about anymore when one cited the cleverness of PR men and women; it was pseudo-life.

Yet not even pseudo-life did full justice to the modern condition. That's because the media were not just passively recording the public performances and manipulations of others, even when life was nothing but manipulations. Having invited these performances in the first place, the media justified covering them because they were receiving media attention, which is every bit as convoluted as it sounds. The result was to make of modern society one giant Heisenberg effect, in which the media were not really reporting what people did; they were reporting what people did to get media attention. In other words, as life was increasingly being lived for the media, so the media were increasingly covering themselves and their impact on life.

That we intuitively know life has become a show staged for the media may explain why by the 1970s there was such a fascination with the mechanics and logistics of entertainment: with conventional performers' hirings and contracts, with movie budgets and grosses, with television ratings, with backstage dramas and turmoil as well as with press agents, spin doctors, speechwriters and anyone else whose job was to contribute to creating an effect. (Of course the backstage drama often constituted a movie that rivaled

or surpassed the movies on-screen.) It is almost as if having lived
for so long with the idea of the suspension of disbelief for conventional entertainments, we demanded a confirmation of disbelief
for the unconventional entertainment of life to prove to ourselves
that we weren't being fooled, that we knew life was all a scam.

Attributing the sudden increase in show business news to
television's preoccupation with entertainment, Neil Postman
called it a "ricochet effect," meaning that the entertainment
values of television bounced off the other media and then got
deflected back into television. "Whereas television taught the
magazines that news is nothing but entertainment," Postman
wrote, "the magazines have taught television that nothing but
entertainment is news." He concluded: "Both the form and
content of news become entertainment"—to wit, *Entertainment
Tonight, Access Hollywood, Show Business Today* and a half dozen
other programs that by the mid-1990s were reporting entertainment news, not to mention regular features on network and local
news broadcasts and the E! cable channel dedicated exclusively to
entertainment.

For all the attention focused on the process, however, the
essence of the pseudo-life was not the fact that it was manufactured. The media's lust—the audience's lust—was for entertainment, and the pseudo-life was manufactured in the name of
entertainment, which made that its real essence. What everyone,
it seemed, was trying to discover was the most exciting, provocative, sensational way to package whatever it was he was doing so
that he might gain shelf space in the crowded media supermarket
where good entertainment was the fastest-selling product, more
often than not the only product sold. If the wares were synthetic,
it was because one was always having to test new methods, apply
new techniques, in the quest for audience approval.

It stood to reason that the more dependent an enterprise or
industry was on public exposure, the more rapidly its practitioners

would learn how to transform it into entertainment, which is why politics was among the very first arenas, after journalism itself, to adopt the stratagems of show business. According to Plutarch, Cicero was trained in public speaking by Roscius the comedian and Aesop the tragedian. Napoleon took instruction from the actor Talma in the art of small talk and carefully calculated everything from his rages to his poses. In antebellum America political orators like Daniel Webster, John C. Calhoun and Henry Clay studied theatrical declamation, prompting Washington, D.C., theater managers to complain that their own presentations couldn't compete with those of the politicians. The theatrical tradition only intensified through the remainder of the century, culminating with Theodore Roosevelt, whom cultural historian Leo Braudy described as the "fruit of nineteenth-century theater" and a "man as comfortable as Mark Twain or any performer with being on stage, where he played not the part of another so much as a larger-than-life version of himself."

But however much the theater may have affected politicians, no entertainment form would theatricalize politics more powerfully than television. In politics, as in all things, television demanded action and it demanded personality. "[T]he reality of politics is boring—committees, hassles with bureaucrats, and the like," Richard Sennett observed in *The Fall of Public Man*. "To understand these hassles would make active interpretative demands on the audience. This real life you tune out; you want to know 'what kind of person' makes things happen. That picture TV can give you while making no demands on your own responsive powers if it concentrates on what the politician feels."

Watching Dwight Eisenhower's presidential campaign, sociologist David Riesman drew a similar conclusion. As Riesman saw it, "wherever we see glamor in the object of attention, we must suspect a basic apathy in the spectator." Essentially he was saying that in the benumbed America of the 1950s, glamour was a political sales device just as it was a sales device in most conventional entertainments, a way to engage people and bestir them from their state of inertia. What they were bestirred to, however, was obviously not political action; it was the pleasure of entertainment. The politician had simply become another kind of star, the political process another form of show, and television its best stage.

Of course Riesman was writing before John F. Kennedy's ascension taught us all how much glamour really counted in the new political environment. With his father's background in Hollywood, where the elder Kennedy had once owned the RKO studio, with his own frequent forays into the film community and with his matinee idol good looks, Kennedy was the harbinger of a new kind of politics that was predicated on star appeal. "What we are dealing with here," Richard Schickel wrote of Kennedy's effect on American politics, "is a recognition on the part of the candidate and his managers that traditional debts and alliances within the party and among various outside interest groups were, in the age of television, of less significance in winning elections, and in governance itself, than the creation of an image that gave the illusion of masculine dynamism without sacrifice of ongoing affection. Which is, one hardly need add, exactly what a successful male movie star recognizes his job to be."

It was with Kennedy in mind that Norman Mailer in 1960 prophesied that "America's politics would now be also America's favorite movie." If not favorite, it would certainly become one of the biggest and longest-running. Candidates were the putative stars, the primaries open casting calls, the campaign was an audition and the election itself the selection of the lead, while the handlers served as drama coaches, scriptwriters and directors. As for substantive issues, though they couldn't be purged entirely, they largely became what film director Alfred Hitchcock, in a discussion of his plotting, once called macguffins—that is, they are the excuse for setting the whole process in motion though they have virtually no intrinsic value. And the purpose of the process?

Ostensibly, of course, it was to provide leaders and set policy. But the reality was that it could make for truly swell entertainment.

Even before politicians came to understand that they were performers, the media, with their penchant for turning everything into entertainment, began repackaging the political process along the lines of show business. If campaigns were largely bouts of dull rhetoric, television coverage simply compressed them into sharp images and sound bites. In a study of the evening network news programs' campaign coverage, Professor Kiku Adatto of Harvard found that the average length of an uninterrupted sound bite declined from 42.3 seconds in 1968 to 9.8 seconds by 1988, with none in the latter election exceeding a minute. And if government itself was a series of bloodless policy decisions, the media simply shifted their focus to politics, so that everything a president did was seen not in terms of its effect on the public, which was boring, but in terms of its effect on his candidacy, which lent government the drama of an ongoing contest. It was, wrote editor and press critic James Fallows, as if every medical advance "boiled down to speculation about whether its creator would win the Nobel prize that year," which is exactly how the media *would* cover medicine if the public showed any interest in it.

Better yet for the political entertainment, once the Watergate scandal erupted in 1972, coverage of the presidency was consumed with disclosures of personal fallibility, not, one assumes, because the press suddenly decided to hold public servants to a higher ethical standard but because public servants were now being held to a higher standard of entertainment. They now were expected to star in an elaborate film noir of corruption and/or sex rather than the standard fare of political one-upmanship. Indeed, the job of the president, his family and his entourage, wrote columnist Russell Baker of the new media scandalmongering, was to "provide a manageably small cast for a national sitcom, or soap opera, or docudrama, making it easy for media people to persuade themselves they are covering the news while mostly just entertaining us." Kurt Andersen of *The New Yorker* labeled President Clinton the "Entertainer-in-Chief."

While the public now accepts that politics is what one journalist called "politainment," it is difficult for us to appreciate just how startling the idea once was that politicians themselves had come to think of the political process as entertainment and had discovered ways to make themselves appear to be what they believed voters wanted them to be. When the writer Joe McGinniss was given access to the innards of Richard Nixon's 1968 presidential campaign and then spun his observations into *The Selling of the President* the next year, his book almost seemed like a revelation. Never before had anyone exposed from the very belly of the beast just how cynically the political process could be manipulated into a media event.

In McGinniss's account, Nixon and his media advisers were the supreme cynics, crafting an image for the candidate and then crafting him to fit it. Harry Treleaven, Nixon's creative director of campaign advertising, even enumerated each of the candidate's flaws and then the corrective for it. No sense of humor. "If we're going to be witty, let a pro write the words." Lack of warmth. "Give him words to say that will show his emotional involvement with the issues." Lack of spontaneity. "He should be presented in some kind of 'situation' rather than cold in a studio. The situation should look unstaged even if it's not."

To effect the last, Nixon's advisers turned the campaign into a series of meticulously staged "spontaneous" television programs produced by Roger Ailes, the executive producer of *The Mike Douglas Show*, a popular afternoon television talk program at the time. "The whole day was built around a television show," McGinniss wrote of the Nixon campaign. "Even when ten thousand people stood in front of his hotel and screamed for him to greet them, he stayed locked up in his room, resting for the show." At the same time that his campaign was beholden to television, Nixon was to denounce the medium and other media manipulations. Said the

Nixon media strategy guide: "[T]he sophisticated candidate, while analyzing his own on-the-air technique as carefully as an old pro studies his swing, will state frequently that there is no place for 'public relations gimmicks' or 'those show business guys' in this campaign."

But if the main vehicle of the campaign was television, the main thrust of television itself was to disassociate content from image, words from feelings, cogitation from reflex, so that the audience would react rather than think—*inter tenere* rather than *ekstasis.* "Voters are basically lazy, basically uninterested in making an effort to understand what we're talking about," Nixon speechwriter Raymond Price emphasized in a campaign white paper that echoed Riesman and anticipated Sennett. "Reason requires a high degree of discipline of concentration; impression is easier. Reason pushes the viewer back, it assaults him, it demands that he agree or disagree; impression can envelop him, invite him in, without making an intellectual demand. . . . The emotions are more easily roused, closer to the surface, more malleable." In short, sensation, the very basis of entertainment, was now to be the very basis of politics too.

And so, following Price's prescription, the campaign advertising did not feature candidate Nixon discussing policy or announcing his vision for America or making any substantive comments whatsoever. Rather, it featured Nixon's voice delivering what even one of his own advisers called "incredible pap" while quintessentially American, Rockwellian images flashed across the screen and forged a subliminal association between the disembodied Nixon and the positive values conveyed by the pictures. *What* he said was irrelevant. As an assistant working on these campaign spots said, "The words are given meaning by the impressions created by the stills."

Ploys like these that caused such a stir in Nixon's day became the very stuff of politics scarcely twenty years later. Americans took it for granted that political commercials were as deceptive and vacuous as any other commercials and that campaigns themselves were shows. Joan Didion, writing of the 1988 presidential contest, which matched the Democratic candidate, Massachusetts Governor Michael Dukakis, against the Republican candidate, Vice President George Bush, observed that everything they did was staged for television and called the traveling campaign "a set, moved at considerable expense from location to location" for the purpose of generating images and sound bites for the media. "There was the hierarchy of the set: there were actors, there were directors, there were script supervisors, there were grips," Didion continued. "There was the isolation of the set, and the arrogance, the contempt for outsiders. . . . There was the tedium of the set: the time spent waiting for shots to be set up."

Specifically, Didion cited Dukakis playing catch on the tarmac at the San Diego airport—a re-creation, it turned out, of an earlier game of catch in Ohio that only the Cable News Network had managed to capture. The ball-tossing, a seemingly casual interlude, was actually staged for the media, and on an otherwise newsless day assumed a symbolic life of its own, a movie vignette to be interpreted by the critics, who variously found the tossing a sign of Dukakis's being "downright jaunty" (Joe Klein, *New York* magazine), an occasion for toughness (Michael Kramer, *U.S. News*) or a moment to limber up (David Broder, *Washington Post*). Didion concluded: "What we had in the tarmac arrival with ball tossing, then, was an understanding: a repeated moment witnessed by many people all of whom believed it to be a setup and yet most of whom believed that only an outsider, only someone too 'naive' to know the rules of the game, would so describe it."

It was *all* a setup now between the politicians and the press. Every speech; every campaign stop; every idle moment between stops like the ball-tossing; every buss the candidate planted on his wife's cheek; every blink and smile and frown and tear—it was all for the camera. A behind-the-scenes documentary on the 1994 Senate campaign in Virginia of Oliver North, former deputy national security adviser in the Reagan administration, showed his strategists weighing which of North's daughters read the Tele-PrompTer best and showed North himself choking up on cue. "We're all caught up in the entertainment value of politics," said North's senior adviser. In the same vein, an adviser to 1984 Democratic presidential candidate Walter Mondale admitted that in preparing for a televised debate, "We spent more time talking about ties than East-West relations."

And it was not just individuals who adopted the trappings of theater; it was institutions. Perhaps most obviously and egregiously, the party conventions became television extravaganzas, not events to be covered by the media but programs staged expressly for them. The time of the opening gavel and the length of the sessions were set to accommodate the media. Color schemes for the rostrum were chosen with the television camera in mind. Speakers were scheduled either to grab the media spotlight or, in the case of a potential embarrassment like Republican renegade reactionary Pat Buchanan, to avoid it. Demonstrations were strictly limited so as not to cut into television time. And the delegates themselves were regarded, in Didion's words, as "dress extras."

Since the media were a party to the sham, they were placed in the peculiar position of having to judge how effectively a politician used them, which, in this political version of the Heisenberg effect, meant that the media weren't really covering politics at all. They were covering themselves covering politics.

Take the televised debates—pseudo-events replete with scripted zingers like 1988 Democratic vice-presidential candidate Lloyd Bentsen's "I knew John Kennedy and you are no John Kennedy" when GOP candidate Dan Quayle compared himself to Kennedy, or septuagenarian Ronald Reagan's "I am not going to exploit for political purposes my opponent's youth and inexperience" when asked about the age issue in a 1984 debate with Walter Mondale. The debates were obviously conceived as media events in which the combatants' delivery was of far more importance than the substance of their remarks. But the standard by which debates were judged was not even the candidates' poise in presentation. The standard was how that presentation was perceived by the media, their sense of who had won. Each debate was followed by a media postmortem to determine which candidate had most impressed the press, since that is what the analysts were really talking about (who impressed *them*); and because the sense of "who won" was all anyone seemed to care about, the media's postmortem became the real story, regardless of what actually happened during the debate or even how the public itself felt. Which is to say that, in a Pirandellian twist, the media reaction to the debate always supplanted the debate.

But because the media were taking their own pulse and then reporting on it and because the pulse became the real story, one really needed *another* report to report the media reaction in order to assess and then convey how the debate actually changed the political race. And because the report of the report now would become the real story with its own inflection and interpretation and influence, one needed yet *another* report on the report of the report . . . and so on into an infinite progression of the media covering the media covering the media.

Of course the media were fully aware that the campaigns were being staged for their benefit and that they were conduits through which manipulations like Nixon's would reach the public. But they also prided themselves on their superiority to those manipulations, and that may explain why they began placing the stagecraft itself at the center of so much of their reportage. "The language of political reporting was filled with accounts of staging and backdrops, camera angles and scripts, sound bites and spin control, photo opportunities and media gurus," Kiku Adatto found in her study comparing the 1988 campaign coverage with that of 1968. "So attentive was television news to the way the campaigns constructed images for television that political reporters began to sound like theater critics, reporting more on the stagecraft than the substance of politics." By her count, 52 percent of the campaign reports on the evening network news programs were devoted to stagecraft, which placed the media coverage at yet another remove from what once was thought to be real: from covering the political pseudo-events staged for them to covering their own reaction to those events to covering the techniques devised to elicit their reactions.

In fact, one could say that in large part the purpose of a presidential campaign was now not just to provide a striking set of images and events for the media to cover but to show the media how efficiently and effectively the politicos had created these images and events, just the opposite of what Ailes had tried to do. That is why during the course of a campaign one could watch the bizarre phenomenon of a political handler like Republican operative Ed Rollins or Democratic adviser Dick Morris explaining to the press how he is using them to manipulate an image even while, as he speaks, he is using them to manipulate an image: the image of his campaign's mastery of the media.

At the same time that the media were reporting on stagecraft, they were also at pains to demonstrate their imperviousness to it—or at least their imperviousness to the worst of it. They always seemed eager to reveal how the manipulations could misfire, as they did, famously, when Dukakis, in a photo opportunity intended to convey his strength and commitment to defense, perched himself atop a tank and wound up looking ridiculous, largely because of the obviousness of the attempt. According to Adatto, this trivial incident appeared in one form or another eighteen times on the network news, always as an example of Dukakis's failure—that is, his failure to provide convincing images for the media. But what it really demonstrated was the extent to which the media, realizing that campaigns had become movies, now applied the critical standards of movie reviewers to judge them. Did the candidate look good and did he perform well? Were the production values first-rate? Were the manipulations well hidden from public view, or could one see the hand behind the "special effects"? Above all, was the audience sufficiently entertained in the way the director intended? The result: Whoever provided the best show received the media's imprimatur, which, in the two-dimensional entertainment society, was almost tantamount to election.

II

ENTERTAINER-IN-CHIEF

ONE CAN CERTAINLY understand how and why the election process turned into a quadrennial movie given the inherent horserace aspect, the need for a candidate to project a likable image to the electorate just as movie stars had to project likability on-screen, the general hoopla and the importance of holding the public's interest over the course of many months. But government had been something else. In the past, once the race was over and the new president had settled into the White House, the overt politicking ended and real policy making began, which isn't to say that presidents didn't deploy public relations techniques, only that those techniques didn't constitute the sum and substance of the presidency as they had constituted the sum and substance of the presidential campaign.

Or at least that is how it was before presidents realized the centrality of perception to governing. This realization is usually attributed to John Kennedy, who had a wonderful flair for the dramatic and a keen awareness of his own charisma, but the pioneer, once again, may have really been Richard Nixon, who lacked Kennedy's natural ease and needed to compensate. According to political analyst Jonathan Schell, Nixon, borrowing a page from his own campaign playbook, "began to frame policy not to solve real problems but only to appear to solve them. . . . " What Nixon comprehended is that since the presidency no less than the campaign is played out in the media, one could provide them with set pieces—staged rallies, an early-morning visit with Vietnam protesters at the Lincoln Memorial, a trip to Red China—that presented you as having achieved what you had said you wanted to achieve whether or not you had actually achieved it, just as during the campaign one provided set pieces that showed you were what you said you were whether or not you actually were. It was government of, by and for images.*

Despite his discovery, Nixon had no real talent for this kind of government, not only because he wasn't a very polished actor but because he couldn't help regarding his own machinations as public relations, just on a grand scale. Ronald Reagan, on the other hand, thought of presidential image-making strategically rather than, as Nixon did, tactically. Reagan intuited that in a society where movies are the central metaphor, everything boiled down to perception and that therefore there was nothing but perception. "What he wanted to be, and what he became, was an accomplished presidential performer," wrote Reagan biographer Lou Cannon in *President Reagan: The Role of a Lifetime*. Other presidents, of course, have been consummate performers; Franklin Roosevelt comes immediately to mind. But for Roosevelt the performance was always a function of the presidency, a means of selling his policies. For Reagan the presidency was a function of the performance. What he was selling was good vibes.

Needless to say, it helped that Reagan had been a movie actor and that virtually all his professional training had been in the arts of performance. He understood the affinity between politics and acting, and he never hid that understanding from public view. He once told the television journalist David Brinkley, "There have been times in this office when I've wondered how you could do

---

* Actually the first modern politician to have arrived at this conclusion may have been German Chancellor Adolf Hitler. Hitler certainly realized the political power of aesthetics, as his parades and rallies attest. According to Hans Jürgen Syberberg's film *Our Hitler,* he would also spend hours watching American movies, not for entertainment but apparently for pointers he could incorporate in governing.

the job if you hadn't been an actor." And when he was asked during his first gubernatorial campaign what kind of governor he would be, he quipped only half-jokingly, "I don't know. I've never played a governor." His lack of guile was part of his charm. Whereas other politicians may have seemed to come to acting through some kind of mendacity, Reagan, as a professional actor, came to it naturally. An actor acts. It is what he does, and that made it extremely difficult for the media to deconstruct his performance as a performance.

But if Reagan thought of himself as a politician /actor, he also thought of his presidency as the movie in which he was starring. According to Lou Cannon, literally everything was scripted for him on half-sheets of heavy bond paper in oversized type, even his own private conversations—a habit that once ignited an explosion from House Speaker Tip O'Neill because Reagan insisted on reading from his notes rather than speaking extemporaneously. (Whether, in retrospect, this could be attributable to the onset of his Alzheimer's disease, no one will ever know.) Advisers learned to use Hollywood terminology to communicate with him, and Secretary of State George Shultz once coached him for a meeting with Soviet leader Mikhail Gorbachev by telling the president how to act "in this scene." Reagan himself compared his daily routine at the White House with the routine of an actor: preparing at night for the next day's scenes, "running lines" during briefings with his advisers in the terminology of movie actors rehearsing dialogue, then going before the cameras in the morning. He would even criticize Nixon's line-readings, with the disdain of a seasoned pro for the amateur.

What separated Reagan's technique from that of a Nixon or even a Kennedy was that Reagan had so thoroughly internalized the cosmology of the movies that he now lived entirely within it— his reality displaced by the movies', his own memories displaced by our collective memory of the movies. He would frequently recount movie plots as if they had actually happened, like the story of a B-17 commander during World War II who comforted a wounded young turret gunner as their plane was going down by taking the gunner's hand and saying, "Never mind, son, we'll ride it down together." (It was in fact a scene from *A Wing and a Prayer.*) On another occasion, delivering a tribute to the dead of the Normandy invasion, he asked, "Where do we find such men?," not realizing that he had taken the line from the admiral in *The Bridges at Toko-Ri.* Advisers often found him addressing issues by applying solutions he had seen in the movies that he screened every weekend at the White House or at the presidential retreat, Camp David. During one arms control meeting with congressional leaders, he began retelling the plot of the film *WarGames.*

It may have seemed surreal—reconceptualizing the presidency as a movie, right down to the scripted conversations—but it was surprisingly effective, both because in invoking movies Reagan was drawing on a deep reservoir of allusion, symbol and emotion in the electorate and because it was obvious that he himself devoutly believed in the values of those movies he invoked. (In fact, his much-vaunted "traditional values" owed much more to the Metro-Goldwyn-Mayer films of the 1930s than to the America of the nineteenth century.) Though Reagan hadn't been a Method actor in Hollywood and hadn't dredged his own life for the "sense memories" that Stanislavsky, the father of the Method, saw as the basis for performance, he became one in the presidency. It was just that the life he dredged was the sum of his movie roles. "There are not two Ronald Reagans," Nancy Reagan once said of her husband. She meant apparently that Reagan believed everything he said, but she also meant, perhaps without intending it, that the actor had subsumed the man.

If so, it couldn't have made for a better presidency in the age of entertainment. Summarizing Reagan's first administration, the political columnist Morton Kondracke rhapsodized that he "has cast a kind of golden glow over the past 4½ years, his programs representing a return to bedrock American values and his optimism shielding the country from bitter realities such as burdensome debt, social inequity and international challenge. Reagan is a kind of magic totem against the cold future."

This genial reassurance was often cited as the primary source of Reagan's appeal, but what was both less obvious and more significant was that it was also his primary presidential objective. For Reagan, the presidency was a movie not only in the sense that it was scripted from Hollywood conventions to play better on the media screens but because it had the same exact function as the majority of Hollywood movies: escapism. Ronald Reagan was the first president to see politics not as a means of addressing problems but as a way of distracting the public from them, the first to design his presidency for the express purpose of making people feel better the way they seemed to feel better watching an entertaining film. (Even substantive policies like shrinking the government or challenging the Soviets as an "evil empire" were framed in movie rhetoric as simple panaceas.) With Reagan in the White House, it was always, to use his 1984 campaign slogan, "morning in America," even though in this theater the lights never came up.

And if Americans readily acquiesced in the illusion, it was not because they were credulous enough to believe that there were no problems in the nation but because Reagan's presidency was a pretty good movie as movies go: well executed, thematically sound, coherent, deeply satisfying and, above all, fun. It made people feel how they wanted to feel. "You believed it because you wanted to believe it," President Reagan once told a columnist who insisted he had seen the young actor on the set of the movie *Brother Rat,* even though Reagan had not been there. "There's nothing wrong with that. I do it all the time."

Though it would take as good and sincere an actor in the White House to replicate this achievement, President Reagan nevertheless left a powerful legacy even for those without his histrionic gifts. In the first place, he made the movies the model for public policy. It was because Reagan had paved the way with science-fiction movie plans like his "Star Wars" antimissile system, and with B movie pronouncements like "They can run, but they can't hide" when Arab terrorists hijacked the *Achille Lauro* luxury liner and killed an American passenger, that House Speaker Newt Gingrich could talk seriously of solving the welfare problem by invoking the old MGM movie *Boys Town* or that George Bush, in accepting the Republican nomination for the presidency, could use Clint Eastwood's line "Read my lips" to swear that he would endorse no new taxes.

It was also because Reagan had demonstrated the power of government as a form of entertainment that his successor, George Bush, could (to some degree) anticipate the movie *Wag the Dog*, about a Hollywood impresario who produces a phony war to deflect criticism of the president, by staging a military campaign to rout Iraqi troops from Kuwait in 1991 as if it were a multibillion-dollar movie blockbuster. There would be no Vietnams in the post-Reagan era, no long, logy, hallucinatory movies in which the good guys were indistinguishable from the bad and the plot dribbled away to entropy. Rather, the Gulf War was formulated like a World War II picture from Reagan's Hollywood heyday. It was meant to be short and sharp, its narrative lineaments clean, its heroes heroic and its mustachioed villain, Iraqi dictator Saddam Hussein, an evil mastermind right out of the hoariest anti-Nazi propaganda. As broadcast by the conventional media, the war even ended like a World War II movie, with the troops parading triumphantly down Broadway or Main Street, showered by confetti and basking in the gratitude of their fellow Americans while the credits rolled. Nor was that all to the analogy. Even after it was over, the Gulf War, like every blockbuster, had its ancillary markets: trading cards, T-shirts, videocassettes of the action.

Nevertheless, there was an important distinction between this "movie" and the conventional movies that had helped keep the home fires burning during World War II, other than the obvious one that those played in theaters and this one played in the medium of life. Those World War II movies had been designed to mobilize support and forge a consensus for the real war being fought overseas. But when the war itself is a movie, when its real-life objectives are murky and mercurial, what exactly is the war movie mobilizing support for?

Once again it was Reagan, after having taught his successors the value of feel-good as a policy goal, who provided the answer. It mobilizes support for itself, which is why the real point of the Gulf War may not have been to liberate occupied Kuwait, insure the flow of oil or eliminate Saddam Hussein, each of which had been adduced as a possible objective. Though President Bush may not have realized it himself and though it discounts the legitimate risks of the war to say so, the real point may have been simply to make us feel good by allowing us the exhilaration of a happy ending, which is, of course, traditionally the function not of warfare but of entertainment.

Turning the presidency into a movie and policy into escapism are no small accomplishments, but Reagan's most enduring legacy may be that in doing so, he also wound up establishing a new measure of presidential success: the president's skill before the media. Affable and supremely self-confident no matter what crisis befell him, Reagan was so deft a performer that he was always able to refocus attention from the matter at hand to his coolness in handling it until the coolness obliterated what it was he was being cool about. The media, which were much more intrigued with theater than policy anyway, happily abetted him because next to drama, performance was what they most admired in a public official. They loved to gush about Reagan's ability to soar above the action and regarded it with something like awe; the Teflon president, they called him after the no-stick surface, because nothing bad ever stuck to him.

But by fixating on Reagan's theatrical skills, the media had not only merged their preoccupations with his but merged their standards with the standards of government. Before Reagan, when one

spoke of a president's performance in office, one meant the effica-
ciousness of his policies. After Reagan, one was more likely to
mean it literally—that is, his movie rather than his management.*
Or, as one young aide to President Clinton put it while complaining about negative press coverage, "We know how to govern. We
just don't know how to give the perception of governing."

In managing to create such a powerful perception of governing, Reagan raised the bar for every political performer who followed. A president or presidential candidate now had to be
smooth or suffer the wrath of the press. This forced poor, verbally
challenged George Bush into scripting supposedly extemporaneous answers to questions just the way Reagan had and then turning snappish when, during a closed-circuit television address to
the convention of the Association of Christian Schools International, his questioners hadn't followed the script. "We've got to get
this sorted out here," he blurted over a live microphone to his
aides. "It happened last week, too. Something's gone awry here."

Nor was it just a president's performance in the role of president that Reagan revised; he created an expectation that politicians possess what in acting is called range. Before his presidency,
a politician making an appearance on a television program might
at most be prompted to play the piano as a way of revealing his
humanity without also compromising his dignity. After his presidency, politicians were expected to appear on talk shows with the
facility of seasoned entertainers, relating anecdotes, telling jokes
and bantering with the host. (Comedian Jay Leno once described

---

* Just as America's conventional movies influenced the rest of the world, so did its government movie. When Russian President Boris Yeltsin made a state visit to Washington in
1991, an aide to President Bush remarked at the makeover Yeltsin had undergone since his
last visit. "He's polished some of the rougher edges from two years ago," said the aide. "He
understands public presentation now, the importance of symbolism as a message" (*New
York Times,* June 23, 1991). Similarly, when Russian Prime Minister Viktor S. Chernomyrdin was campaigning during the 1995 parliamentary elections, he enlisted American
rap star Hammer to headline his rallies, and almost every party list included pop stars and
actors as candidates. Asked why he was running, one singer answered, "Honestly speaking, who the hell knows?" (*New York Times,* November 16, 1995).

politics as show business for ugly people.) When Vice President Albert Gore appeared on *The Late Show with David Letterman,* a segment producer pressed him to balance a broom on his chin, though Gore demurred, preferring to discuss government waste instead. (He did, however, bring a Top Ten List.) Said the disappointed producer: "Let's try to get through this stuff as fast as possible. It's going to put America to sleep."

That was the point. It wasn't only the politicians who suddenly found themselves in the entertainment whirlwind. It was the public itself. By converting politics into show business, President Reagan had also helped convert an electorate with responsibilities into an audience with demands—primarily the demand to be entertained—and thus provided the final element in what was the real political revolution of the 1980s: not the much-bruited-about demise of postwar liberalism and the rise of conservatism but the triumph of entertainment over political ideology of any sort. Indeed, to the extent that ideology mattered at all, it had become just another plot device to fire up the audience, conservatives against liberals, liberals against conservatives, not much different from cowboys against Indians in the movies of yore. As President Reagan himself mused after leaving office in what may have been an expression of his own overriding ideology, "You like the audience. You want to please the audience."

Perhaps the final confirmation of how thoroughly political life had been transformed in the post-Reagan era was that the media started treating it exactly the way they treated any conventional entertainment. Standard tabloids were now as likely to feature the president in some lurid headline as they were an entertainer like Madonna or Michael Jackson, while supermarket tabloids began covering Washington with the same salacious zeal with which they covered Hollywood. The *National Enquirer* even opened a Washington bureau. "We refer to Washington as Hollywood East around here," said the paper's editor.

Meanwhile, John F. Kennedy, Jr., son of the late president,

read the portents and launched a political magazine titled *George* that explicitly embraced politics as politainment. "We want to make politics sort of entertaining," Kennedy told the *New York Times*, and called it "another aspect of cultural life, not all that different from sports and music and art." Kennedy took some criticism for *George*'s flippant attitude toward the sacred institution of politics, but it was probably because he had revealed what political journalists had generally tried to conceal. Politics wasn't any different from anything else in the popular culture. It was just show business for ugly people.

III
MACGUFFINS

POLITICIANS HAD simply caught on faster to the lesson everyone would eventually learn: that people could hardly resist the impulse to turn virtually everything into entertainment when entertainment was what everyone seemed to be demanding. Some things easily conformed because they already had a genetic predisposition to entertain. Sporting events, for example, rapidly evolved from competitions to exhibitions, though until the late twentieth century they had resisted the more blatant invasions of show business gimmickry. When chorus girls took the field during the opening ceremonies of the 1924 World Series, they were seen as interlopers and were pelted with oranges and pop bottles. By the 1970s baseball stadiums had mascots roaming the stands and scoreboards cueing fans when to cheer, and only the most diehard of traditionalists would have thought twice about it.

The reason for these additions, of course, was that baseball was a long, pastoral and contemplative game born of the nineteenth century and now trying to survive in a twentieth-century entertainment society that prized fast, hyper and sensational. The confused lords of the sport were just trying to adjust. The new sports of choice were football and basketball, which were better suited both to the aesthetics of television and to the ever-growing demand for bigger, faster, louder that was the entertainment equivalent of a new drug high. In the end baseball would surrender not only to mascots and scoreboards. It would sacrifice the very fabric of the game to entertainment: lowering pitching mounds, shrinking strike zones, quickening playing surfaces, replacing pitchers with designated hitters, juicing the baseball— all designed to increase the number of runs on the assumption, no doubt accurate, that for most fans high-scoring games were far more entertaining than low-scoring ones.

Still, it remained for the Walt Disney Company to mine the deeper affinities between sport and movies. Disney had made a popular film titled *The Mighty Ducks* about a ragtag group of youngsters who are molded into a championship hockey team. The company then bought a National Hockey League franchise, named it the Mighty Ducks, used for its logo the Ducks' logo in the movie and called its arena The Pond. In a brilliant stroke of cross-merchandising, the movie (and its sequels) sold the hockey team while the hockey team sold the movies and both sold the products bearing that duck insignia. Later the Disney Company, having released a remake of the old film *Angels in the Outfield*, repeated the strategy by purchasing a controlling interest in the California Angels baseball team and redesigning its uniforms to conform with those in the movie. It only underscored what one Cub fan said of his team, which was owned by the *Chicago Tribune* newspaper and television company: "Just remember: It's not a team, it's a TV show." (He might have said a "movie.")

But the movie was more than logos and merchandising. In planning its coverage of the 1996 Summer Olympics from Atlanta, NBC television devised a strategy based on extensive research that was meant to ensure higher ratings. "Story" was research director Nicholas Schiavone's discovery as he told it to *New Yorker* contributor David Remnick. "Viewers want a narrative momentum, a story that builds." Schiavone added other ingredients: reality ("unscripted drama"), possibility ("the rise of individuals from ordinary athletes and their humble beginnings to the company of the world's elite"), idealism (the "purity and honor" of the Olympics) and patriotism ("National honor and Olympic tradition seem to go hand in hand"). But, said Schiavone, "What they [viewers] really want is not live but alive; not sports but stories about sports," a finding that accounted for why so much of the Olympics' coverage revolved around profiles of athletes rather than around the athletic events themselves.

Essentially what Schiavone was saying is that just as policy positions were the macguffins of political campaigns, so athletic events were the macguffins for sports coverage. The competition was an excuse and a denouement for the movie, and the movie was the athlete's melodrama. Here is a figure skater whose father was killed just before the competition, and another who was orphaned. Here is a downhill skier who wasn't thought good enough to make his country's team and was laying bricks when he finally was rediscovered and called to action. Here is a football player who overcame a youth of gang violence, a basketball player whose sisters died of AIDS and a baseball player who returned to the field after having been diagnosed with and treated for cancer. Who needs the sporting events when the athletes themselves are walking inspirational soap operas?

With athletic events subordinated to the athlete's story, it is no wonder that Deion Sanders, both a professional football cornerback and a professional baseball outfielder, began calling himself an entertainer. Obviously all professional athletes are entertainers in the sense that what they do entertains us, but one suspects that was not exactly what Sanders meant. More likely he meant that he provided a certain extra panache on the field beyond that required by the assignment itself and that he provided a certain panache off it too. He was, in short, aware that his performance transcended athletics and that he had a persona to maintain.

Though Sanders's life was not exactly the stuff of inspirational tearjerkers, he did have his own "movie," shaped by him and his image-makers and presented by the media, in which he starred as an ostentatious high-liver and fast-talker who loves money and sprouts dollar signs to prove it. (There was even a music video to go with it.) Later he underwent a religious conversion, which gave him a new movie to promote. Similarly, basketball's Charles Barkley starred in his movie as a lovable curmudgeon, Shaquille O'Neal in his as a gentle giant, boxer Mike Tyson in his as an implacable force of nature and basketball player Dennis Rodman in his as an outrageous, cross-dressing, gender-bending, rule-breaking, tattooed bad-ass, a role that got him far more attention from the media than anything he did on the court, unless it was something, like head-butting a referee or kicking a courtside photographer, that reinforced his off-court image. Only the most exceptional athletes, a Michael Jordan, Wayne Gretzky or Joe Montana, were able to act out their movies on the actual court, ice or playing field, which is precisely what made them exceptional.

If sport didn't have a difficult time transforming itself into entertainment, neither, it turned out, did religion. Evangelical Protestantism, which had begun as a kind of spiritual entertainment in the nineteenth century, only refined its techniques in the twentieth, especially after the advent of television. Televangelists like Oral Roberts and Jimmy Swaggart recast the old revival meeting as a television variety show, and Pat Robertson's 700 *Club* was modeled after *The Tonight Show,* only the guests on this talk show weren't pitching a new movie or album; they were pitching salvation.

But it wasn't just on television that religion appropriated the methods of entertainment to keep a flock that was everywhere inundated by show business. It was in the churches themselves. The movement toward a more vernacular liturgy and more contemporary music may have seemed like simple modernization of an aging religious institution; not incidentally, however, they were also ways of making services more entertaining. One young minister in Waco, Texas, boasted that his congregation had the best rock music in town, describing the sound as a "cross between Pearl Jam and Hootie and the Blowfish." The popular megachurch movement of the 1990s, which attracted thousands of worshippers to cavernous auditoriums, even implemented the same devices as any rock group trying to fill a stadium: not only the music but light shows and huge overhead projectors illustrating sermons or showing video clips. Some even had cappuccino carts and food courts.

Yet one didn't have to be a member of a new religious movement to appreciate the value of entertainment as a spiritual force. Colm Tobin, reporting in *The New Yorker,* described a dramatic visit that Pope John Paul II made to Czestochowa, Poland, in 1991. The pope, who, like Ronald Reagan, had acting experience from his student days, mounted the platform gingerly as if he were too frail to continue, then turned wanly to gaze upon the crowd. "He did not wave or make any gesture," wrote Tobin.

> The television lights were on him, and his face was alert to all the tricks of light. He turned again and walked up to the altar, wandering from side to side, as though in deep reverie and contemplation. The crowd held its breath. The young people cheered him; they were ready to do anything he said. Later, he sat with his hands covering his face, as though the burden of his office were too much for him. And later still, when a young girl from the Sudan who had been reading some of the prayers during the ceremony tried to run toward him and was held back by security guards, he gestured to them to let her go, and she came up to him and wrapped her arms around him. The crowd was spellbound.

It was clearly a great and deeply moving performance, this ebb of strength and flow of resolve, but what the celebrants may not have realized is how closely it resembled the signature climax of soul singer James Brown's act, where Brown stumbles and collapses only to be helped gently to his feet by his acolytes and draped with a protective cape, a man stricken by the burdens of rock and roll but forcing himself to soldier on as the pope at Czestochowa soldiered on through the heavy burdens of the papacy.

PERHAPS THE MOST DIFFICULT adjustments to the imperatives of entertainment were those undergone by the arts, which had, by definition, been arrayed against entertainment and had denied its sensationalist aesthetic. These had tried to hold the line even as everything else seemed to be succumbing around them, but not even art could finally resist the siren call of show business. The arts were forced either to surrender or to be marginalized to the point where they would cease to matter to any but a handful of devotees.

In literature the erosion of will began early. Some critics blamed paperback books for driving publishing into the arms of entertainment, seeing them, in effect, as the television of literature; they made books available, but they also cheapened them. One publisher, complaining about sensational paperback covers, opined, "The contents of the book . . . were relatively unimportant. What mattered was that its lurid exterior should ambush the customer." Others traced the decline even further back to the rise of magazine serialization as a major source of book revenue and the need for books to adapt themselves to this method of distribution, which entailed bold characters, strong plots, cliffhangers and other sensationalist appurtenances.

Still others saw the decline of serious literature in direct proportion to the rise of commerce in publishing. When the Book-of-the-Month Club, itself a commercial institution dedicated to selling books rather than promoting literature, eased out its editor in chief in 1996 and transferred his duties to the head of marketing, a former club juror, Brad Leithauser, dejectedly said they could just as easily be selling kitchen supplies now. It was an increasingly common plaint among writers that books had become another commodity to be marketed, but the blame on commercialism was misplaced. Since no one expected publishing to be an eleemosynary institution, the problem wasn't commercialism per se; it was the kinds of books that commerce demanded. What empowered the forces of marketing was entertainment because quite simply, entertaining books were more likely to sell than nonentertaining ones, or more accurately, books that could become part of an entertainment process were more likely to sell.

In a way the real entertainment hurdle for literature, even trashy popular literature, was the fact of the word. Words, as Neil Postman has written, demanded much more effort than visuals, and even if one were to expend that effort, there were obvious limitations to the sensation generated by words compared with the seemingly limitless sensation generated by the visuals and sounds of the movies, television and computers. None of this was lost on publishers. Just as newspapers realized their insufficiency versus television news, so publishers realized their insufficiency versus the entertainment competition, and they sought to do something about it.

What publishers discovered was that given the right circumstances, a book was ultimately incidental to its own sales. It was yet another macguffin for a larger show. What publishing houses were really selling was a phenomenon—something the media would flog the way media flogged any Hollywood blockbuster. The object was to get people talking about a book, get them feeling that they had missed something if they didn't know about it, even though they were responding not to the book itself, which few of them probably had read or would read, but rather to the frenzy whipped up around the book—a controversy or novel feature or eye-catching angle like a seven-figure advance to the author or a big-money sale of the film rights. The frenzy assumed a life of its own even as the alleged object of the frenzy kept receding further and further into the background. The novelist David Foster Wallace, bemused when the media began championing his immense novel *Infinite Jest* and making Wallace himself a literary star, called this the "excitement about the excitement." It was one of the principal marketing tools for anything in the Republic of Entertainment.

As far as literature went, most of the initial excitement was stirred not by the book but by its author, whose life movie would promote the book the way Olympic athletes' life movies promoted the Olympics for NBC. The tradition actually stretched back at least as far as Byron, who was canny enough to cultivate a bohemian persona as the Romantic poet and then actively exploit it. As Dwight Macdonald described it, "Byron's reputation was different from that of Chaucer, Spenser, Shakespeare, Milton, Dryden and Pope because it was based on the man—on what the public conceived to be the man—rather than on his work. His poems were taken not as artistic objects in themselves but as expressions of their creator's personality."

Walt Whitman did the same and to the same effect. He wanted to be seen as a character whose personality would advertise his poetry. A friend once described him as a "poseur of truly colossal proportions, one to whom playing a part had long before become so habitual that he ceased to be conscious that he was doing it." In fact, the idea that celebrity could create a best-seller more easily than a best-seller could create celebrity was enough of a commonplace by the end of the nineteenth century that the protagonist of *New Grub Street,* an 1891 novel, could say, "If I am an unknown man, and publish a wonderful book, it will make its way very slowly, or not at all. If I become a known man, publish that very same book, its praise will echo over both hemispheres."

However true it was then, it became even truer in the age of mass media. No one, though, seemed to have as ready a grasp of this as Ernest Hemingway, who was actually compared to Byron for his flagrant self-promotion. Just as thoroughly as any fictional character he created in his novels, Hemingway created a persona for himself and authored a life movie in which he could star on the screens of the media. This was Hemingway the artist roughneck, expatriate war hero, bullfight lover, big-game hunter, deep-sea fisherman, world-class drinker, womanizer, brawler—a man so outsized that he dwarfed the writer and his books even though this movie was the main reason anyone but litterateurs was likely to pay his books any heed. Critic Edmund Wilson churlishly called this persona "the Hemingway of the handsome photographs with the sportsman's tan and the outdoor grin, with the ominous resemblance to Clark Gable, who poses with giant marlin which he has just hauled off Key West," as opposed to Hemingway the writer.

Of course Hemingway knew the value of all this, and though critics continued to lament that he had sacrificed his art on the altar of celebrity or that he was, as Leo Braudy put it, "the prime case of someone fatally caught between his genius and his publicity," he realized that there might have been very little art if it weren't for the celebrity—at least very little art that anyone would buy, much less read. As he metamorphosed into "Papa Hemingway," the grizzled macho icon with his beard stubble and peak cap, he became more popular than ever and even gained a certain immunity from the critics, who now routinely disparaged his work. The public who defended him didn't really care whether he was a good writer. They cared that he was a bold personality—a movie's idea of a good writer.

In the end, Hemingway would be one of the most influential writers of the twentieth century, but it was not as the proponent of lean literary modernism; it was as the proponent of literary celebrity. Where he led, virtually every writer trying to make his mark followed. "The way to save your work and reach more readers is to advertise yourself, steal your own favorite page out of Hemingway's unwritten Notes from Papa on How the Working Novelist Can Get Ahead," Norman Mailer wrote in *Advertisements for Myself,* thus acknowledging his debt to Hemingway while also granting that he himself had a "changeable personality, a sullen disposition, and a calculating mind" that would seem to disqualify him from celebrity. (Of course, far from being disqualified, Mailer turned these very qualities into his own salable persona.)

Still, Hemingway and Mailer had talent, and their personas as brawling artists ultimately depended upon it. A more impressive feat was to create a persona so entertaining that there didn't have to be any talent. Editor Michael Korda credited writer Jacqueline Susann with this advance. Having emerged from public relations—Susann's husband, Irving Mansfield, was an old PR man— she hawked her books by hawking herself as a celebrity, though she had done nothing to earn that status. "When we expressed anxiety about the manuscript," Korda wrote in a reminiscence of Susann, "Irving told us that it was Jackie (and the example of 'Valley [of the Dolls],' then approaching ten million copies sold) that he was selling, and not, as he put it indignantly, 'a goddam pile of paper.'" His point was that the book was absolutely irrelevant once the name was on the cover.

It was a relatively small step from this to designer publishing, in which the author's name, like a fashion designer's label, sold the book even if the author hadn't written the book. This in fact was what technothriller author Tom Clancy achieved. In 1995 Clancy signed to publish a line of paperback thrillers targeted at teenagers, the first of which was to be titled *Tom Clancy's Net Force.* Despite the possessive case, however, Clancy wasn't necessarily going to write the story. As the *New York Times* put it in its announcement of the deal, his role would be to "oversee the book's production"—in the event, the byline read "created by Tom Clancy"—which gave the author an entirely new function. He was no longer a writer; he was an imprimatur.

With all this effort devoted to creating personalities who could sell books, the next logical step was to drop the middlemen—that is, writers—entirely and go directly to celebrities themselves, as publishers increasingly did through the 1980s and 1990s. Actors and actresses, singers, comedians, war heroes, anchormen and protagonists of scandals signed huge publishing contracts clearly not because anyone expected them to produce great books but because they carried ready-made entertainment value from other media which they could vest in this one. They were, in show business parlance, "crossover artists."

As it turned out, it was no guarantee. The trouble with celebrity as a sales device was that it was volatile, as Random House discovered after giving aging television-soap-opera diva Joan Collins $4 million to write a novel. Collins, however, delivered what the publisher deemed an unacceptable manuscript, and Random House sued to recover $1.2 million of the advance it had paid. Collins's editor, Joni Evans, testified that the novel was "very primitive, very much off base. . . . it was jumbled and disjointed"—as if she had been expecting Collins to submit a real book and not just put her name on the jacket. Collins told reporters afterwards, "They were begging for me!" and quoted Evans as having told agent Irving "Swifty" Lazar, "I want Joan Collins in my stable so much I can taste it!" But that was when Joan Collins was still a marketable name. By the time she submitted her manuscript, her star had fallen, and from the perspective of some outsiders at least, Random House seemed to be placed in the uncomfortable position of rejecting her for her decline. Or to put it another way, the book itself seemed to become relevant only when Collins wasn't.

With publishers essentially selling so many books on the backs of their authors' lifies because these were the only things that could trigger the conventional media's interest, it almost became a requirement that noncelebrities have great life stories or be condemned to midlist, the Siberia of publishing. Even a dense and difficult literary novel like Salman Rushdie's *The Satanic Verses* became a best-seller when Iran's Ayatollah Ruhollah Khomeini issued a *fatwa*, or religious edict, imposing a death sentence on the author for allegedly having insulted the Muslim faith in the book. The *fatwa* thrust Rushdie into a terrifying life movie and forced him into hiding, but it also gave him a name recognition that very few literary novelists could possibly hope to match. When he appeared publicly in New York to promote a new novel, the cognoscenti showed up in force as they never would have had Rushdie been just an author rather than the celebrity star of his very own thriller. Columnist Frank Rich called the display "*fatwa* chic."

But Rushdie, a serious novelist, was simply the most glaring example of a publishing industry in hostage to entertainment, an industry in which authors' own stories superseded their books. Poet Ted Hughes's *Birthday Letters* became a best-seller because the poems addressed the suicide of his wife Sylvia Plath. A slender volume of verse titled *Ants on the Melon* by Virginia Hamilton Adair, an eighty-three-year-old blind woman who had gone largely unpublished, made Adair a minor celebrity and won her a *New Yorker* profile, though the poet J. D. McClatchy, unimpressed by the quality of the poetry, said, "Her story seems to be the story, not the work," which could also have been said about so many of the new literary phenomena. Even Adair herself agreed: "I think part of it is this old nut, a character."

Or there was Michael Palmer, the doctor who, inspired by the example of medical suspense novelist Robin Cook, decided to try his hand at a medical thriller. When he was about to embark on his book tour, however, he realized he wasn't getting what he called high-profile bookings. So Palmer decided to reveal that he was a recovering alcoholic and Demerol addict and was now helping other, similarly afflicted physicians. His publicists beamed over the disclosure, knowing it would generate press. Palmer's addictions thus became what he himself called a marketing device.

Slightly more savvy writers decided that if they were going to make their lifies their marketing tools, they might as well make the lifie the book too. In part this may explain the craze for literary confessions in which writers divulge their deepest and occasionally dirtiest secrets—the autobiographical equivalent to the entertainingly lurid biographies dedicated to detailing a subject's pathologies. No matter how high-minded their professed motives, one suspects these memoirists also know the entertainment value of their tales: a poet who is a sex addict and child molester, a mopey young woman who is committed to a mental institution and another who battles anorexia, a young novelist addicted to anxiety inhibitors, another attractive young novelist who had an incestuous relationship with her father. Needless to say, plots like these make every bit as good entertainment as similar stories in the supermarket tabloids—which is to say that while confession may be good for the soul, it is also good for book sales.

But the final surrender of literature to entertainment may have come with the discovery that a book needn't even be a vehicle for its author's lifie; it could be a vehicle for the author's photo. Publishers had long preferred writers who were telegenic and glib, able to hawk their books where it counted: on television. By the mid-1990s, however, there was a group of young author pinups—Paul Watkins, Douglas Coupland, Tim Willocks, movie star/novelist Ethan Hawke—whose basic selling point was their appearance. "He had a rock-star type aura that these young women project onto the author," was how a promotions director at the Waterstone bookstore in Boston described Coupland's reading there before a large audience. Playing off his aura, Tim Willocks's publisher enclosed a photo of the writer with an invitation to a promotional lunch. "He's definitely a cute author," a features editor at *Mademoiselle* enthused. "We're definitely biased toward cute guys."

Perhaps it was inevitable that with literature drawn into the entertainment vortex, it would also generate ancillary merchandise just as movies generated toys, clothing, books and other products. Robert James Waller, whose *The Bridges of Madison County* became the very paradigm of a publishing phenomenon, wound up issuing a compact disc of himself singing his own compositions inspired by his own novel. Following his trail, novelist Joyce Maynard released a compact disc of music to accompany her book *Where Love Goes*, Elizabeth Wurtzel planned to provide a CD sound track for the paperback edition of her memoir *Prozac Nation*, James Redfield's inspirational book *The Celestine Prophecy* spawned *The Celestine Prophecy: A Musical Voyage* and Warner Bros. signed self-help writer Deepak Chopra to a recording contract. "Each of Deepak's seven spiritual laws of success could be distilled into a song," explained a record executive. "Then the theme of each law could be distilled into a mantra."

Viewing these developments with concern, the critic Jack Miles predicted that publishing would eventually find itself divided between a very small audience of readers seeking knowledge and a much larger audience seeking entertainment—in effect, another sacralization of the sort that had divided culture in the late nineteenth century. "What is offered for everybody will be entertainment and entertainment only, and then only at a level that excludes nobody," Miles wrote. "What is offered as knowledge, by contrast, will be offered, usually not for everybody but rather for professionals who will 'consume' it as (and mostly at) work." Extrapolating from Miles's vision, one could even imagine a day when there would be for everyone what had already long existed in Hollywood: designated readers to summarize plots, so that no one would ever have to tax himself by reading more than a few pages, as Hollywood executives were never taxed.

But even these divisions were not as clean as Miles suggested, because entertainment could not be kept so easily at bay. Books that purported to be informational were increasingly invaded by entertainment, so that one had to make a new distinction between real or traditional information and entertainment in the form of information—what has been called faction. The latter was the sort of thing in which best-selling celebrity biographer Kitty Kelley specialized. When she revealed in her 1997 biography of the Windsors that the queen mother was artificially inseminated, to cite just one example of many, her evidence seemed to be that everyone knew the king's brother Edward was impotent, that impotency ran in the Windsor family and so that therefore the logical conclusion was the one she drew. It was certainly a stretch, but Kelley could get away with it because she knew accuracy was of little consequence to her readers; entertainment was. The most important thing in the Republic of Entertainment was that the "facts" be provocative enough to provide a sensational show.

IV

ART FOR ENTERTAINMENT'S SAKE

IF ANYTHING, the relationship between entertainment and the visual fine arts was even more complex. On the one hand, fine art had a very small patronage, which meant both that it received less interest from the general media than literature and that it had some degree of protection against the encroachment of entertainment. After all, how many people really cared about fine art? On the other hand, in a country where entertainment value was now the highest value, any artist or gallery owner with even a nodding acquaintance with popular culture had to realize the financial benefits as well as the status that attended getting on the media's screens. The question was how to gain that attention without compromising the art.

Since those who bought art usually had advisers to guide them, celebrity attained outside the art world hadn't conferred the same degree of value on a work of art that it conferred, say, on a book. That is why the prices paid for canvases painted by entertainers like Frank Sinatra, Red Skelton or Tony Bennett didn't match the prices paid to serious artists. Nor, with the rare exception of a painter like Grandma Moses, the Virginia Hamilton Adair of the visual arts, had artists used their lifies to create value for their work. (In fact, it was the "deathies" that were more likely to drive up a painter's prices; suicide was an artist's best career move.) This meant that visual artists were thrown back on the devices of the art world to make themselves known and to establish artistic identities that they could convert into notoriety and money.

Some were fortunate enough or talented enough to establish their identities through style. Picasso, who was probably the most successful at doing so, created a style so distinctive that even an artistic ignoramus would instantly recognize it as the artist's trademark. At the same time, he used the very oddness of his work, its sharp departure from the traditional representational painting with which the general public was most familiar, to define himself with that public as an artistic caricature, a sort of rarefied bird who painted paintings for rich idiots who didn't appreciate the representational genius of Norman Rockwell. It was a highly marketable identity—*the* painter who played to all the prejudices against modern art—and it served him remarkably well throughout his life.

But it was not an easy status to achieve. Other artists, through luck or design, attracted media attention by turning the process of making art into a spectacle. This was the triumph of the so-called "action painters" of the 1940s and 1950s, who used their canvases as a kind of movie screen for the creation of the art and made themselves into romantic action heroes, bounding, thrashing and raging their way across that canvas/screen and leaving art in their wake. (Jackson Pollock, the most recognizable of the action painters, talked of literally being "*in* the painting" as if he were an actor in a film.) It was highly visual and provocative—"How can these drips be art?" the unschooled wanted to know—and it proved marketable to the general media, providing, as it did, controversy, sensation and star appeal. It also wound up making Pollock the Ernest Hemingway of art: a man whose rugged, masculine, untamed image was as large as his frenetic canvases.

Yet as entertaining as the idea of an action painter was, barriers still remained between the entertainment provided by the creative process, which had given rise to Pollock's romantic image, and modern art itself, which was difficult and inaccessible for most people—just a mess of squiggly lines. It was Andy Warhol who smashed those barriers or, as the art critic Harold Rosenberg put it, "liquidated the century-old tension between the serious artist and the majority culture." By replacing the hot romanticism of the creative act with a sense of cool detachment and the abstraction of modern art with an art so accessible that many pondered whether it was really art at all or just him putting them on, Warhol began to demystify the entire art world and drag it squarely into popular culture.

Or, what may have been the same thing, he dragged popular culture into the art world. For Warhol art wasn't a celebration of God's handiwork, as it was for so many nineteenth-century painters, and it wasn't an expression of the artist's sensibility, as it was for most twentieth-century painters. He was among the first to think of art as the culture's handiwork and the product of the culture's collective sensibility, which is why he celebrated soup cans, soap pad boxes, Mickey Mouse and the other effluvia of modern American life.

Of course, popular art was nothing new; it was just that until Warhol the art establishment had always disdained it. Warhol's trick was that he was able simultaneously to demystify high art and to take the stigma out of the popular—a trick that allowed artists to appeal to and even solicit the general public without necessarily losing cachet. "I want to have an impact in people's lives," artist Jeff Koons told *Vogue* magazine in 1990, comparing his work to the Beatles' music. "I want to communicate to as wide a mass as possible." Keith Haring, who provided a trope for his entire career by making chalk drawings on blank New York subway advertising billboards and thus advertising himself, talked about his sculptures the same way: as "visual and physical entertainment" for ordinary people. He had no qualms about opening a Pop Shop that sold his T-shirts, baseball hats, pencil cases, backpacks and con-

dom cases. Mark Kostabi, who mass-produced his paintings on an
assembly line, went Haring one better: He dreamed of franchising
Kostabi Worlds as if they were McDonald's.

Why, after loosing this force of mass commerce, Warhol was
still tolerated by the art establishment, may have had to do with
the deep cultural chord he struck in acknowledging that popular
culture had prevailed over high culture and that its junk, which
was the subject of his paintings, now occupied the resonant center of American life. (A simpler reason may have been that he
taught a grateful art world how to entertain and gain all the financial and media rewards that accrued to entertainers.) Ever dead-
pan, Warhol never let on whether he was being ironical or not, but
he seemed to invite the viewer to regard his canvases as cross-
cultural transactions between the rapidly converging worlds of art
and entertainment, transactions in which he made the popular
into art and art into the popular. In doing so, what he seemed to be
saying is that it wasn't only those soup cans that were pop cultural
artifacts; it was his own paintings of them as well. Both were part
of a new monoculture where entertainment and art blended.

More, Warhol realized that in the monoculture people themselves could be pop cultural artifacts and that celebrities were
basically human soup cans—instantly recognizable products.
That was why, along with his Brillo boxes, he could paint portraits
of Elvis Presley, Marilyn Monroe or Jacqueline Kennedy Onassis
without altering his fundamental theme that nothing, not even art,
could escape the gravitational pull of popular culture and that art
finally would have to embrace this fact or find itself the victim of a
hostile takeover.

The media loved the idea that trash could now be art—it was
an entertaining hook—and it loved Warhol for providing it. Conversely, Warhol loved the media. Not for him the old pose of the
tortured artist wresting art from his soul in a lonely battle with his
daemon. Instead, Warhol fully and happily embraced the celebrity

culture and his own status within it as media star. He adored parties and hobnobbing and attention, and he was deliberately crass when it came to wealth. He once placed an ad in the *Village Voice* newspaper saying he would do anything for money and listed his phone number.

His stardom, however, was ultimately less a by-product of his art than a higher form of it. What Warhol realized and what he promoted in both his work and his life, if it is even possible to separate them, was that the most important art movement of the twentieth century wasn't cubism or surrealism or fauvism or minimalism or op or pop, to which he himself nominally belonged. No, the most important art movement was celebrity. Eventually, no matter who the artist was and no matter what school he belonged to, the entertainment society made his fame his achievement and not his achievement his fame. The visual art, like so much else in American life, was a macguffin for the artist. It was just a means to celebrity, which was the real artwork.

Few artists would ever have admitted this, even to themselves, much less publicly, but Warhol trumpeted it and made it the foundation of his own new school, which would include artists as disparate in style as Keith Haring, Jean-Michel Basquiat, Julian Schnabel and Jeff Koons. What united them under Warhol's umbrella is that all of them understood the value of publicity, the necessity of wresting attention from the general media if they were to succeed as artists, the necessity, really, of making themselves into entertainment. As Haring put it, Warhol "reinvented the idea of the life of the artist being Art itself. . . . He blurred the boundaries between art and life so much that they were practically indistinguishable."

For some traditionalists, this just meant hiring public relations firms to promote them in the media. (Los Angeles artist Ed Ruscha's PR firm landed him appearances in magazine ads and in bus-shelter displays modeling clothes for Barney's and The

Gap.) For others, it meant using the art as public relations—what Boorstin might have termed "pseudo-art," since like pseudo-events, the art was constructed for the media. This was Jeff Koons's tack. Declaring himself the creator of "some of the greatest art now being made," Koons produced such works as a basketball suspended in water, a new vacuum cleaner mounted in Plexiglas and huge casts of himself and his then-fiancée (later wife) Ciccolina, an Italian pornographic film star, in flagrante, surrounded by giant photos of the same—all intended not so much to be displayed or collected as to be written about.

Meanwhile, Koons announced he was preparing a movie in which he would star with his wife,* was undergoing a bodybuilding regimen recommended by actor Arnold Schwarzenegger, was having his hair done by rock singer David Bowie's stylist and was starting his own advertising agency. When he said, "My art and my life are totally one," he meant it, though he also made himself liable to a charge Harold Rosenberg had leveled against Warhol: that for him, in contrast to most artists, art was "something to do for gain." The media ate it up.

Koons wasn't alone. There were dozens like him: sensationalists like Damien Hirst, who attracted the media by displaying decaying animal carcasses and other grotesqueries; shock artists like Andres Serrano, who drew attention, and provoked conservative wrath, by thrusting a photograph of a plastic crucifix into a beaker of his own urine; performance artists like Joseph Beuys, who made himself the artwork; minimalists and conceptual artists who did away with the visual art altogether and left only the celebrity. Since Warhol, the whole art world seemed to be in the

---

* Visual artists obviously had a deep attraction to the movies. Not only Koons but Warhol, Schnabel, David Salle, Cindy Sherman and Robert Longo all made films. One might think it simply a matter of a visual artist in one medium trying his hand at another, though it is equally likely that it was a matter of visual artists gravitating toward the primary source of celebrity. In entertainment culture, the movies were still the light and everyone was a moth.

entertainment business, every artist desperately searching for ways to get his movie exhibited and reap the rewards that only stardom in an entertainment medium can bestow. Fine art became that medium.

But the secondary effect didn't end with the artist. What was true of the artist was finally becoming true of the art museum as well. Museums had long existed, in the words of historian Neil Harris, "to project cultural authority." If anything, they were an elitist redoubt against entertainment. Yet museums also found themselves needing to attract patrons to justify their existence and their budgets, and the surest lure was entertainment. (In some ways this was actually a return to the museums of the early nineteenth century, which had housed an eclectic mix of art, natural history and various oddities.) Already in the 1920s designer Lee Simonson was calling for museums to redefine themselves in light of the competing experiences being provided by the theater and movies. "Its role is not that of a custodian," Simonson wrote of the art museum, "but that of a showman."

As it turned out, museums soon found themselves hosting artistic extravaganzas in which the mounting of the show often overshadowed the artwork in it. "It has become a low-rating mass medium in its own right," art critic Robert Hughes observed of the transformed museum. "In doing so it has adopted, partly by osmosis and partly by design, the strategies of other mass media: emphasis on spectacle, cult of celebrity, the whole masterpiece-and-treasure syndrome." After one multimedia exhibition, the critic Hilton Kramer sneeringly spoke of "the art museum as indoor theme park" and complained that "[w]hat dominates is the overall atmosphere, the momentum of a contrived environment that gives us a new, quick, disposable sensation at every turn. . . . The point, in other words, is pop entertainment." The real point, however, was not that entertainment had invaded these sacred precincts. It was that the entertainers, like the Bolsheviks raiding the Czar's palace, were now occupying the citadel of the old art establishment.*

THE ONE AREA of American culture that might have seemed absolutely impervious to the assaults of entertainment would have been ideas, since entertainment is basically packaged sensation and ideas are by definition a product of ratiocination: the kryptonite to entertainment's Superman. Nevertheless, education, a prime conveyor of ideas, felt the tug of entertainment as soon as child development experts began researching ways to make learning more fun. The outcome was inevitable. What could possibly be more fun than entertainment? It was this effort that gave birth to *Sesame Street* with its skits, songs, jokes, cartoons, puppets, commercials and hyperkinetic tempo, all designed to stimulate even the most incurious and apathetic preschooler, and that would later yield educational computer software which was designed to turn learning into a game.

But however valuable entertainment may have been as a vehicle to convey information to very young children, the movement didn't stop at primary or even secondary education. Having grown up within the bubble of entertainment and having been educated at least in part through the methods of entertainment, more and more university students were arriving on campus with the expectation that their college educations would be entertaining as well. And since universities, in the fallow years after the matriculation of the postwar baby boomers, needed students, they frequently obliged. "That usually meant creating more comfortable, less challenging environments," wrote Mark Edmundson, an English pro-

* And not only museums. Sotheby's auction house announced that it had commissioned the artist and set designer Robert Wilson to devise a multimedia show at a presale exhibition of medieval mosaics. "These pieces are breathtaking," said a Sotheby's vice chairman. "But medieval works have a small, defined audience. To broaden that audience we had to make these things more timely so that people would see them differently" (*New York Times*, November 6, 1997).

fessor at the University of Virginia, "places where almost no one failed, everything was enjoyable, and everyone was nice." It was the campus as theme park.

Still, this was an institutional adjustment to satisfy customers who naturally preferred a show to study. (Who didn't?) Over the years, though, entertainment came to modify intellectual discourse itself by changing the common conception of what intellectual discourse was. The media had always favored provocative ideas because those were the ones that provided the best show. Among the television talk show regulars in the 1960s and 1970s, when TV sought controversy to hike ratings, were atheist Madalyn Murray O'Hair, American Nazi George Lincoln Rockwell, Black Power advocate Stokely Carmichael, LSD champion Timothy Leary, anarchist Abbie Hoffman and libertine Hugh Hefner, each of whom had a single, clearly defined dogma to espouse and usually good one-liners to go with it. When the talk shows couldn't find provocateurs, they settled for razor-tongued eggheads like Gore Vidal, William F. Buckley, Jr., Mary McCarthy, John Simon and Norman Mailer, who did for intellectuals what Picasso did for painters: caricatured them according to the prevailing prejudices and made them entertaining.

Of course this wasn't really about ideas; it was about opinions. There was great entertainment value in intellectuals' delivering tart opinions, an even higher value if they were snide about it. More entertaining still were two or more ideologues with opposing opinions thwacking one another with insults, as in the staged fights on *Crossfire* or *The McLaughlin Group,* two programs of political opinion that resembled professional wrestling more than any sort of reasoned debate. Yet, with argument as a televised blood sport, one didn't really need politics for a fight. The format of dueling opinions was flexible enough to fit any subject: movies, sports, religion, sex. All that mattered was the passion of the argument, so that even someone railing against entertainment invariably became an entertainment.

This was largely the media's doing. But wherever one finds the primary effect, the secondary effect is almost certain to follow, and it was no different for intellectual discourse. No more able to resist the blandishments of entertainment and the celebrity that accompanied it than writers or artists were, intellectuals began searching for ways to turn themselves into the sorts of figures whom the media liked to celebrate, apparently in the hope the media would discover them too.

It didn't help that the academic world had established a pecking order of its own that seemed to be modeled on Hollywood's star system, with universities bidding for "academostars," as one critic called them, the way Hollywood studios bid for talent. The star analogy was apt. Academostars like Frank Lentricchia, Stanley Fish, Cornel West and Henry Louis Gates, Jr., built their reputations the way stars usually did: by gaining media attention, in this case writing articles for newspapers and magazines and appearing as experts on television programs, or glomming onto the latest academic fad or controversy. Moreover, universities encouraged the process for the same reason movie executives lured stars: because they attracted an audience (students, especially graduate students), created a buzz (school rankings) and put money in the coffers (alumni contributions and endowments).

Though this was an insular form of celebrity, primarily for internal consumption, it wasn't long before some intellectuals began to figure out what it took to grab the mass media ring rather than settle for the paltry academic variety of celebrity. Art historian and cultural critic Camille Paglia was often cited as a prototype of the academic self-promoter, and she would have been the first to agree. Playing off the stereotype of the pompous man or woman of letters, Paglia, decked out in leather and flanked by muscular young bodyguards, may have been the first intellectual to assume the pose of rock star. Her mission, she once said, was to put "the bomp back into the bomp-de-domp."

If Paglia's intention was to get attention—and obviously it

was—her tactics worked. For a while in the early 1990s she seemed to be everywhere. But it wasn't just because of her image that the media adored her. Paglia understood the value of ideas the way Warhol understood the value of art—that is, as "something to gain from"—and she knew that simply articulated, controversial ideas were the ones with the highest salability in the entertainment market. The 1990s alone saw the general media retailing not only Paglia's own theory about the defeminization of women but Naomi Wolf's about women's servility to beauty, Francis Fukuyama's about the end of history, Charles Murray's about the genetically determined intellectual inferiority of blacks, Frank Sulloway's about the centrality of birth order to leadership qualities, Daniel Jonah Goldhagen's about the complicity of ordinary Germans in the Holocaust and Abigail and Stephan Thernstrom's about the failure of affirmative action policies. Regardless of the intrinsic quality of these ideas, which ranged from highly questionable to clearly serious and important, what they all had in common is what this paragraph demonstrates: However complex they may have been in their full formulation, the media could conveniently reduce them to condensed sound-bite versions.

It was Marshall McLuhan who once advised Timothy Leary that he would have to find "something snappy" to promote his philosophy of pharmacological freedom, as McLuhan himself had done in promoting his own theories of communication with the slogan "The medium is the message." That is how Leary said he came up with "Tune in, turn on, drop out." But times changed. By the end of the twentieth century no one needed that advice anymore, because everyone already knew that ideas had to be accessible and provocative to survive in the Darwinian jungle of intellectual entertainment. Hot ideas had become the intellectual equivalent of the "high concept" film.

This is certainly not to say that most intellectuals consciously sought ideas that met these criteria and thus might land them profiles in *The New Yorker*, *Vanity Fair*, the *New York Times Magazine* or even *People*. The arcane and obscure still had their rewards on the campus, including academic celebrity. Nor is it to say that a hot idea was necessarily a bad or a superficial one. It is to say, however, that the idea of hot ideas was now part of America's cultural environment and that it was virtually impossible for anyone to disregard it entirely and categorically, any more than one could entirely disregard celebrity, which was the tangible reward for a hot idea. Even if only through the intellectuals' subconscious, entertainment had infiltrated intellectual discourse. Once there, it would begin to commandeer this last bastion of opposition to it and do so with its opponents' complicity. For how could anyone, even the most hermetic of intellectuals, resist entertainment?

Chapter Four

The Human Entertainment

I

FIFTEEN MINUTES OF ANONYMITY

AS CONCEPTS GO, it may have been the most pervasive and dominant popular idea of the late twentieth century, though no one really seems to know when or where or how it originated, other than that it was apparently of fairly recent vintage. "Forty years ago, when I was growing up," wrote the critic Richard Schickel, "the word 'celebrity' was almost never used in print, in conversation, in any sort of discourse, civilized or casual. Most of the people one read about in the papers or heard about on the air, or who were the subject of magazine profiles were 'successful' or 'famous.'" Those were the old adjectives of choice.

Even before celebrity, fame had always had a certain luster in America that it had nowhere else. The country had arrived festooned with the fame of its revolutionary creation, and the Founding Fathers seem to have been extremely conscious of their own fame in having whelped the new nation. One historian saw what Alexander Hamilton referred to as that "love of fame which is the ruling passion of the noblest minds" as a motive force in the Founding Fathers' own nobility, while another believed that they were seeking in part to create a country "where new kinds of men and therefore new kinds of fame would be made possible"—a fame drawn from the greatness of the nation and available to everyone in it.

Celebrity may have been the twentieth-century incarnation of this democratic fame, but it was, as Schickel recognized, fame with a difference. Traditionally fame had been tied, however loosely, to ability or accomplishment or office. Celebrity, on the other hand, seemed less a function of what one did than of how much one was perceived. As Daniel Boorstin put it in his famous tautological formulation, "The celebrity is a person who is known for his well-knownness," making the real achievement of the celebrity the fact of his public recognition. The greater the recognition, the bigger the celebrity.

Given that celebrity was predicated on public awareness and that few arenas offered as much visibility as show business, it was only natural that show business and celebrity would become intertwined, especially once the movies arrived. What the producers of movies observed very early on is that audiences recognized their favorite featured players and would assign them affectionate nicknames—Florence Lawrence was the "Biograph Girl," Mary Pickford the "girl in the curls"—when their actual names weren't posted. It didn't take long for producers to exploit this public fascination with personalities by giving these actors billing, or for the audience to regard their favorites as the surest guarantee of entertainment.

But star appeal leached beyond the screen and into the other media, which became the multiplexes where the life movie played. Even before the emergence of the movie star, newspapers had begun placing a heavy emphasis on personalities, especially the rich and famous, giving readers what the cultural historian Leo Braudy has described as a "fascinating blend of empathy and control: empathy with the successful; control through information about them and their world." One survey of the *Saturday Evening Post* and *Collier's* magazines showed that the average number of biographical stories per year nearly doubled from the period of 1901–1914 to the period 1922–1930 and nearly doubled again from 1922–1930 to 1940–1941, while the portion of biographical stories with entertainment figures as subjects rose from 26 percent in the first survey period to 54 percent in the second, suggesting the growing interest both in personalities generally and in show business personalities specifically.

In time, movie stars' images and interviews would be so widely disseminated that the stars would seem to rule popular culture. "[S]tories about the stars were fed by public-relations agents to gossip columnists, whose columns whetted the public's appetite for the movies in which those stars were appearing," cultural analyst Louis Menand wrote, describing the later stages of this process. "[T]he newspapers sold the stars, and the stars sold the columns." As a result of this symbiosis between the movies and the other media, Menand said, "a vast portion of the commercial culture now slipstreams along behind the publicity for Hollywood movies," which is essentially the publicity for its stars.

A by-product of this process was that the movie star as personality superseded the movie star as performer and gradually became divorced from him. Dwight Macdonald believed the concentration on personality was a way for audiences of mass culture to connect themselves to a work, the same way that an athlete's backstory connected fans to a sporting event or a writer's backstory connected readers to his book. "[T]he individual buried in the mass audience can relate himself to the individual in the artist," Macdonald observed, "since they are, after all, both persons. So while Masscult is in one sense extremely impersonal, in another it is extremely personal." And Macdonald adduced the example of a drunken John Barrymore playing to packed houses in Chicago for more than six months because he kept departing from the play's text to discourse on whatever happened to come into his mind at the moment, and audiences complaining only on those rare nights when Barrymore played it straight.

By any definition movie stars are celebrities, more so when, like Barrymore, they are able to step out of character and play themselves. But because entertainment had become America's cosmology, the world as show, and the movies had become a metaphor for the new life movie, movie stars were more than embodiments of fame. They were also living, breathing tropes who demonstrated that what was true for one entertainment medium (film) was equally true for another (life)—namely, that entertainment needed identifiable and magnetic personalities to maximize the audience response to sensation. Movies had stars. Life had celebrities.

The idea that celebrities were the stars of the life movie necessitated an amendment to Boorstin's definition. Celebrities weren't only known for their well-knownness. In what was an entirely new concept, celebrities were self-contained entertainment, a form of entertainment that was rapidly exceeding film and television in popularity. Every celebrity was a member of a class of people who functioned to capture and hold the public's attention no matter what they did or even if they did nothing at all. The public didn't really seem to care. The stars' presence, the fact that they deigned to grace our world, was sufficient. That is why newspapers could run pages of photos of celebrities at parties, sitting in restaurants, attending benefits or arriving at premieres and why a magazine like *Vanity Fair* could devote long sections to what it called photo portfolios, which were nothing more than pictures of celebrities whom we had already seen dozens of times.

But while most of these media celebrities had won some degree of fame through show business, the life movie long ago had begun generating celebrities of its own—people who had starred nowhere but in life. One typical example was Evelyn Nesbit. Nesbit was an exceptionally attractive fifteen-year-old girl who had moved to New York with her mother at the turn of the twentieth century and suddenly found herself the cynosure of newspaper and magazine photographers. To them Nesbit personified the "artist's ideal of feminine beauty," and she was soon featured in Sunday magazine stories. "That blast of notoriety was frightening," Nesbit would later write in her autobiography. "We didn't know what it was all about, what Sunday Magazine stories meant." What they meant, she quickly discovered, were full-page photo layouts with "hardly any 'story.'" In short, Nesbit had become an image.

Shortly thereafter Nesbit was approached to appear on the stage, where her beauty bewitched architect Stanford White, more than thirty years her senior and married but no less a world-class sybarite for it. White wound up seducing her. When Nesbit eventually married an erratic and tyrannical Pittsburgh coal-and-railroad heir named Harry K. Thaw, her new husband kept pressing her for details of her past relationship with White. On June 25, 1906, in a fit of rage, Thaw shot White to death while the architect dined at the new Madison Square Garden rooftop restaurant. "Newspapers the country over were in an uproar," Nesbit would write "Wild and garbled stories appeared. Lurid headlines." Nesbit was now not just an image but a protagonist. She would testify in her husband's behalf—his defense attorney had pleaded temporary insanity, what he called "dementia Americana"—and Thaw would eventually be acquitted by reason of mental instability, but Nesbit was sentenced to celebrity. "I became public property forever as the price of saving Harry Thaw from conviction and the electric chair."

Nesbit's transformation would be repeated thousands of times by thousands of others in the succeeding decades as the media sifted life to determine whom to anoint with publicity. But having both exploited celebrity and created it, the media would soon find themselves in servitude to it. Celebrity was the force to which nearly everything deferred because human entertainment seemed to interest people more than any other entertainment. By the 1980s virtually every general-interest magazine in America—and in the rest of the world for that matter—featured a celebrity on its cover and one celebrity story after another inside. Anyone who cared could discover what celebrities did in their spare time, whom they romanced, where they lived, what they wore, how they did their hair and applied their makeup, their recipes for success, their secret anguish, their philosophies of life. As the legendary magazine consultant Alexander Lieberman put it, "Presenting personalities is the obsession of our time."

Celebrity was so emblematic of the period that if every era has its archetypal magazine—the *Saturday Evening Post* with its home truths in the first decades of the twentieth century, the snappily sophisticated original *Vanity Fair* in the 1920s, the photo-laden *Life* in the 1940s and 1950s which perceived life as a theater of the eye—then the archetypal magazine of the late twentieth century was the aptly named *People*. Inspired by a section of *Time* magazine that chronicled celebrity milestones—marriages, divorces, births, deaths—*People* expanded the concept to include anything a celebrity did, on the canny principle that ordinary people were fascinated by extraordinary ones. Within ten months of its launch on March 4, 1974, the magazine had a circulation of 1.25 million. Within eighteen months it was turning a profit.

Though *People* made a point of including noncelebrities in its pages—among them, good Samaritans, outstanding teachers and doctors, philanthropists, individuals in extremis—its success was unmistakably a testament to the enchantment of celebrity. In its first twenty years its most frequent cover subjects were Diana, Princess of Wales (fifty-five appearances), Elizabeth Taylor (twenty-six), Sarah Ferguson, the former Duchess of York (nineteen), John Travolta (nineteen), Madonna (seventeen) and Cher (seventeen). *People* editor Richard Stolley even devised a set of rules for a successful cover: Young is better than old. Pretty is better than ugly. Rich is better than poor. TV is better than music. Music is better than movies. Movies are better than sports. Anything is better than politics. And nothing is better than a celebrity who has just died. It was a bracing description not only of what sold magazines but of what values the media now sold to the country.

Those values were, if possible, even more aggressively promoted in *Vanity Fair*. Like the original magazine of that name, which under editor Frank Crowninshield set the standard for urbanity before and during the Jazz Age, the resurrected version aimed to capture the zeitgeist of its time, especially as expressed in arts and ideas. In that vein the new *Vanity Fair's* first editor, recruited from the *New York Times Book Review*, called the magazine "an ongoing cultural enterprise." But it wasn't long before the ongoing cultural enterprise yielded to the real zeitgeist: celebrity. The eventual editor, Tina Brown, who was the daughter of a movie producer and came over from the caustic, gossipy British *Tatler*, described her *Vanity Fair* as "sort of an intellectual MTV," though it might be seen as just a fatter, glossier, more pretentiously written *People*—a modern high-tech multiplex for the life movie, compared to *People's* rather plain and boxy theater.

But while *Vanity Fair* and *People* were essentially running most of the same lifies, with the same faces making regular appearances in both magazines, there were nevertheless real differences, even apart from the degree of gloss in each. One was in their respective attitudes toward celebrity. Though the importance of fame was implicit in its pages, *People* in its rather old-fashioned way still took celebrity at face value as the product of publicity. Brown, on the other hand, understood that in the new entertainment state celebrity was a form not only of prominence and glamour but of exaltation and sanctification—the bond that connected anyone who mattered regardless of what they had done to matter. In Brown's pages, movie stars sat sheet to jowl with world leaders, criminals with fine artists, the latest self-help gurus with great thinkers. In fact, it seemed a point of pride in *Vanity Fair* that celebrity was the paramount value of modern America, the only important value. Good Samaritans, outstanding teachers or doctors, individuals in extremis, had no place in the magazine because they hadn't crashed the gates of fame.

And there was another difference that may not have been apparent to ordinary readers but *was* apparent in the magazines' reputations among advertisers and cognoscenti: *Vanity Fair* had managed to "celebritize" itself while *People* remained a vehicle for its subjects' celebrity. *People* was certainly the more popular magazine; its circulation climbed above three million while *Vanity Fair's*, even after Brown's accession, never exceeded one million. And it was obviously the more profitable; one reporter doubted that *Vanity Fair* had even turned a profit at all under Brown. Yet Brown made *Vanity Fair* seem hot in a way that *People* never was by somehow convincing the other media that her magazine was *the* place where celebrity was certified. In fact, said one *Vanity Fair* editor, "Tina almost created the whole idea of being hot at the same time she created the idea that Tina is hot."

Hot had of course existed before Tina Brown, though it is possible no one had ever regarded it with quite the same reverence as she. If celebrity was the highest state to which a human being could aspire, hot was the highest state of celebrity. Even tepid was treated like leprosy by *Vanity Fair,* which is why there would never be repeated Elizabeth Taylor covers for Tina Brown. Celebrity had constantly to be renewed, reinvigorated, made relevant. As a consequence, almost every *Vanity Fair* subject was cast in terms of superlatives. In *Vanity Fair's* pages Andrew Dice Clay was "Hollywood's Hottest Comedian," Anjelica Huston "One of Hollywood's Classiest Acts," Harrison Ford "Hollywood's Sanest Star." Even the wife of Romania's dictator Nicolai Ceauçescu was labeled "The Most Despised Woman in Eastern Europe."

It was by no means incidental that as one of the chief arbiters of what was hot, Brown became, as that *Vanity Fair* editor had said, hot herself. "The Most Powerful Woman in Journalism" a *Vanity Fair* profile on Brown might have been titled, this time without exaggeration. Celebrities invested their heat in *People*. Having turned herself into a celebrity, Brown brilliantly reinvested her own celebrity and that of her magazine into *Vanity Fair*'s subjects so that the magazine, in the Möbius strip of modern America, created celebrity even as it subsisted on it. It was the media manifestation of Boorstin's tautology: Anyone who was hot got into *Vanity Fair;* anyone who was in *Vanity Fair* was hot.

But for all this, it wasn't as a creator of celebrity that *Vanity Fair* rated the interest of any cultural anthropologist analyzing the American movie; it was as one of the most extreme purveyors of the new religion of celebrity. Whereas even *People* maintained some perspective on celebrity and occasionally—like its middle-class, middle-American readers—recognized competing values to it, *Vanity Fair,* in its almost deranged obsession with fame, wealth, beauty, status, aesthetics and heat, was like the heroine of its namesake. As Becky Sharp in William Makepeace Thackeray's novel embodied the excesses of nineteenth-century bourgeois culture, so Tina Brown's magazine was itself among the excesses of the twentieth-century entertainment state: It was all about celebrity; it was only about celebrity; there was nothing worth talking about but celebrity. Celebrity was everything.

WHILE THE PRINT MEDIA moved effortlessly into celebrity through profiles and photos that featured stars in civilian life, television had a much more difficult time developing a format to accommodate the idea of human entertainment. Back in the 1930s and 1940s gossip columnist Walter Winchell, a former vaudeville hoofer, suggested one possible approach by freely interlarding celebrity items with dramatically delivered news on his radio broadcasts, turning news into entertainment and celebrities into news. In the late 1950s CBS's Edward R. Murrow, a distinguished correspondent who had memorably reported World War II from the European theater over CBS radio, further elided news into celebrity while hosting a popular television program titled *Person to Person* in which he interviewed stars ensconced in their homes and implicitly blessed the proceedings with his own journalistic integrity, even as he made it clear that he was slumming.

Yet Winchell and Murrow were primitives compared to their true heir, Barbara Walters. No figure in late-twentieth-century journalism was more representative of the merger of news and celebrity worship, and none, not even Tina Brown, may have done more to advance it than she. The daughter of the owner of the Latin Quarter nightclub in New York City, Walters, like Winchell, came by her show business instincts honestly. Though she first appeared on the national scene as cohost of the NBC morning program *Today,* which was itself an amiable blend of news and light features, Walters posed as and was accepted as a newswoman. She would even hold the distinction of being named the first female network news anchor in America, an appointment that lent her credibility even as, in her critics' eyes, it diminished the position itself.

But Walters made her reputation less as a news anchor than as a celebrity interviewer. With a shamelessness that a traditionalist like Murrow would have found unseemly if not contemptible, Walters disdained the pose of disinterested objectivity and instead conducted her interviews in the manner of an earnest high school guidance counselor talking to a fragile charge. She prefaced personal questions by averring her obligation to ask them, and then listened to the answers in wide, almost misty-eyed agony, emoting as much sympathy as anyone could possibly have mustered. When she prodded her subjects about their failed marriages, drug and alcohol addictions, improprieties, peccadilloes and crimes, she was at pains to show she got no joy from prying these secrets from them, that she was actually there for succor. (She was also at pains to show that she herself had ascended to celebrity, that she was one of them.) Her trademark was the sobbing celebrity broken by so much sensitivity, while Walters sat with her face frozen in deep, empathic hurt.*

Inimitable as it may have seemed, Walters's overwrought yet nonjudgmental style of interviewing would in time become the industry standard. Network news interviewers like Jane Pauley, Connie Chung, Diane Sawyer and scores of lesser-knowns would all adopt the Walters attitude, some of them even the patented Walters tics: the interrogator's anguish, the cocked head, the gentle prodding, the exaggeratedly chatty "You know what people are going to say" that preceded the most intrusive questions. It was simply the way one now approached the famous on television, be they movie stars or heads of state: personally but reverently, probing for dirt but respecting the celebrity. (It would be left to interviewer Larry King to push this reverence into sycophancy and provide a forum for celebrities that was virtually public access but one where, in King's defense, celebrities always felt secure enough to lower their guard because they knew they would never be challenged.)

Even more important than Walters's style, however, was her substance. Writing in 1996 on the occasion of Walters's twentieth anniversary at the ABC television network, Caryn James in the *New York Times* called her a "journalist as good-tempered diva" and cited her central achievement as conflating Washington celebrity and Hollywood celebrity by invading the private lives of both politicians and movie stars, thereby placing them on exactly the same smarmy valence.

That she had certainly done. As *Vanity Fair* mingled individuals

---

* Walters had so patented this style that when ABC acquired the rights to broadcast a 1995 BBC interview with Diana, Princess of Wales, the network promoted the program as "introduced by Barbara Walters," as if Walters were a designer label. The intent clearly was to inform potential viewers that even though some unknown had done the actual interviewing, Walters had bestowed her blessing upon it and that it would provide the same entertainment value.

in the great Mixmaster of celebrity, so did Walters on television. But this slighted an even greater accomplishment, one without which there could have been no mingling. Walters had managed to smuggle celebrity past the journalistic guard dogs and into a network news organization without making the distinction that Murrow had made between his serious reportage and *Person to Person*. For Walters, celebrity *was* serious reportage, and that was why on her 20/20 news magazine program an interview with a movie star shilling his latest picture could be followed by hard news like an exposé on, say, radiation leakage from a power plant or inadequate meat inspection, as if the interview and the exposé were of equal gravity.

For those who even recognized what had happened—and few seemed to—this was cause for consternation. "No one expects a commercial TV network to forgo the ratings race or superstar interviews," *New York Times* columnist Frank Rich complained when ABC newswoman Diane Sawyer lobbed softball questions at singer Michael Jackson on *Prime Time* on the occasion of Jackson's new album which was said to contain anti-Semitic lyrics. "The question raised by Ms. Sawyer's show is why it is postured as news—complete with the interviewer gratuitously calling herself a 'serious journalist'—when journalistic standards were so promiscuously abandoned."

The short answer to Rich's question was Barbara Walters, the pioneer who enabled "journalists" like Sawyer to treat every subject from the president of the United States to the latest hunky movie star as a melodrama waiting to be revealed on national television news. For all her professions of seriousness, Sawyer was clearly not a serious journalist in the traditional sense, just as a Michael Jackson interview was not news in the traditional sense. Stamped in Walters's image, Sawyer was a new kind of hybrid: a performer who purported to be a journalist and who had the network's imprimatur as a journalist but who had successfully crossed the line into celebrity entertainment without raising too much commotion because, frankly, journalists in glass houses couldn't really throw stones at her. In the entertainment state, they were all becoming entertainment reporters.

In fact, at least one colleague of Rich's at the *Times* had come perilously close to the kind of television celebrity "new news" for which Rich had scolded Sawyer. It occurred when O. J. Simpson, shortly after his acquittal for murder, agreed to be interviewed by NBC's Tom Brokaw and Katie Couric on the newsmagazine *Dateline*. In the best tradition of celebrity appearances, the NBC News president, Andrew Lack, promised that Brokaw and Couric would act "as journalists, not as prosecutors," and that they would be "very tough but very fair." (These were of course the Barbara Walters guidelines for interviews.) Despite these assurances, Simpson reconsidered, canceled and then phoned *Times* reporter Bill Carter, who allowed him to expatiate for forty-five minutes as if he were on the Larry King show. "I'm an innocent man," Simpson insisted. "I don't think most of America believes I did it." Putting the best possible spin on his interview, Carter called Simpson "affable and personable, even laughing about reports that his legal bills had left him broke."

By letting Simpson have his way with them, the *Times* provided further evidence, if any was needed, of the power of celebrity to mesmerize even those who should know better. In the 1980s, as a kind of corrective to this bewitchery, a few young apostate journalists started an impudent magazine called *Spy* that ridiculed celebrity in equal measure to *Vanity Fair's* and Barbara Walters's deification of it. Firing a satirical howitzer at the celebrated gained *Spy* a small portion of fame as well as a devoted following, but in the end it became an object lesson in the ineluctable force of celebrity to bulldoze everything in its path, including the howitzer. As the acquisitive 1980s turned into the recessionary 1990s, both the magazine's cachet and its subscriptions plummeted, and it fell upon hard financial times. Meanwhile, its founding publisher and first editor wound up respectively at *Vanity Fair* and *The New Yorker,* which at the time was edited by, of all people, Tina Brown. The infidels had been converted.

IT WAS REALLY an issue of supply and demand. The public demanded; the media supplied. But as the demand for celebrities kept growing beyond the capacity of the finite number of movie stars, singers, athletes and other conventional entertainers to satisfy it, the media had to find or create new figures. Fortunately, since celebrity was a function of publicity, all the media had to do to make more celebrities was widen the beam of their spotlight, though doing so also snapped whatever may have still attached celebrity to achievement, fame to ability. The only ability that mattered in the expanding universe of celebrity was the ability to get one's name in the media. That is why Walter Winchell could once promise Doris Lilly, an attractive friend of his, that he would make her a star even though Lilly had no apparent talents that could bring her stardom. He could promise because he understood that publicity conferred stardom every bit as much as stardom conferred publicity.

With publicity as both means and end, anyone could qualify. Take business. Whereas the only businessmen previous generations may have known were inventor/entrepreneurs like Thomas Alva Edison or Henry Ford, or billionaires like John D. Rockefeller or Andrew Carnegie, by the last quarter of the twentieth century there were dozens of businessmen being profiled routinely in the media. Corporate chiefs like Lee Iacocca of the Chrysler Corporation, Ted Turner of Turner Broadcasting, William Gates of Microsoft, even Victor Kiam of Remington shavers, and financiers like Malcolm Forbes, Armand Hammer, Michael Milken and Henry Kravis were suddenly starring in boardroom dramas of high finance, presumably because the public enjoyed the genre.

Of them all, though, the one with the most perspicacity about celebrity and the one most representative of the new celebrity businessman may have been Donald Trump, a relatively minor New York real estate mogul whom the media made a household name in the 1980s. To the media, the brash, bloviating young Trump was the perfect symbol of the avarice, rapaciousness and ostentatiousness of new business wealth, and they loved to report his grandiose exploits. But what really made Trump a symbol of the 1980s was less his showy greed than his willing compliance with the secondary effect of the media—namely, that in order to compete with entertainment, one had to turn oneself into entertainment.

Trump understood that in an entertainment-driven society celebrity was among the most effective tools of salesmanship and that consequently a businessman's job was not only the management of assets but the management of image. By the same token, the media didn't care that Trump wasn't in the same financial league with other business superstars; his life was a good act for them to exhibit, as Trump ensured it would be. His best-selling books, his gaudily appointed apartment in the Trump Tower, his oversized yacht, his glitzy, elephantine Atlantic City casinos and, one might have added, even his divorce from a onetime Czech figure skater and his marriage to a buxom young beauty queen were all what Trump once called "props for the show," which he admitted was "Trump" and which he crowed had enjoyed "sold-out performances everywhere," meaning, presumably, the media.

Trump's blockbuster was so good a show that not even failure could close it. When his investments went sour and creditors began circling, Trump stayed afloat by selling assets and renegotiating loans and then, with his customary temerity, celebrated his survival in another book—*The Art of the Comeback.* (That he was able to get bank loans on the collateral of his name was just another testament to his celebrity.) But the true measure of the success of Trump's act may have been that his ex-wife Ivana's life became a kind of spinoff with its own ancillary industries: not only continuing press coverage but a novel and a fragrance and fashion house. "I'm not an actress," Ivana told the *New York Times* in what was as good a description of the celebrity condition as any. "I can't dance or sing. I'm not a superstar. Maybe what I am is a personality. I'm traveling extensively, and wherever I go the perception of me helps to sell the products. Maybe I'm selling me."

Just as Trump's movie spun off Ivana's, and even his teenage daughter Ivanka's, virtually every lifie had its celebrity spinoffs, and a big lifie, like former football star O. J. Simpson's 1995 murder trial, could turn into a cottage industry of celebrity. Even the supernumeraries at the trial seemed to bid for stardom. Simpson houseguest Kato Kaelin, who testified that he heard a thump which some construed as Simpson clambering over the fence after the murders, hired a publicist, planned a Las Vegas act (it fell through) and became a radio talk show host. Prosecutors Marcia Clark and Christopher Darden, defense attorneys Johnnie Cochran and Robert Schapiro, rogue policeman Mark Fuhrman, who was accused of having tried to frame Simpson, and the Los Angeles Police Department detectives who investigated the case, Simpson's former girlfriend Paula Barbieri and even his niece, all negotiated book deals, and both Barbieri and one of the jurors posed nude for *Playboy* magazine. Meanwhile, two other defense attorneys, Barry Scheck and Peter Neufeld, signed a development deal with CBS television for a series based on their lives.

Similarly, those who only served celebrities now found themselves regarded as celebrities by association: hairstylists, fashion designers, interior decorators, cooks, gardeners, physical fitness instructors, spiritual advisers and speechwriters who had previously concealed their work but who now openly boasted about which lines they had contributed to a presidential address. *Vanity Fair* even ran a lengthy profile of Robert Isabell, a so-called "power" florist, whom the magazine breathlessly described as "New York's premier party impresario—the good time guru of A-list celebrities, society matrons, and Wall Street moguls." For good measure, the article added that the florist had the "hands of an artist" as well as the looks of "Warren Beatty's younger brother."

And there was yet an even more attenuated form of celebrity, one for which the celebrity didn't even need a name. On the cover of its December 11, 1995, issue, that cover where a celebrity photo usually resided, *People* magazine featured a swimsuit-clad young woman and the banner "Murder of a Model"—not a famous model or a once-famous model or even an up-and-coming young model on the fringes of the glam fashion world. Linda Sobek was basically a catalog model, but "model," with its signifiers of sex and beauty, was the operative celebrity word, and in a media culture hungry for entertainment, it lifted her murder from the police blotter to the *People* cover and onto television tabloid programs and local television news broadcasts across the country. In death Linda Sobek became a generic celebrity.

It was an ever-growing fellowship to which she belonged. Now that the requirements for initiation had been relaxed, there were thousands of people who had joined the class of celebrities. In addition to traditional entertainers and their attendants, there were fashion models, bodybuilders, self-help hierophants, chefs, popular authors and artists, scientists and social theorists, economists, religious leaders, diet counselors (consider the phenomenon of diet spokesperson Richard Simmons), lawyers, doctors, journalists, criminals, adulterers like Long Island car mechanic Joey Buttafuoco, whose teenage paramour shot his wife (years later he was still signing autographs and had been given a cable television talk show), umpires and referees, cartoon heroes and animated figures on the Internet. The list was as endless as the number of stories the media needed to generate.

And even stories that the media *didn't* need to generate. There were underground celebrities at the edges of the media radar whose only function was to be trendily obscure enough to make anyone who knew them seem knowing. There were business executives and physicians (about 60 percent of whom in Los Angeles, by one estimate in the early 1990s, had hired public relations firms) and even otherwise ordinary and unexceptional individuals who paid PR men to make them celebrities. There were also celebrities who actively resisted celebrity by declining publicity, as reclusive authors J. D. Salinger and Thomas Pynchon did. Rather than void their celebrity, however, their abnegation practically voided Boorstin's definition of it: They became famous for not wanting to be famous.

Indeed, the profusion of celebrity was so overwhelming that it also seemed to void another oft-quoted dictum. In the future everyone would not be famous for fifteen minutes, as Andy Warhol had prophesied. In the future, it seemed, everyone would be *anonymous* for fifteen minutes.

II
THE ZSA ZSA FACTOR

NOW CAME the problem. With so many celebrities, the media had to distinguish between the stars and the character actors, between those who commanded the media spotlight and those who had only been grazed by it. A new nomenclature was required. Andy Warhol claimed that a friend of his named Ingrid had coined the word "superstar" in the early 1960s, when she began using it as her surname to grab media attention. It got her the recognition she sought—she became a minor celebrity—but it also became a handy label to sort celebrities, and it led to an Orwellian hierarchy that could have occurred only in the age of entertainment: In the life movie all celebrities are equal, but some celebrities are more equal than others.

For conventional entertainers, however, there was a much larger problem than taxonomy. There was competition. Before the expansion of celebrity, when they were the only ones acknowledged by the media, it had been easy. After the expansion, when it seemed everyone had become a celebrity and every celebrity was an entertainment, conventional entertainers suddenly found their *work* having to compete with the *lives* of presidents, criminals, fashion designers, florists, recluses, other entertainers, even generic models. "Metaphor has left art and gone into current events," film director Mike Nichols once lamented. "Who in the fuck is going to compete? Where is there a hero who can fall from greater heights than Michael Jackson? Where is there more naked rivalry than between Tonya Harding and Nancy Kerrigan? What couple can you write about that is a stronger metaphor about relations between the sexes than the Bobbitts?"* This was a whole new world of entertainment, and it demanded new configurations between work and life, between traditional entertainment and the life movie.

One of the early trailblazers in this process of discovery was a statuesque showgirl named Peggy Hopkins Joyce. Joyce had been born in 1893 into poverty in Norfolk, Virginia, but escaped it at sixteen, when she ran off with a vaudeville bicyclist. She eventually found her way onto the stage as a Ziegfeld girl, and she even appeared in a handful of films. Still, it wasn't much of a career, and in 1928 it effectively ended with her appearance in the play *The Lady of the Orchids.* By that time, however, she had already discovered a new vocation: divorcée. Joyce was married six times and divorced five, after the first marriage always to and from wealthy men and always with great media fanfare. Even those who had never heard of the actress Peggy Hopkins Joyce knew the bride (in her last film, *International House,* in 1933 she pointedly played herself), and though her profession had originally fueled interest in her life, her life easily overshadowed her work, making her one of the first performers who successfully negotiated the transition from the stage to the life movie.

Zsa Zsa Gabor's achievement was much more complex than

---

* Claiming that he had sexually assaulted her, Lorena Bobbitt severed her husband's penis while he was sleeping, took a drive and then dumped it out her car window.

Joyce's and constituted a considerable advance over hers because Zsa Zsa had no work to kindle an interest in her life. Gabor had been born in Budapest, Hungary, where her father was a prosperous jeweler and her mother a frustrated actress who, Zsa Zsa would write, made "everyday life a stage for herself, a spectacular in which she was the star." (Fittingly, Zsa Zsa had been named for her mother's favorite Hungarian actress.) A great beauty who discovered early that "the press liked to write about me," Zsa Zsa in short order married a Turkish diplomat at fifteen, divorced him, met and married hotel magnate Conrad Hilton during a visit to Hollywood, then divorced him and married actor George Sanders. If it sounded like a movie, it was. "In time I was to discover that I saw things not as they were but as a play within a play, in which I was always the heroine, waiting for the prince to awaken me with a kiss," she wrote in the first of her two autobiographies without seeming to realize that she had inherited her mother's fantasies.

Up to this time she was essentially a professional beauty, a trophy wife with a reputation for saying whatever happened to pop into her head. But in the fall of 1951, while Sanders was away on a film assignment in England, Zsa Zsa was asked by a producer friend to become a panelist on a television program called *Bachelor's Haven,* in which she was to dispense extemporaneous advice to the lovelorn. Her uninhibited and often unintentionally hilarious responses to questions made her an instant personality and the center of what she described as an "avalanche" of publicity. Suddenly, heads turned when she entered a nightclub. Women stopped her in the street to talk. After four programs she was put on the cover of *Life* magazine, and within a year she had made five films, though she hadn't acted since she had been a child. "I realized," she later admitted, "that my fame was much greater than my acting ability at this time."

It was, as realizations go, a major one. Gabor had become a celebrity in Boorstin's definition of the word. She had no talent save a talent for being herself, but this was quite enough to un-leash such a torrent of attention that fifty years later Zsa Zsa Gabor would still be a household name, though virtually no one could tell you what she did or why she was famous. This made Zsa Zsa one of the first and easily among the most outstanding ex-emplars of what might be called in her honor the "Zsa Zsa Factor" that undergirds so much of modern celebrity. It was a fame that required having to do no work to get it, save gaining media exposure.

If one were to plot the Zsa Zsa Factor on a grid, one would mark one axis "fame" and another "achievement." Those who best exemplified modern celebrity would be those who, like Zsa Zsa Gabor herself, had the greatest fame with the least achieve-ment—in entertainment terms, those who could entertain simply through the fact of their existence, as the mere mention of Zsa Zsa's name would bring a smile to our lips. At the end of the ray along the fame axis would be the coordinate for the ultimate celebrity accomplishment: to be known by everyone for having done absolutely nothing.*

In many ways, as Zsa Zsa herself recognized, she was the pre-cursor of Elizabeth Taylor, who may be as close to a theorist of the life movie as there has ever been. Like Zsa Zsa, Elizabeth Taylor grew up in a fantasy, only hers was provided not by a starstruck mother but by the Metro-Goldwyn-Mayer studio, for which she worked as child actress. The studio arranged everything from her dates to her first wedding, so that the fiction on-screen seamlessly extended into her life. "I liked playing the role of a young woman in love," she said suggestively, explaining why she married Nicky Hilton, son of Conrad.

---

* There were in fact aspirants. A huge-breasted young woman named Angelyne posted billboards of herself around Los Angeles, but the billboards advertised nothing but Ange-lyne, who was neither a singer nor an actress nor a performer of any kind. "She wants to be famous for simply being Angelyne," her assistant explained to sociologist Joshua Gamson. (Gamson, *Claims to Fame: Celebrity in Contemporary America* [Berkeley: University of California Press, 1994], p. 1.)

But it wasn't only the romance Taylor borrowed from film. One of her biographers theorized that she also imitated the melodrama of her movies to lend her own life drama. This explained the serial marriages, the fights and divorces, the addictions and binges, the brushes with death. By 1958, when her third husband, producer Michael Todd, died in an airplane crash, Taylor's life was rivaling her work on-screen and probably had a much larger audience. As she described Todd's funeral in Chicago, ten thousand fans had turned out at the cemetery to see the show. "And they were sitting on tombstones with blankets spread out," she wrote in a memoir. "I remember seeing bags of potato chips in the wind. And empty Coca-Cola bottles. And children crawling over tombstones. And as the car pulled up, they all broke away from their picnic lunches, came screaming like black-gray birds to the car—all squawking and screaming and yelling in our ears as if it were some sort of premiere." During the interment fans yelled, "Liz, Liz. Come out, Liz. Let's have a look."

Her life wouldn't disappoint them. In succeeding years she would marry singer Eddie Fisher, carry on a public affair with her *Cleopatra* costar Richard Burton before finally divorcing Fisher and marrying him, would divorce Burton, remarry him and marry twice more. For all this, she understood the fate that eventually awaited her. "Once you're up there on that last rung, your head splitting in two," she wrote, "you can only go down." And though she said she was looking forward to retirement, to the time when she would no longer be famous, what she was describing was really the tragedy of celebrity.

As Leo Braudy explained it in his study of fame, *The Frenzy of Renown*, the tragedy of celebrity was that fame always doubled back on those who possessed it, making them a creature of it. Ultimately they had to measure up to the image or be stripped of the fame. Daniel Boorstin viewed it more starkly. "The very agency which first makes the celebrity in the long run inevitably destroys him," he wrote in *The Image*. "He will be destroyed, as he was made, by publicity," meaning that publicity is perishable; once the celebrity passes from public view, there are no lasting accomplishments to survive him. "No one," he added, "is more forgotten than the last generation's celebrity."

But Elizabeth Taylor discovered that one need never pass from public view, that one could keep unraveling the long skein of one's own life, that one could make one's own life a movie and that so long as it was entertaining, one would never be passé. "I am my own commodity," she once declared, and she was absolutely right. Taylor had learned to commodify her life. By the 1990s no one went to see new Elizabeth Taylor films anymore because there were none to see, yet she still managed to attract the media by starring in the saga of her life, so that her "movie" played everywhere. In other words, her new career was living.

Taylor's early appeal as a life performer was her willingness to expose her private sexuality, first with Fisher and then with Burton, and to provide a voyeuristic charge for those who read about her. Her later appeal, when she was no longer a sex symbol, was her willingness to expose her dysfunctions as melodramatic entertainment: her ballooning weight and subsequent diets, her drug problems, her vexed marriages and romances, her various illnesses. "One can only enjoy oneself, or suffer, for the entertainment of others," Goethe once wrote, "and in the greatest rush, this is communicated from house to house, from town to town, from empire to empire and at last from continent to continent." It was a perfect description of Elizabeth Taylor's new function.

Yet the self-consciously produced celebrity life movie was not only her creation; it was her legacy. Taylor taught other waning celebrities that intimacy was the best publicity when there was nothing else to publicize and perhaps the only way to snag starring roles, even if it was only their own lives in which they were starring. (Appropriately, the test issue of *People*, dated August 23, 1973, featured Taylor on the cover with news of her impending divorce from Burton.) Thus, in addition to stories about the usual romantic entanglements, we got young actress Drew Barrymore revealing that she had been addicted to drugs; another young actress, Kristy McNichol, and singer Paula Abdul admitting that they had suffered nervous breakdowns; figure skater Tai Babilonia confessing that she had attempted suicide; Beatle Ringo Starr, actress Mary Tyler Moore and former baseball star Mickey Mantle divulging that they were alcoholics, and another alcoholic, Kitty Dukakis, wife of Democratic presidential candidate Michael Dukakis, acknowledging that she had drunk cleaning fluid in desperation; comedienne Roseanne Barr disclosing that she had been molested as a child; a Miss America claiming that she had been battered by her boyfriend; actor Rob Lowe baring that he was a sex addict, comedian Jerry Lewis that he was a Percodan addict, director Mike Nichols that he was a Halcion addict—to name just a very few from a seemingly endless list of calamity. Some horrible revelation was virtually a prerequisite for celebrity.

Presumably one could have continued recycling these plots as movies themselves do, were there not someone to push the edge of the life movie envelope. That became one of the responsibilities of the singer/actress Madonna. Taking what might be called a postmodernist view of celebrity, Madonna was less interested in the basic plot elements of the life movie, as Elizabeth Taylor was, than in the manipulations required to create them. Self-reflexive where Elizabeth Taylor was literal, Madonna added a Pirandellian twist to the life movie: She made her life movie *about* her life movie.*

Daniel Boorstin once attributed flimflam artist P. T. Barnum's success not—as the conventional wisdom had it—to his discovery that people could be easily fooled, but to how much the public

---

* In some ways President Clinton was the first politician of the Madonna age. Unlike Ronald Reagan, he clearly didn't live within his movie, but unlike Richard Nixon, who was a covert Machiavellian until his cover was blown, Clinton took real pride in his machinations. The public knew that he was a manipulator; they had just learned to appreciate the quality of the manipulations. His presidency functioned within what one historian, speaking of circus impresario P. T. Barnum, had called an "operational aesthetic."

enjoyed being fooled, especially if one could see the mechanisms. The same could be said of Madonna. In the 1991 documentary *Truth or Dare*, which follows Madonna on tour, she admits that she is not the best singer, dancer or actress and adds disingenuously, "Who do I think I am, trying to pull this off?" But even that comment was a kind of in-joke with the audience. She and we knew exactly who she was. She was a conceptual performance artist whose truest art was the art of promoting Madonna. Like Barnum, Madonna let us know we were being manipulated. She luxuriated in it. Unlike Barnum, however, she invited us to see the mechanics behind her tricks until all we saw were the mechanics. It was the brazenness of it that made it so entertaining. As her then-boyfriend actor Warren Beatty says in the film, "She doesn't want to *live* off-camera, much less talk."

So while Elizabeth Taylor just kept adding scenes to her movie, Madonna kept reinventing herself every few years and kept the public guessing what she would be next. One year she was a sexy street urchin, then a begowned siren à la Marilyn Monroe, then a futurist idol out of Fritz Lang's *Metropolis*, then a retro 1940s movie star, then a dominatrix, then a mother. None of these, save possibly the last, purported to be "real," in the sense that Elizabeth Taylor's life was actually being lived out even as it was being played out—that is, she was actually getting married and divorced. Madonna was an actress whose life had become a series of orchestrated roles with the overriding role that of Madonna pulling the strings, whereas Liz Taylor, like most celebrities, was an actress whose life was one ongoing role: herself.

But whether it was Zsa Zsa, Liz or Madonna, what each confirmed is that celebrity was the hot entertainment of the late twentieth century, and the hottest stars in it were those who seemed to live for us, who opened their lives to us, who suffered and survived for us. They were those who either leaped from the screen or never even bothered with it because they had come to the profound realization that there really was nothing there for them anymore—or for us. As poet Randall Jarrell once said, celebrities had become "our fictional characters," and life was their medium.

III
CELEBRITY WITH A THOUSAND FACES

TO CALL celebrity lifies entertainment is not merely to say that they provided the same sensational pleasures as good melodrama; it is to say that they also served the other functions of conventional entertainment. Where movies and television provided distraction and escape, lifies now provided them as well. It was what the literary scholar Mark Edmundson, writing about popular forms, called "easy transcendence" because it required so much less of us than the transcendence one experienced from art or religion, only that we let ourselves be transported.

Where movies and television provided a sense of community forged from the shared symbols of popular culture, lifies now provided community as well from shared gossip and trivia about celebrities. And where popular culture empowered the audience by sticking a thumb in the eye of high culture, celebrity lifies empowered the audience by investing it with a degree of collective control over the stars of the lifies. As Elizabeth Taylor wrote, "The public seems to revel in the imperfections of the famous, the heroes, and to want to be in a position of attacking—which I guess makes them feel a little bit superior."

On the evidence, Taylor seemed right. There was obviously no point in reveling over the imperfections of fictional characters. Gossiping about real people, on the other hand, could have consequences for their careers, especially since celebrities had no institutional means to redress public opinion, which is why the sociologist Francesco Alberoni called them a "powerless elite." Would actor Hugh Grant be pardoned for having been caught with a prostitute in the back of his limousine? Would Eddie Murphy be pardoned for having picked up a transvestite? Would Michael Jackson be pardoned after allegations that he had molested a young boy? As these tridents were poised at the celebrities' throats, the answers rested in the audience's mercy. One couldn't say that about conventional entertainment.

But lifies functioned as more than ongoing serial entertainments; they coalesced into something very close to social myths that gave them an importance out of all proportion to their seemingly inconsequential origins. As the literary historian Richard Slotkin described the process of cultural mythopoesis, it began with a story or stories. Over time, these stories, if repeated often enough and made familiar enough, accreted into myths—that is, larger tales with bolder lineaments. Over more time, the myths accreted into, or rather were distilled into, an archetype—a single, simple narrative idea that, in Slotkin's view, expressed the soul of the culture.

So it is with celebrity lifies. They begin as individual stories about Tom Cruise or Sylvester Stallone or Julia Roberts or Princess Di or Oprah Winfrey in the tabloids or in *People, Vanity Fair, Us* and other publications or on television newsmagazine shows. Through repetition, these eventually become myths about the celebrities: Cruise's professionalism and unpretentiousness, Stallone's constant tension between his working-class roots and his Hollywood status, Julia Roberts's doomed search for love and independence, Princess Di's battles with an obdurate and inhumane monarchy, Oprah Winfrey's continual crises and her continuing triumphs over them. Finally, and this is an ongoing process, all these various myths begin to resolve themselves into a single fundamental theme or set of themes about American life.

What these myths provide, in addition to their obvious entertainment value, is instruction in how to deal with our own adversity. "It has always been the prime function of mythology and rite to supply the symbols that carry the human spirit forward in counteraction to those other constant human fantasies," wrote Joseph Campbell in *The Hero with a Thousand Faces,* his classic study of cross-cultural narratives. Though he was speaking of classical myths, he could just as well have been speaking about modern celebrity. As Campbell saw it, the central heroic myths of virtually every culture follow the same three stages: "A hero ventures forth from the world of common day into a region of supernatural wonder; fabulous forces are there encountered, and a decisive victory is won; the hero comes back from this mysterious adventure with the power to bestow boons on his fellow man."

Perhaps it was with Campbell in mind that the actor Bruce Willis told the novelist Jay McInerney in a 1995 interview for *Esquire* magazine, "There's only four basic stories they can write about you. One: You hit the scene. Two: You peak. Three: You bomb. And four: You come back." Though Willis added a third stage—bombing—his schema was essentially the same as Campbell's. Like Campbell's hero, the celebrity hero arrives from what Campbell calls the "world of secondary effects," that is, the world of everyday reality. Thus celebrities come from the same places their audience comes from, but they are also different, endowed, as Campbell says of the hero, "with extraordinary powers from the moment of birth," in this case the powers of talent and charisma. Next, they hit the scene, entering the "region of supernatural wonder" that we call Hollywood, where they encounter fabulous things: wealth, glamour, fame, sex, drugs, you name it. Many of them must also survive a "road of trials" and a "woman as temptress," in Campbell's words, before they finally triumph, though unlike Campbell's hero, the celebrity doesn't vanquish evil forces; he vanquishes his own anonymity. At this point in the original monomyth, the victorious hero returns to share what he has learned with those he had left behind. In Willis's adaptation, the celebrity loses it all, a victim of his own hubris or of the public's fickleness. Only then, after he has been forced to win back his fame, does the celebrity reemerge from Hollywood, if only figuratively, in magazines and books and television talk shows, sadder but wiser, to tell the rest of us what he has learned.*

As Campbell described the archetype or basic meaning of his monomyth, the hero's journey was a voyage into the psyche to wrestle with and ultimately defeat his childhood fears. What he learns in the process is that the hero and the god, the seeker and the found, the ordinary world and the supernatural world are really one. And when he returns from his journey and his contest, he bears his enlightenment as a gift to everyone else. In the end it has been his function to show us the continuity between the natural world outside us and the spiritual world within. "The essence of oneself and the essence of the world: these two are one," concludes Campbell.

Whether we consciously realize it or not, this is also the subtext of the standard celebrity profile. Tom Cruise, writes Kevin Sessums in *Vanity Fair*, came from humble beginnings before he entered Hollywood. But once in Hollywood, despite the wondrous things he found there, he also had to rediscover himself: "I became famous at a very young age and didn't know who I was." Fortunately Cruise fights through his uncertainty and returns to tell us what he has learned—namely, that it is all right to be famous and successful, that the celebrity and the person are still one. "I used to feel really, really uncomfortable about it," he told Sessums of his success. "I definitely still wake up in the middle of the night sometimes, and Nic[ole Kidman] and I will be talking, and I'll say, 'Look at this . . .' " in apparent amazement.

Vanity Fair also found that Sylvester Stallone's "spirit is soaring" and his "career is back on track." Unlike Tom Cruise, Stallone had won his first victory over anonymity only to be confronted

---

*It should be noted that some get lost in their celebrity and never return because they would have nothing to tell us if they did. A case in point was the model/actress Margaux Hemingway, Ernest's granddaughter, who descended into drugs, drink, bulimia and abusive relationships. "She was just a gentle loving soul who got lost in fame and fortune," said a friend after Hemingway committed suicide in 1996 at age forty-one ("A Life Eclipsed," *People* [July 15, 1996]).

with Willis's stage three: bombing. "I was being wrapped up in old newspapers," Stallone told *Vanity Fair.* "I coulda walked around here on flame and nobody woulda put a marshmallow on my body. It was pretty dismal." But Stallone survives what he calls the "barroom brawl" of life by rediscovering his younger, truer self. "It took me many years to find out the real joy is probing the unknown— getting back to naivete, getting back to the place where you feel so safe, so innocent, so juvenile. . . ." The article is Stallone's boon to us.

Then there was Julia Roberts. Roberts was only twenty-two when she starred in the hit film *Pretty Woman* and became, again in *Vanity Fair*'s words, "Hollywood's Cinderella, the belle of the box office." But then she too withdrew from the star trip to tackle her identity. "I've discovered certain things," she told Kevin Sessums, celebrity's Homer. Like Cruise and Stallone, what she seems to have discovered was her true self inside her godhood. "It's unbelievable that someone so physically beautiful could also have this 'everyperson' quality about her," film executive Joe Roth told *Vanity Fair,* "but that's exactly why she's a movie star." And, he might have added, a mythic hero.

Even that old polymorph Madonna found herself battling her psyche in the wilderness after the failures of her book *Sex,* her album *Erotica* and her film *Body of Evidence.* She had hit "rock bottom," she told *Vanity Fair*'s Ingrid Sischy. "What was happening on the outside was happening on the inside," meaning that she was racked by self-doubt. This led to a bout of introspection. "I think people are turning more inwards, going, 'Who am I? What am I?'" What Madonna discovered during her mysterious adventure was that she didn't need the fame and glory that had always seemed to sustain her. What she discovered was little Madonna Ciccione inside the brassy superstar.

Of course it was exactly the same story again and again and again. Only the names changed, and sometimes not even those, since the myth was frequently repeated with the same celebrity having undergone a different trial or having been interviewed at a different stage in his career. What did this archetype teach us that made it worth recycling so often? It taught us that celebrities originate in our own daily reality before they cross over into the rarefied world of Hollywood. It taught us that they too must suffer their trials and tribulations on the road to success, and often even after having arrived there. It taught us—and this was Bruce Willis's modern democratic interpolation in Campbell's schema—that celebrities often have to be humbled, even humiliated, before they can be reintegrated both psychologically and socially. Finally, it taught us that everything worthwhile is in the kingdom of our own selves, not in Hollywood. Or, as Campbell said, each "carries within himself the all; therefore it may be sought and discovered within."

Campbell's archetype addressed primal fears extant in all societies: the anxiety of separation; the terror of the unknown; the dread of forces larger than ourselves; death. The celebrity archetype addressed social fears extant in modern America: the anxiety of losing one's identity or never finding it at all; the terror of having too little amid plenty; the dread of anonymity; the awful suspicion that some people were blessed and some were not and that most Americans were among the latter. What the celebrity archetype offered, then, was reassurance. Reinforcing the subversive, anomic subtext of entertainment, it told us that the whole idea of celebrity elitism was something of a chimera. As actress Loni Anderson put it in her memoir, "There was a time when I thought I'd lost everything. Here's what I actually lost: bicoastal homes and household staffs; private jets; too many cars; a glamorous life; a public face; busy-ness; naivete; fear." And what did she find? "I guess what I really found was myself."

WHAT CAMPBELL CODIFIED was the basis not only for cultural myths but for systems of religious belief as well. Moses,

Jesus, Buddha and Muhammad all underwent a trial and transformation similar to the hero's, and each returned with an instruction to impart as the hero did. In imposing the same mythic matrix on celebrity, the entertainment culture was also providing a system of belief. The spirituality, the alternative reality, the easy transcendence, the celebrity homilies, the gospels inspired by celebrities' deaths, the icons on their way to apotheosis—all these edged entertainment, as incarnated by celebrities, ever closer to theology, in a way, turning the tables. If religion had become entertainment, entertainment was now becoming religion.

It has often been said that movie stars are the royalty of America. (The better analogy, really, is that the royals are the movie stars of Britain.) But stars and other celebrities seem to be much more like devotional objects than royal figures, and they inspire devotional language. When Richard Schickel in his book on celebrities, *Intimate Strangers,* talks of fans' having "internalized them, unconsciously made them a part of our consciousness," he is really describing communion. Or when people say, as many did after the death of Princess Diana, that they feel they have a "personal relationship" with a celebrity, they are invoking the same term that evangelists use to describe their relationship with God.

Most of this is of course figurative, and most of it, as Schickel indicates, lurks beneath the crust of consciousness. But there are times when the religious imagery becomes explicit. Singer Michael Jackson wrote a letter to *People* magazine in 1987 unmistakably casting himself in messianic terms: "I MUST achieve[.] I MUST seek truth in all things. I must endure for the [power] I was sent forth, for the children[.] But have mercy, for I've been Bleeding a long time now." Though he would have never described himself as a deity, basketball superstar Michael Jordan nevertheless also evoked religious imagery; the Nike symbol of Jordan, arms and legs splayed as he soars for a dunk, looked suspiciously like an athletic crucifix, and Jordan's exploits, his "walking on air" as he elevates for a shot, his resurrection and NBA championship after two years of retirement, his inspirational performance in the 1997 NBA finals against the Utah Jazz while battling the flu, all invited religious analogies. Asked once by a journalist if he were a god, Jordan blushingly answered, "I play a game of basketball. . . . I try to entertain for two hours and let people go home to their lives. . . . I could never consider myself a god."

Testing the proposition that celebrities had attained godhood, a hoaxster in Portland, Oregon, organized a rally for a Church of Kurt Cobain, the lead singer of the rock group Nirvana, who had committed suicide, and found willing congregants. But it was no hoax that every year thousands of pilgrims made their way to the gravesite of rock-and-roll pioneer Elvis Presley on his death anniversary, many of them halt and lame, seeing Graceland as a kind of American Lourdes where they could be healed. It was what journalist Ron Rosenbaum called a "fusion of our longing for spirituality and our lust for celebrity." (Needless to say, Presley's life had conformed perfectly to the monomyth.)

Indeed, death, especially an untimely death like Presley's, seemed to complete the religious analogy. Always there were the grand effusions of grief, the processionals and testimonials that canonized the deceased, even the hymns. (Elton John's "Candle in the Wind" served double duty for both Marilyn Monroe and Princess Di.) Always there was the sense of victimization, as if every celebrity had died for society's sins, whether it was Presley, victimized by the excesses that celebrity forced upon him, or Marilyn Monroe, victimized by the exploitation of her beauty, or Princess Di, victimized by the media's vulpine attentions. And always there was the deification as affection apotheosized into worship, with fans making pilgrimages to gravesites as if these were shrines, buying artifacts as if they were relics and seeking exegeses of the lives as if they were sacred texts.

Yet perhaps even more meaningful than these superficial resemblances between the trappings of entertainment and the trappings of religion, between the worship of celebrity and the worship of God, was the moral equivalence between the two. Like a religion, entertainment promulgated a set of values and had even become, arguably, the single most important source of values in late-twentieth-century America. To say this is not to restate the obvious—for example, that violence in films and television programs may incite violence in life or that sex on-screen may promote promiscuity off-screen. It is to address something much more fundamental, something that brings us back to cosmology.

In the first place, what the movies endowed to the life movie and what the life movie endowed to those of us who perforce live within it is that entertainment is the primary standard of value for virtually everything in modern society. Those things that entertain are, with rare exceptions, the most highly prized. In the second place, as is becoming increasingly evident, the movies made entertainment the new measure of individual worth as well. Again, this is true not only of people who provide conventional entertainment, though they are among the best remunerated and most highly regarded individuals in American society, but also of those people who have become human entertainment: celebrities.

Despite the celebrity archetype that denied the exceptionality of the famous, to be a celebrity is widely regarded as the most exalted state of human existence, and not just by *Vanity Fair*. As Los Angeles Deputy District Attorney Christopher Darden said of O. J. Simpson, "[T]here are no rules for celebrities." Nor are there any limits. Celebrity gives one entrée into that secular heaven where there are money, sex, beauty, glamour, power, respect and affection as well as the small perks of life, like the best tables at restaurants or the best seats at sporting events or invitations to the most chic parties or even honorary degrees. "I am famous," actor Jason Alexander said by way of explanation for why he was asked to deliver the 1995 commencement address at Boston University's School for the Arts. "I would like to think that it's because I'm a pretty good guy and I'm passionate about my craft and my business, but it's not. It's because I'm famous. . . ."

For all that, the greater value of celebrity may be not what it could get one but what others naturally assumed about one who had it. As early as 1898 the narrator of novelist Winston Churchill's *The Celebrity* averred, "Far be it from me to question the talents of one upon whose head has been set the laurels of fame." Then the assumption was that celebrity was the reward for accomplishment. Writing fifty years later, and much more cynically, the sociologist C. Wright Mills called celebrity the "crowning result of the star system in a society that makes a fetish of competition. . . . It does not seem to matter what the man is the very best at; so long as he has won out in competition over all the others, he is celebrated." This may have been true when Wright was writing in the 1950s, but by the 1980s the converse was actually true. It was the celebrity itself, not any competition for it, that bestowed the superlatives, and that meant that anyone wanting to be regarded as the best would have been well advised to seek celebrity first.

This furtive elision from one's entertainment value in the media to one's human worth placed the anointed in a perpetual nimbus of superlatives. Take a *New Yorker* profile of the British advertising executive Charles Saatchi that is a fairly typical example of the interchangeable value language of celebrity: One size fits all. Describing Saatchi in his younger days, the profile says: "Very quickly, Charles became a leading copywriter, notable for his rock-star hair, his Carnaby Street clothes, and his obsession with cars." (Note: He is notable for his image rather than his work.) Then: "The ads were controversial, but they changed advertising. . . . They also made Charles a star." (Note: The real point!) Now, however, must come the transition from stardom into genius: "In America, Charles had seen a celebrity culture coming alive, and he sensed what many of his competitors did not—that such tawdry Yank values as 'personality' and 'sex appeal' could translate into revenue." Meanwhile, Saatchi's brother, Maurice, is described as "the most attractive man in London." (Note: Not *one* of the most attractive men but *the* most attractive.) Finally, there is the illustration of genius. Saatchi is just sitting in his office one day idly scribbling when he produces an ad for Silk Cut cigarettes the way Picasso might have casually produced a sketch for *Guernica*. As the deputy chairman of the Saatchi board recalled the scene, "He said, 'What do you think of that?' And it was a piece of silk with a cut in it. So he said, 'There it is, there's our ad.' The brand had been too effeminate, and this ad had a sort of violent streak in it. And it doubled their market share."

After decades of reading hundreds of similar accounts of celebrities' offhanded brilliance, we have been conditioned to take these reports at face value. *Of course* Saatchi could scribble a dazzling ad campaign in minutes. But when you move just a half step back, when you regard this brainstorm in the cool light of reason rather than in the hot spotlight of celebrity, you realize that there is nothing brilliant about Saatchi's ad at all, that in fact, in any context other than celebrity it might even be considered idiotic. Just imagine a civilian submitting a picture of a piece of silk with a cut in it and declaring, "There's our ad!" In the great inversion of human entertainment, the act has been given value by the celebrity of the person who performed it.

What the profile of Saatchi really demonstrated, then, was not his genius—though he may very well be one—but the fact that celebrity was like a bank reserve upon which one could draw and spend on anything one did. Or to paraphrase artist Jenny Holzer's maxim that "Money creates taste," one might say that "Celebrity creates value." Thus the artist Julian Schnabel can draw upon his celebrity to record an album of lovelorn country-and-western songs he has composed, while singer Tony Bennett can draw upon his celebrity to exhibit paintings he has done. And actor Ethan Hawke can draw on his celebrity to write a novel, while novelist Norman Mailer can draw on his celebrity to appear in films.

How much value can celebrity create? Though this may seem a somewhat amorphous transaction, once businessmen came to appreciate the importance of celebrity in the corporate world, its value could be quantified. When Alex J. Mandl, the former president of the American Telephone & Telegraph Company, was given a $20 million signing bonus to head an obscure wireless phone company in 1996, the firm justified the fee on the basis that a big name attracts investors exactly the same way a big-name movie star attracts an audience. As it turned out, the company was right. Within forty-eight hours of Mandl's appointment, each share rose $6.75, covering his bonus six times over—and suggesting that the economic value of the celebrity of a corporation's chief executive officer might even exceed the value of its material assets. Or, as Marshall McLuhan once said, "[E]ntertainment pushed to an extreme becomes the main form of business and politics."

In their book *The Winner-Take-All Society*, economists Philip J. Cook and Robert H. Frank even translated this process into an economic theory that accounted for the growing disparity in the 1990s between the highest- and the lowest-paid within a single profession. They believed that the increasing globalization of markets had created a giant set of bidders for services, in effect turning every employee into a free agent. While multinational corporations could pay more, employees at the tops of their professions could also demand more. The best way for an employee to succeed in such a market, however, was to establish some unique value, and the most easily appreciated value was celebrity. Celebrity status could drive up the bidding for investment bankers, engineers, lawyers, doctors and businessmen because it gave a job seeker what Cook and Frank called mental shelf space in a market where many products were bidding for that space. What employers were really bidding for, though, was the celebrity a well-known figure could invest in the company.

Nor was it only in his own performance or products that a celebrity could invest the value of his fame. He could invest it in anything with which he came into contact because, apparently, people felt that the residue of his celebrity adhered to these places and objects. That was why celebrity restaurants became hot eating places and why areas in which celebrities settled suddenly became hot residential real estate. It was why artist Jeff Koons could sign $6 Nike posters, frame them and sell them for $900, and why there was a run on the clothes of designer Gianni Versace the week after he was murdered by a serial killer. It was also why the $40 plastic Swatch watches that Andy Warhol had collected eventually sold for thousands of dollars at auction, and why the various knickknacks and gewgaws of Jacqueline Kennedy Onassis fetched such staggering prices at her estate auction: $772,500 for a set of President Kennedy's golf clubs (858 times Sotheby's estimate); $453,500 for a rocking chair (Sotheby's estimate: $3,000 to $5,000); $574,500 for a cigar humidor that comedian Milton Berle had given to John Kennedy; $12,650 for a pair of Kenneth Jay Lane earclips. The woman who purchased the last gushed, "I get to be a princess every time I put them on." But it wasn't the rush of royalty that she really got; it was the rush of minor celebrity as the woman who had overpaid for Jackie Onassis's earrings.

It was with the Onassis auction in mind that the families of the victims of serial killer Jeffrey Dahmer hatched a plan to auction Dahmer's instruments of torture and divide the proceeds. "Look at what Camelot brought," said an attorney representing the families. "We have two sides to our psyche, the Camelot side and the Dahmer side. You can only imagine what people would pay for some of this stuff. And the sicker the connotation, the bigger the bucks." The reason these instruments had value, however, was not what they had been used for but, once again, who had used them. Dahmer's celebrity inhered in his tools.

But this was hardly the most extreme case of how the value of celebrity could be transferred. The most extreme may have been the assassin who sought to absorb his victim's fame the way primitive hunters sought to absorb the anima of their prey. The target was almost immaterial so long as he was celebrated. Arthur Bremer, the assailant of 1972 presidential aspirant George Wallace, had stalked President Nixon first, and singer-composer John Lennon's assassin, Mark David Chapman, had considered killing talk show host Johnny Carson, Jacqueline Onassis, actor George C. Scott, Elizabeth Taylor and Beatle Paul McCartney, among others, before settling on Lennon. Chapman admitted that he almost walked away from Lennon with an autograph rather than with Lennon's life; it was an admission of the continuity between wanting to own a small piece of a celebrity and wanting celebrity itself. Had Chapman walked away with his signed album, he would have faded into oblivion. Instead, he became a permanent character actor in the life movie.

IT IS WITH criminality, perhaps, that one can best see just how the values of human entertainment usurped other, more traditional values. Judged by traditional values, criminals are objects of reproach and scorn. But judged by the values of entertainment, which is how the media now judged everything, the perpetrator of a major, or even a minor but dramatic, crime, was as much a celebrity as any other human entertainer. Timothy McVeigh, later convicted of setting off a bomb outside the Alfred P. Murrah Federal Building in Oklahoma City, Oklahoma, and killing 168 people, received the kind of glamour treatment from *Newsweek* magazine that was usually only accorded movie stars. The cover photo of McVeigh staring off dreamily into space, his lips resolute but also soft, was pure Hurrell, the romantic photographer of Hollywood's golden age. (McVeigh had joked with the photographer Eddie Adams not to let any of the trashy magazines get the photos.) Meanwhile, the interview inside was pure *Photoplay*: gushy, reverent, excited. McVeigh looked, wrote *Newsweek*, "a lot more like a typical Gen-Xer than a deranged loner, much less a terrorist. His handshake was firm, and he looked his visitors right in the eye. He appeared a little nervous, maybe, but good-humored and self-aware. Normal." He was also "a subtle and intriguing figure, at once more clever and [more] ingenuous than his tabloid personality." Asked about the children killed in the blast, McVeigh was, said *Newsweek,* "horrified" and muttered, "It's a very tragic thing."

The interview, which was reported in the familiar language of celebrity rather than news journalism, was part of a campaign by McVeigh and his attorney to, in the attorney's words, "present our client to the public as we believe he really is"—that is, to present a more flattering image of him. In furtherance of his campaign, McVeigh petitioned the court to permit him to grant a one-hour interview to the questioner of his choice from a list that included Barbara Walters and Diane Sawyer of ABC, Tom Brokaw of NBC and Dan Rather of CBS. He also requested that the interview be broadcast during television's fall sweeps week that November, when the ratings are determined. Finally, giving equal time to the print media, he asked that he be allowed to be interviewed by one of the nation's leading newspapers and again submitted a list of possibilities.*

At the time, McVeigh clearly didn't see himself as an indicted suspect in a heinous crime. He saw himself as a celebrity promoting a new movie. In 1963, after Lee Harvey Oswald allegedly killed President John F. Kennedy in Dallas, Texas, Oswald provided a great oxymoronic metaphor by escaping into a movie theater, finding the source, so to speak, for the obsession with celebrity even as he was attempting to hide from it. Yet that sort of behavior would become inconceivable in the evolving celebrity culture. Why hide? "Nowadays if you're a crook you're still considered up-there," Andy Warhol wrote. "You can write books, go on TV, give interviews—you're a big celebrity and nobody even looks down on

---

* A year and a half later Barbara Walters revealed that she had actually auditioned for McVeigh in his jail cell and got the impression of a "pleasant young fellow" (*Cochran & Co.,* Court-TV, February 6, 1998).

you because you're a crook. . . . This is because more than anything people just want stars."

Whether or not people wanted criminal stars, criminals certainly wanted celebrity. McVeigh was bidding to be on the television screen. John C. Salvi III, who was accused (and later
convicted) of murdering two receptionists on December 30, 1994,
at two different abortion clinics, told his attorney that he wanted
to be interviewed by Barbara Walters, a recurrent theme apparently among criminals. The so-called Unabomber, who killed
three and wounded twenty-three in sixteen separate bombing
attacks, not only delivered a manifesto to the *New York Times* and
Washington Post that he demanded be published—else he would
kill again—but was clearly concerned about his image, confiding
to his journal that if he were caught, as he later was, he would be
wrongly dismissed as a "sickie." He may have been worrying about
his billing too. Psychologists speculated that he issued his manifesto shortly after McVeigh's bombing because he was afraid of
being upstaged and hoped, in their words, to "regain his position
as the country's most infamous bomber."

If the Unabomber lifie sounded like a typical movie thriller
featuring a criminal mastermind playing cat and mouse with the
authorities, it may not have been a coincidence. It is entirely possible that Unabomber Theodore Kaczynski, and McVeigh for that
matter, were intentionally doing in the life movie what got film
directors attention in conventional movies: blowing things up.
Shortly before his bombing, McVeigh had in fact rented a video-
cassette of *Blown Away,* a film about a former IRA terrorist baiting
an old colleague who is now on the bomb squad of the Boston
police. More, McVeigh seemed to have scripted his caper along
the lines of a movie: the scheme itself; his apparent motive (little
guy against the system); his preparation, which was right out of
a thriller; even the idea of a getaway car. Obviously he had
not scripted his capture, but he improvised the role as he went
along, again using the movies as a paradigm. In custody McVeigh

became Rambo, the silent, stalwart hero refusing to give the enemy any information.*

Other celebrity criminals may not have designed their crimes for the media quite this way, but some of them did design the aftermath. John Lennon's assassin, Mark David Chapman, had left a tableau in his hotel room—a photo of Judy Garland with the Cowardly Lion, a Bible inscribed to Holden Caulfield (the protagonist of J. D. Salinger's *The Catcher in the Rye*), a photo of himself with refugee children—that he thought would suggest a motive behind his crime. In short, he was providing a theme as well as an act. Later in jail, Chapman, still media-conscious, lost fifty pounds for a *People* magazine photo shoot. In the same vein, a psychiatrist who examined serial killer Theodore Bundy speculated that Bundy wanted to be caught so that he could orchestrate the real show: his trial. "Mr. Bundy is the producer of a play which attempts to show that various authority figures can be manipulated, set against one another," said the analyst. "Mr. Bundy does not have the capacity to recognize that the price for this 'thriller' might be his own life."

But the textbook case of a young ne'er-do-well plotting to grab celebrity through a homicide movie may be Arthur Bremer. Bremer explicitly saw himself as an actor in a film, so much so that while stalking President Nixon, his initial target, he missed a chance to kill him when he raced back to his hotel to change into a black suit. Later Bremer ruefully told his diary that he had been "overly concerned with my appearance & composure after the bang bangs. I wanted to shock the shit out of the S[ecret] S[ervice] men with my calmness." At another point, still thinking of how his movie would play, he scripted what he was going to say after he fired: "A penny for your thoughts."

---

* Even more slavishly indebted to the movies was a crew of bank robbers who had attempted a heist in North Hollywood, just a stone's throw from the studios. The calm daytime sally, the automatic weapons, the black body armor all evoked immediate parallels with Michael Mann's 1995 movie thriller *Heat*. When one of the robbers strode into a fusillade of bullets, it was a scene that could only have been inspired by the movies.

When his plans to assassinate the president were foiled, Bremer decided to target George Wallace instead, fully realizing it was a comedown. "SHIT! I won't even rate a T.V. enteroption [*sic*] in Russia or Europe when the news breaks—they never heard of Wallace," he writes. And acknowledgment was clearly the objective: to exorcise the ghosts of anonymity. "FAILURES," he scrawled in one diary entry. "Felt like an utter failure," he wrote at the bottom of another page. But contemplating his assassination plan fortified him: "I'm as important as the start of WWI. I just need the little opening & a second of time." Once he had accomplished his mission, he would sell his diary to the movies, eventually winding up in "Hollywood (I KNOW IT SOUNDS INSANE, SO DON'T THINK IT) & making my fortune on the old sivler [*sic*] screen." That of course was the nub of it. You killed George Wallace because killing George Wallace would make Arthur Bremer a movie star. You killed him because it was the shortest and surest path to celebrity in a society where celebrity was the object of desire.

IV

THE OTHER SIDE OF THE GLASS

WHAT HAD BECOME apparent to Bremer had also become apparent to virtually everyone living in America in the late twentieth century: that if you weren't part of the life movie itself, then you were relegated to being part of its vast anonymous audience. To many, this was too terrifying a prospect to contemplate. Not to be in the movie, not to be acknowledged, was the profoundest form of failure in the entertainment state. As the writer George W. S. Trow analyzed the situation in *Within the Context of No Context,* America was now divided into two grids. One was the grid of the popular—the grid, broadly speaking, of entertainment. The other was the grid of the intimate—the grid of one's personal life. Everyone belonged to one or the other—everyone, that is, except celebrities. "Celebrities have an intimate life and a life in the grid of two hundred million," Trow wrote. "For them, there is no distance between the two grids in American life. Of all Americans, only they are complete."

But everyone naturally sought completion. "I know I'm nothing," longtime pornographic film star Nick East told Susan Faludi of *The New Yorker*. "Though most of the world has seen my face, I'm nothing because I didn't do anything." Still, East looked forward to a day when he would make himself "worthy" of public recognition, a day "when I'm on the talk shows—the next O. J. Simpson, not that I'm going to kill somebody, but the next media sensation—when all the 'Hard Copy' shows, when the world is going to pay attention." It was the new American Dream. As director/choreographer Michael Bennett once said, "Unfortunately in America today, either you're a star or a nobody."

"Everybody wants to be famous," actor Bruce Willis told Jay McInerney in his *Esquire* interview, following Bennett's line of reasoning, but Willis doubted it had always been that way and he attributed the change to what he called television culture. On television ordinary Americans daily saw the benefits of celebrity and the adoration that celebrities received. At the same time, television helped nurse Americans' own sense of inadequacy, not only in the face of celebrity but in the ordinary course of life where dissatisfaction was one of the major engines of advertising; you bought things because you had to compensate for what you didn't have. In a society that often encouraged a lack of self-worth, if only to force people to spend money to ameliorate the situation, "the 'star' provided an accessible icon to the significance of the personal and the individual," as cultural analyst Stuart Ewen put it. Indeed, the subliminal message of every movie icon in every movie was the importance of being important.

The trouble was that the icon didn't live in our quotidian space. Despite the insistence on the basic democracy of celebrity and despite the fact that the public could exercise its power to drag celebrities back across the threshold, it was a central tenet of the mythology of celebrities that they inhabited their own special world. Leo Braudy called it a "mystic community of other famous people, a psychic city of mutual respect for each other's individual nature." Writer Tom Wolfe, labeling it the "Center," described it as "the orbit of those aristocrats, wealthy bourgeois, publishers, writers, journalists, impresarios, performers, who wish to be 'where things happen.' . . ." And Andy Warhol cited access to this world as the "best reason to be famous": "so you can read all the big magazines and know everybody in all the stories." As far as the general public was concerned, its existence was never doubted, only envied. "I know who they are," novelist Jacqueline Susann once said of her readers, "because that's who I used to be. They want to press their noses against the windows of other people's houses and get a look at the parties they'll never be invited to, the dresses they'll never get to wear, the lives they'll never live, the guys they'll never fuck."

But that didn't stop them from hoping that they might yet gain access to that world, that they might yet get to the other side of the glass. The question was how. The answer, increasingly, was television, which was itself on the other side of the glass, the glass of the television tube that separated the celebrated from the anonymous. The great unspoken egalitarianism of celebrity was that because it was *human* entertainment, one didn't necessarily need any talent to attain it. All one really needed was the sanctification of the television camera. That was in part why people immediately reacted whenever a television camera caught them, however briefly, in its lens. Even at sporting events fans would leap and wave and mug as the cameras panned the stands during breaks in the action, though it was never clear exactly to whom they were waving or for whom they were mugging. Had they told their dear ones to stay glued to the set on the off chance they might make an appearance? Or was it simply that for one split second they were on the other side of the glass themselves in that blessed world of celebrity?

It was the desperation to get to the other side of the glass, the understanding of what it took to get there and what it conferred once one arrived that director Martin Scorsese captured in his 1982 film *The King of Comedy*. Rupert Pupkin (Robert DeNiro) is an aging celebrity aspirant addled by dreams of fame. He spends his evenings in his basement holding imaginary conversations with celebrities and hosting his own talk show with cardboard cutouts of Liza Minnelli and Jerry Langford (a fictionalized Johnny Carson). When Pupkin actually manages to meet Langford (played by comedian Jerry Lewis) and asks him for an opportunity to do his comedy routine on Langford's television show, Langford delivers the old show business bromides about hard work and tells him he will have to start at the bottom.

But Pupkin knows enough about celebrity to know better. He and an equally addled accomplice, whose dreams are of star romance, not fame, kidnap Langford. The ransom? An appearance by Pupkin on *The Jerry Langford Show*. "That's the only way I could break into show business—hijacking Jerry Langford," Pupkin jokes to the audience, which doesn't know yet that he is not kidding. And Pupkin ends his routine with the new American truth: "Better to be king for a night than a schmuck for a lifetime." Of course, once he kidnaps Langford, Pupkin has in fact broken through the glass. His stunt makes him a celebrity. He graces the covers of *Time, Newsweek* and *People*. He signs a one-million-dollar book contract for his life story, which becomes a best-seller and is sold to the movies. When last we see him, he has served his jail sentence and is making a television appearance as the "king of comedy."

Similarly, in the 1995 film *To Die For* a beautiful young woman named Suzanne Stone (Nicole Kidman), stuck in the improbably named town of Little Hope, New Hampshire, dreams of escaping the monotony some day by becoming another Barbara Walters. "You aren't anybody in America if you're not on TV," she declares as she angles for a job as a local television personality. When Suzanne manages to lasso a dim-witted teenage girl into a scheme to murder her husband so that she can more aggressively pursue her career, the girl compares their friendship to "living in this really great movie," though she finally comes to recognize the paradox of Suzanne's lust for celebrity: "If everybody were on TV all the time, we'd be better people. But if everybody were on TV all the time, there'd be nobody to watch"—unless it is life, not TV, that is the medium.

What Rupert Pupkin had solved, with perverse ingenuity, was the matter of how to get on television. Statisticians speak of a cocktail party effect, by which they mean that in order to get heard at a cocktail party, a guest must talk more loudly. This in turn prompts another guest to talk even more loudly, which prompts yet another guest to talk more loudly still and so on, until there is cacophony. In a sense, Americans at the end of the twentieth century lived within the cocktail party. Anyone wanting to be heard had to adopt the celebrity variant of the bigger, louder, faster aesthetic that drove conventional entertainments, but this set off a chain reaction of one-upmanship, forcing would-be celebrities to become ever more outrageous to be seen amid the clamor and heard above the din.

As Scorsese had dramatized, some people were willing to do almost anything to get to the other side of the glass for their moment of beatification, and the media were just as eager to grant it. One drunken fan who fell twenty-five feet while catching a point after touchdown at a Chicago Bears game appeared on *The Late Show with David Letterman* and had already signed with an agent for speaking engagements and commercials. Others, who had absolutely nothing to barter for fame but their private lives, closed the gap between the grids and passed to the other side of the glass by revealing their innermost secrets on daytime television exploitation talk shows. Since there were nearly two dozen of these programs in the mid-1990s, and each program consumed roughly eight guests an hour, some one thousand people each week were engaging in the cocktail conversation, trying to shout over the others, with thousands more waiting in the foyer. The truth was, though, that shouting was no longer sufficient. Real entertainment demanded combat. As one producer admitted, "For a show on rape, it used to be enough to interview the victim. Now you need the victim and the perpetrator. You need her to come face to face with her rapist."*

And these thousands ready to expose the worst of themselves, ready to endure humiliation for a visit to the other side of the glass, were not even the most devout flagellants. Others gave more to celebrity. Appreciating the entertainment value of death, they gave their lives. Comedian Freddie Prinze committed suicide because, according to a friend, he saw it "as a way of becoming immortal—you know, getting your face on the front page of every newspaper. He planned it." In the same way, pornographic film star Cal Jammer killed himself because, surmised a former girlfriend, he saw the attention the media devoted to the suicide of a female porn star. "I wonder if Savannah reached such a high level of fame after her suicide that he thought that was the way to do it," said the girlfriend. But unfortunately not even the tabloid television shows picked up his story. He gave his life for fame and still didn't make it to the other side of the glass.

It was in truth an occupational hazard for putative celebrities. No one knew exactly what it took to pass. You could kill yourself and not make it. You could look sensational and not make it. You could do outrageous things and not make it. You could commit unspeakable crimes and not make it. ("How many times do I have to kill before I get my name in the paper?" a serial murderer once

---

* The progenitor of these programs, *Donahue*, left the air in 1996 after thirty years, conceding that the entertainment envelope had been pushed beyond its ability to compete. Said an executive of *Donahue*'s television syndicator, "The kind of show he [Phil Donahue] wanted to do is not the show the average person wants to watch anymore. They want to be entertained and not his way. They want more craziness" (*New York Times*, January 18, 1996, p. A19).

complained.) There was so much caprice involved, just as there was so much caprice involved in determining which conventional entertainments succeeded. And the most exasperating part of it for those who wanted to become human entertainment was that the celebrities and the celebrity wannabes really were often indistinguishable from one another. With talent no longer a prerequisite, it was luck as much as anything that put some people on one side of the glass and some people on the other, making celebrity yet another example of chaos theory.

Yet even for those who were lucky enough to make it, there were perils. In 1987 Robert O'Donnell was a thirty-seven-year-old fireman paramedic in Midland, Texas, when he pulled eighteen-month-old Jessica McClure from an abandoned well in full view of the world watching on the Cable News Network after baby Jessica had been trapped for nearly sixty hours. "It was the greatest moment of Robert's life," said his mother, "and it was the worst thing that ever happened to him." O'Donnell immediately passed to the other side of the glass, becoming a nationally recognized hero who was soon squabbling with fellow rescuers over the movie rights to the story.

What he had not bargained for was that his stay there would be temporary. As *New York Times* reporter Lisa Belkin put it, he was "a man so changed by fame that he no longer belonged in his world, but not changed enough that he could leave that world behind." Angry that his celebrity hadn't brought him greater reward, O'Donnell began suffering severe migraine headaches, for which he sedated himself with painkillers. In short order, he lost his job, was sued for divorce, bounced from one situation to another and then finally killed himself with a shotgun blast on a barren West Texas road. O'Donnell had been addicted to fame, and the true cause of death was his withdrawal from it. As had happened to so many others, his scenes had been left on the cutting room floor of the life movie. In taking away his celebrity, they had taken his reason to live.

Chapter Five

The Mediated Self

I

A NATION OF GATSBYS

AT THE SAME TIME that the public life movies starring celebrities were playing in the mass media, personal life movies, billions of them, starring ordinary people who hadn't passed to the other side of the glass, were playing in everyday existence: on the street, at the office or factory, at a restaurant or shopping mall or local bar, in school, at a party, in the living room, even in the bedroom. These weren't necessarily high-concept pictures like the public lifies; they were frequently no more than a conversation or a gesture or a glance. These didn't have audiences in the tens of millions as the public lifies did; sometimes they had only an audience of one. And these didn't provide metaphors and myths as the public lifies often did; usually they provided only the modest joy of performance.

Though the personal lifies were no less, and possibly even

more, influenced by the movies than the public celebrity lifies,
they had actually been in performance long before the movies
arrived, in fact since people first became aware of the power and
pleasure of self-presentation and perhaps even before then. An
obscure Russian playwright of the early twentieth century named
Nicolas Evreinoff, who was a pioneering theorist in the interplay
between reality and imagination, believed theatricality was an
"instinct" and called it a fundament of life, just as Johan Huizinga
in *Homo Ludens* had called play one of the essentials of human
existence—that is, an instinct to entertain as well as be entertained "The birth of a child, education, hunting, marriage was
the administration of justice, religious ceremonies and funeral
rites— every important event in life is made by the primitive man
(and not by primitive man alone!) the occasion for a purely theatrical spectacle," wrote Evreinoff. "His entire life is a succession of
such 'shows.' "

But whether showmanship was a natural instinct or not, it
was certainly useful in negotiating one's way through the world. As
the urban sociologist Richard Sennett saw it in his book *The Fall of
Public Man*, appearance and self-presentation were the very bases
of social relations in Europe in the eighteenth century. In Sennett's
analysis, people, particularly the upper classes, dressed like actors
and behaved like actors on the unstated assumption that public
life was basically a performance in which you projected to others
how you wanted to be perceived even though everyone understood
that the role had very little to do with anything other than role-
playing. It was as if all social intercourse were an elaborate show
and all the world a stage, as the cliché went.

While this form of interaction leaped the Atlantic Ocean,
Americans nevertheless had a different, if no less acute, appreciation for acting and appearance in everyday social life from Europeans. There was something about this country, especially on its
raw frontier, that encouraged a theatrical temperament, possibly
as a way to exhibit dramatically the lack of restraint in America

compared to the social constraints of Europe. "These men of the back country seemed born actors," the cultural historian Constance Rourke once wrote; "they had a sense of display." And not only the frontiersmen. The pleasure of performance extended even to the Yankee, who, Rourke said, "apparently enjoyed—as any actor would—creating a sensation by his looks, his lingo, his repartee and even his songs."

If the open American environment energized theatricality, so did Americans' sense of democracy. Democracy meant not only that one could theoretically become whatever one wanted to become (through hard work, of course) but also that there was more social fluidity and fewer overt class distinctions in America than in Europe to betray one's appearance. As a result, how one looked and acted could easily translate into who one was: class by style. In fact, it became so difficult to tell whether one was really what he or she purported to be that everywhere Americans were racked by what Walt Whitman called the "terrible doubt of appearances."

To this doubt was added another ambivalence about social theatricality that Europeans evidently hadn't felt. On the one hand, nineteenth-century Americans prided themselves on their genuineness and had nothing but contempt for affectation, which they identified with decadent European culture. (They had built an entire popular culture from this contempt.) On the other hand, these same Americans, ever pragmatic, put great store in wealth as a measure of industriousness and a signal of social success and importance. That meant that Americans carefully distinguished between the cultural connotations of appearance, which they abhorred, and the material connotations, which they avidly sought to project. The object was to seem rich without also seeming aristocratic, to seem naturally noble without also seeming effete.

In practice, urban nineteenth-century Americans found themselves obsessed with self-presentation. Members of the middle class, at pains to distinguish themselves from the working classes, strove to present themselves as genteel and paid a price for it. One observer writing in 1873 noted their haunted faces showing "unmistakable signs of their incessant anxiety and struggles to get on in life, and to obtain in addition to a mere subsistence, a standing in society." Meanwhile, the working classes, no less affected, devoted inordinate resources to making themselves appear richer than they really were, creating in the process a new class of genteel poor. This was especially true of workingwomen who squandered their meager funds on fancy clothing because, in the words of one historian, "[t]o be stunningly attired at the movies, balls, or entertainments often counted more in the working woman's calculations than having comfortable clothes and shoes for the daily round of toil."

The "modes of externalization," as one contemporary approvingly called them, weren't limited to clothes and other finery. They were also a matter of behavior. So important was deemed the ability to express oneself that by the late nineteenth century elocution had become an obligatory subject in the curriculum of American schools. One popular textbook, *The Delsarte Speaker* (1896), after a French singer and drama teacher, even taught students how specific gestures corresponded to specific emotions—what later generations would call body language. By the end of the nineteenth century almost every American was familiar with the Delsarte System and knew that hands clasped to the breast signaled mother love, a hand clapped to one's forehead remorse, an arm extended with open palm repulsion, both arms extended, one pointing up and one pointing down, patriotism. In short, they knew how to act.

Photographs and later movies would benefit from this obsession with appearances, which is certainly one of the reasons why these technologies surfaced when they did, but they would also serve as propellants for that obsession, making Americans more alert to the impressions they made. In Marshall McLuhan's estimation, the photograph even introduced a new sense of self. It involves, he wrote, "a development of self-consciousness that alters facial expressions and cosmetic makeup as immediately as it does bodily stance, in public or private"—so much so that he thought the "age of Jung and Freud is, above all, the age of the photograph, the age of the full gamut of self-critical attitudes."

But once again it was the movies, as the most popular and powerful entertainment medium, that created the most powerful modes of externalization. "My life was going to the movies. The movies gave me hope," comedienne Carol Burnett once said in a sentiment that could have been expressed by any number of Americans. Over time, after tens of millions of them had watched thousands of motion pictures, the movies gradually began occupying the American imagination like an expeditionary force, not only filling Americans' heads with models to appropriate but imbuing them with an even more profound sense than anyone in the nineteenth century could possibly have had of how important appearances were in producing just the right effect.

In a sense, the movies were the twentieth century's answer to Delsarte. "You know how to brood because you have seen 'Rebel Without a Cause,' " cultural analyst Louis Menand has written. "What better model does the world offer? You know how to ruin your life because you have seen 'Shampoo.' You know how to win because you have seen 'The Verdict'; you know how not to win because you have seen 'Top Gun.' You know how to walk down the sidewalk carrying a can of paint because you have seen 'Saturday Night Fever.' " Even the throngs who lined the Los Angeles Freeway cheering on O. J. Simpson as he attempted to escape in his Ford Bronco had learned to do so from movies in which rebels defied authority and the citizenry lent them vocal support. The movies offered a menu of so many gestures, so many poses, so many attitudes, so many expressions, so many lines that if one chose, one could, observed critic Geoffrey O'Brien, "end up adopting a whole life."

In emphasizing the value of appearance, what the movies reflected and facilitated was not just a theatrical style of behavior but a cultural shift toward a whole new social ideal. As the historian Warren Susman defined it, the old Puritan production-oriented culture demanded and honored what he called character, which was a function of one's moral fiber. The new consumption-oriented culture, on the other hand, demanded and honored what he called personality, which was a function of what one projected to others. It followed that the Puritan culture emphasized values like hard work, integrity and courage. The new culture of personality emphasized charm, fascination and likability. Or as Susman put it, "The social role demanded of all in the new culture of personality was that of a performer. Every American was to become a performing self."

By the 1920s there was already a vast literature in personal aesthetics, everything from self-help books like Orison Swett Marden's *Masterful Personality* to serious novels concerning personal presentation like Theodore Dreiser's *An American Tragedy* and Ernest Hemingway's *The Sun Also Rises*. (One of the biggest bestsellers of the 1930s would be Dale Carnegie's *How to Win Friends and Influence People*.) Perhaps the most powerful articulation of the new American yearning to reinvent oneself, however, was F. Scott Fitzgerald's *The Great Gatsby*. The elegant Gatsby was, of course, actually the prosaic Jay Gatz from North Dakota. "The truth was that Jay Gatsby of West Egg, Long Island, sprang from his Platonic conception of himself," remarked Fitzgerald's narrator, Nick Carraway. "He was a son of God—a phrase which, if it means anything, means just that—and he must be about His Father's business, the service of a vast, vulgar, and meretricious beauty. So he invented just the sort of Jay Gatsby that a seventeen-year-old boy would be likely to invent, and to this conception he was faithful to the end." He was faithful because in this dream, Carraway realized, Gatsby had found a "satisfactory hint of the unreality of reality, a promise that the rock of the world was founded securely on a fairy's wing."

Like the celebrities who would follow, Gatsby was a symbol of twentieth-century America, where so many were discovering the fairy's wing on which to found their own unreal reality. Decades later, advertisers would invent a motto to accompany the symbol. It came from an oft-shown television commercial of the 1980s featuring a soap-opera actor pitching a pain reliever. "I am not a doctor, but I play one on TV," he said. In the same way Gatsby himself might have said, "I was not an Oxford grad, but I played one," or President Reagan might have said, "I was not a president, but I played one," or the once-popular rock duo Milli Vanilli, who were found to be lip-synching other vocalists, might have said, "We were not a rock group, but we played one," or Zsa Zsa Gabor might have said, "I was not an actress, but I played one." In a culture of personality, playing one was just as good as being one, which threatened to make us a faux society of authors without books, artists without art, musicians without music, politicians without policies, scholars without scholarship.

A small but striking example of how performance had overtaken substance was the booming business beginning in the late 1970s in customized college term papers, something which tormented administrators and instructors but seemed to stir little moral anguish in students themselves. "There's a regular customer whose course load would be appropriate for the résumé of a U.N. secretary general," a professional term-paper writer confessed in *Harper's* magazine. "She's taking several courses on developing economies, including one referred to by other clients in the same class as 'Third World Women.' And one on the history of black Americans from Reconstruction to the present." When the writer presented the student with a twenty-five-page paper on the early years of the civil rights movement, the student scanned the paper and cracked, "Interesting course, isn't it?" Another paper for the same client on dowry murders in India elicited, "It's a great course, isn't it?" And a third, on the black leader W. E. B. Du Bois, prompted, "He seems like a fascinating guy. Somebody told me he wound up in Ghana." The point obviously is that the girl wasn't really a student in any substantive sense; like so many others in the life movie, she was just playing one.

FOR MANY CRITICS, particularly critics of capitalism on the left and critics of materialism on the right, the engine that drove modern America was consumption, which in turn was stoked by advertising. In their view, not only had the country attempted to democratize politics and culture, but, much more important and much more successfully, it had democratized desire, and it was the desire that led to the fixation on owning material things. The new generation of Americans, wrote George Jean Nathan and H. L. Mencken in 1921, had put "their inheritance into phonographs, Fords, boiled shirts, yellow shoes, cuckoo clocks, lithographs of the current mountebanks, oil stock, automatic pianos." Economist Paul Mazur, writing just a few years later, saw all this consumption as the product of a growing economy that had transformed America from a "needs" culture to a "desires" culture in which citizens were now "trained to desire change, to want new things even before the old have been entirely consumed."

But even if one accepted the premise that consumption, not entertainment, was the central force of modern America, consumption and entertainment had had a long-standing association, especially when merchants realized that entertainment was among the most effective ways of luring customers. In early-nineteenth-century America entertainment and the selling of goods freely commingled at fairs and bazaars, and pitchmen frequently used entertainers to attract crowds. The new department stores that arrived later in the century were explicitly viewed, in one merchant's words, as a "stage on which the play is enacted," meaning the play of consumption. In time these stores would deploy elaborate window dressing, musical accompaniment, art shows, theatrical lighting and playlets to enhance the sense that shopping was just another form of entertainment.

By the late twentieth century, entertainment and retailing were so intermingled that one could hardly distinguish between them. "People who come to shop want to be entertained," said fashion designer and retailer Ralph Lauren. "They're challenging me. 'Don't let me down, Ralph. What've you got?' " What Lauren had by the mid-1980s was a store on Manhattan's Madison Avenue in the old Rhinelander mansion, which he had dressed like a set with, wrote architecture critic Paul Goldberger, "just the right balance between beautiful objects for sale and beautiful objects placed to enhance the experience," and another store in East Hampton, Long Island, that Goldberger described as "a miniature theme park of Americana, filled with attractive pieces of clothing, any one of which you can have if you only present a credit card." *

In Chicago the Nike athletic shoe and apparel company spent a reported thirty-four million dollars on a sixty-eight-thousand-square-foot flagship complex it called Niketown. It included video theaters, display cases of professional athletes' shoes and jerseys, an aquarium and half a basketball court as well as life-sized sculptures of basketball star Michael Jordan. "My job is to be sort of a film director," Nike's design director Gordon Thompson III told the *New York Times,* "and this store tells a story. It's a mythology, but one for a range of consumers, people who are 7, 27 and 67. . . . I like to think it's part 1939 World's Fair and part theater." Meanwhile, a camping equipment retailer followed Nike's lead by installing a sixty-five-foot artificial rock in its store for climbing, and another sports retailer installed a waterfall and oversized video screens.

It was even harder to tell where the store ended and the entertainment began in the megamalls that began sprouting across the

---

* A poll conducted by Yankelovich Clancy Shulman and reported in the *New York Times* found that shoppers now wanted fantasy and entertainment as well as convenience in their stores (*New York Times,* April 23, 1993, pp. D1, D7).

North American continent in the 1980s. At the 5.2-million-square-foot West Edmonton Mall in Alberta, Canada, there were, in addition to the obligatory movie theaters, a nightclub, an indoor amusement park, a water park, a man-made lagoon with a replica of Christopher Columbus's *Santa Maria* floating atop and submarines gliding below, mechanical jazz bands, real Siberian tigers and a Fantasyland Hotel, where one could sleep in a room with a national decor of one's choice. Inside the even larger Mall of America on the outskirts of Minneapolis, Minnesota, there was a Camp Snoopy theme park with a roller coaster and a Lego Land of giant Lego blocks. Here Snoopy and other *Peanuts* characters greeted shoppers just as Disney characters greeted visitors to Disney World or Disneyland. To create new malls that would further integrate merchandising and amusement, the Sony Corporation formed a division the name of which said it all: Sony Retail Entertainment.

The association of consumption with entertainment didn't end with the shopping experience. There was also the flow of celebrity from the world of entertainment to the world of consumption. As early as World War I actors and athletes were enlisted to give endorsements of products in advertisements, and aviator Charles Lindbergh, even before he successfully completed his solo flight across the Atlantic Ocean in 1927, had already cut deals with Mobil Oil, Vacuum Oil, AC spark plugs and Wright Aeronautical.

In part, of course, these endorsements suggested that a celebrity's aura would rub off on a consumer who used the favored products, thus placing him, in his imagination at least, on the other side of the glass with the celebrity. In part, however, they also suggested that the celebrity's aura had rubbed off on the product too, placing the product itself on the other side of the glass. Since the celebrity was created by publicity, it wasn't long before merchandisers learned that products could be celebritized through promotion, just as people were. "The nationally advertised product is a celebrity of the consumption world," Daniel Boorstin wrote in *The Image,* acknowledging the process. "It is well known for its well-knownness, which is one of its most attractive ingredients."

But just as one looked to celebrities not simply for their familiarity but for their inherent entertainment value, one could now look to "celebritized" products for a form of inanimate entertainment. One could read profiles of certain products in general-interest magazines, watch advertisements about those products, feel the tingle of the excitement and hype about them, even wear clothing bearing the logos of those products as one might have imitated the style of a favorite movie star. (Coca-Cola, for one, had an entire store of licensed merchandise in New York.) This meant not only that products helped create an image for individuals seeking one but that products themselves had an image. "As long as people dislike the anonymity of mass production," product designer J. Gordon Lippincott said as early as 1947, "there will always be added sales appeal in products that have personality." Thus, commodities became personalities just as personalities had become commodities.

While there were dozens, if not hundreds, of examples of products being celebritized—everything from Microsoft's Windows 95 software program, which was launched with enough fanfare to trigger what one computer store manager called "consumer madness," to Godiva's upscale chocolates to Ben & Jerry's ice cream to Mephisto shoes to Ray-Ban and Vuarnet sunglasses to any designer fashion—the most egregious illustration of an otherwise mundane product's being given the celebrity treatment may have been the "Sport Paint Collection" from designer Ralph Lauren. As shilled in its advertising copy, the paints were "A Bold New Concept for the Home—the colors of the sport collection reflect the vitality of active sport and competition." Those colors included yellow (here called catamaran), white (gymnast), gray (sweatshirt grey), turquoise (lap pool blue) and black (hockey puck). Though it sounded like a parody, peddling ordinary house paint in the over-heated rhetoric of *Vanity Fair*, it was really just the celebrity in-version—celebrity creates value rather than value creates celebrity—now applied to the world of products.

Beyond the megamalls and the celebrity products, there was another, more critical interaction between consumption and entertainment, one that put the former squarely in the service of the latter. This had to do with function. Even theorists of con-sumption understood that there was no primal need to own things and that acquisition was itself dependent on something else, pri-marily, they believed, on fabricated, conditioned, Pavlovian want engineered by advertisers. A few theorists, however, saw that acquisition had a purpose other than feeding the capitalist maw. The purpose of acquisition, as they saw it, was exhibition. Thor-stein Veblen had grasped this at the very inception of modern con-sumption in the late nineteenth century. Man works, wrote Veblen in *The Theory of the Leisure Class*, not only to satisfy his needs but "to rank high in comparison with the rest of the community in point of pecuniary strength." The problem, as Veblen saw it, was that "[i]n order to gain and to hold the esteem of men it is not suf-ficient merely to possess wealth or power. The wealth or power must be put in evidence."

Among members of the upper or "superior pecuniary class" this led to "conspicuous leisure," a kind of performance art in which one showed how little one had to work by showing how much time one had to cultivate one's aesthetic sensibility. But because, in Veblen's words, the "norm of reputability imposed by the upper class extends its coercive influence with but slight hin-drance down through the social structure to the lowest strata," even the middle class and the poor felt the need to consume con-spicuously to assert their social worth. This led to Veblen's famous "conspicuous consumption," in which everyone acquired primar-ily to show everyone else what he or she had acquired.

In effect, this reversed the traditional assumption about the relationship between consumption and entertainment. The assumption was that entertainment was a form of consumption, the commodification of leisure in an industrialized capitalist society. In truth, since the act of buying and then displaying goods was often the most efficient and effective way to create a convincing role for oneself in the life movie, consumption really seemed to be a form of entertainment. It was a means of preparing oneself to put on a show.

This in fact was precisely how Americans themselves saw consumption. Already in the nineteenth century they were buying goods in the hope that they would be transformed by them—what advertising historian Jackson Lears called the "desire for a magical transfiguration of the self," which helped account for the enormous sales of patent medicines in the late nineteenth and early twentieth centuries. Nor was the transfiguration limited to appearances; it was also a matter of changing how one felt about oneself. By the twentieth century the idea of transfiguration was so central to consumption that advertisers had largely ceased extolling their products' utilitarian virtues and instead sought to convince consumers how much better they would feel if they owned the product. As Neil Postman analyzed it, "The television commercial has oriented business away from making products of value and toward making consumers feel valuable, which means that business has now become pseudo-therapy."

Writing at a time when social and economic status was the foremost goal of image management, Veblen didn't reckon on the rise of individual personality to challenge it and to provide alternative forms of value to it. But what he had said about the role of conspicuous consumption in demonstrating economic superiority would be equally if not more true for those who wanted to demonstrate their superior personality: their superior sense of style; their superior sense of cool; their superior sense of conformity or nonconformity; their superior sense of being superior. In the personality culture, consumption was a form of personality creation. Or as sociologist David Riesman put it, the "product now in demand is neither a staple nor a machine; it is a personality."

If one considered this role-playing as a kind of entertainment in life, a personal show, one could see how entertainment and consumption were often two sides of the same ideological coin. Entertainment was about release, freedom, transport, escape. Aside from the purchase of necessities—brands of which were themselves often differentiated from one another by their "personality"—so too was consumption. Entertainment was about the power of sensation. So too was consumption, in this case the sensations generated externally by how one looked and internally by how one felt. Entertainment relied heavily on instant gratification. So too did consumption. Entertainment was an expression of democracy, throwing off the chains of alleged cultural repression. So too was consumption, throwing off the chains of the old production-oriented culture and allowing anyone to buy his way into his fantasy. And, in the end, both entertainment and consumption often provided the same intoxication: the sheer, mindless pleasure of emancipation from reason, from responsibility, from tradition, from class and from all the other bonds that restrained the self.

II

PROPS

ACCORDING TO a famous pronouncement of President Calvin Coolidge in the 1920s, "The chief business of the American people is business." But by the late twentieth century the chief business of Americans was no longer business; it was entertainment. Almost everything produced, from automobiles to toothpaste, was a prop in, or a set dressing for, the life movies being enacted by tens of millions of Americans each day. Indeed, as life more and more came to resemble a movie, the entire economy seemed to reorient itself to serve the production, and America's growth industries increasingly were those that were directly tied to conventional entertainments or those that in one way or another enabled people to perform their lives.

Among these was the fashion industry, which one could now think of as the costumer for the life movie. Of course there had always been a segment of society that had been fashion-conscious, not just because these individuals enjoyed wearing fine clothing but because they enjoyed showing off the fine clothing they wore. As Richard Sennett described eighteenth-century public dress in Europe, "[O]ne stepped into clothes whose purpose was to make it possible for other people to act as if they knew who you were." The idea was that the clothes one wore expressed the status one had.

Two hundred years later in America, fashion still served this function, and Tom Wolfe could still call fashion "the code language of status," which explained why individuals wore designer initials on their clothing or paid exorbitant prices for a T-shirt or a pair of jeans just because it bore a designer tag. It was a way of conveying to everyone who saw you that these weren't just any T-shirts or any jeans; they were *expensive* and *tasteful* T-shirts and jeans that allowed the wearer to simulate taste and wealth, whether he really had these or not.

But over that same period fashion had also come to serve another function, one that was imaginative rather than expressive. With designer fashions widely available and thus decoupled from class, clothing was now intended not to signal one's status but to display, once again, one's personality or at least the personality one wanted to project. "To choose clothes, either in a store or at home, is to define and describe ourselves," Alison Lurie wrote in *The Language of Clothes,* and even inattention to fashion, she thought, was a fashion statement—namely, "I don't give a damn what I look like today." Under these circumstances, clothes don't really make the man; clothes *are* the man. Or, in the immortal words of tennis star Andre Agassi, as expressed in a commercial for Canon cameras, "Image is everything." And, conversely, "Everything is image."

Though every fashion designer more or less operated within this idea, none may have done so quite as self-consciously as Ralph Lauren. Like Jay Gatsby, Lauren was a product of his own creation. Born Ralph Lifshitz in 1939 on Mosholu Parkway in a middle-class neighborhood in the Bronx section of New York, he studied business at City College, worked as a salesman at Bloomingdale's department store and Brooks Brothers men's furnishings store, sold neckties for a company named Beau Brummel and eventually wound up designing the ties himself. But Lifshitz, who changed his name to Lauren when he was seventeen for obvious reasons, was no mere fashion maven. He was a young man captivated by a vision, the vision promulgated by the movies he watched. "Whether that world exists or not, I don't know," he once said. "I saw things as they should have been, not as they were."

What Lauren appreciated from his own love of the movies was that people would pay to transform their lives into their cinematic fantasies: safari outfits to make one a colonialist from *Out of Africa*; denim jackets and jeans to make one a cowboy from a Hollywood western; finely tailored English suits to make one an aristocrat from any number of crisp drawing room melodramas. At the same time, he realized that these transformations were more than a matter of costuming. With his home furnishings and accessories as well as his ad campaigns, Lauren was selling an image of life, a kind of collage of movie fantasies that, in his own words, "represent living, not fashion" and that, more specifically, provided the "whole atmosphere of the good life" that movies had always purveyed. One writer called him the first image manager, which is exactly what he was. He gave the middle class what the upper classes and celebrities had always had: a conscious aesthetic.

That it happened to be the aesthetic of the movies only spoke to Lauren's understanding of design as entertainment and entertainment as freedom. "America is a mix, a collection of all kinds of things funneling in together," he told one interviewer, "not isolated, not England, not France. We take all these things we've accumulated and form ourselves. And that's what America is. You're entitled to be whatever you want to be." Lauren was absolutely right: Self-creation was liberation. If totalitarian societies lacked uncensored entertainment, which might have threatened social control, they also lacked style, which might have threatened uniformity. The French sociologist Jean Baudrillard called this form of rebellion practical liberation, as opposed to political liberation, observing that "people in 'totalitarian' countries know very well that this is true freedom and dream of nothing but fashion, the latest styles, idols, the play of images, travel for its own sake, advertising, the deluge of advertising."

As Lauren saw it, what the movies had always done on-screen, which was to provide transport into their world, he could now do in life. Even pasts were available for a price; at Lauren's Madison Avenue store one could buy a silver tobacco canister engraved "To father on the occasion of his silver wedding, 15th October 1910." Moreover, like the movies, the world Lauren offered was far better than anything real from which it might have been struck. As one journalist described it, "His chuck wagon holds silver spoons, not greasy ones. His English Country doesn't have damp walls. The servants dust in the corners. The overstuffed chairs have springs. He's taken the pain out of perfection." Even Lauren's ads of beautifully groomed models posed against idealized sets linked in loose visual narratives of a large loving family or of pristine adventure or of deodorized sex bespoke perfection—life itself as escapism.

But it wasn't enough to have acquired these objects. To realize the dream, one needed to be tutored in how to use them. This is where Martha Stewart came in. What Ralph Lauren was to the materials of image, Martha Stewart was to their deployment. Like Lauren's, Stewart's childhood, in Nutley, New Jersey, as one of six siblings, was humble. Her mother was a homemaker who, in Martha's words, "cooked, cleaned, sewed all our clothes, canned and preserved and got us off to school on time." Her father was a part-time gardener, plumber and carpenter who barely scraped by. Martha herself was graduated from Barnard College, became a stockbroker, quit her job to raise a daughter and later became a caterer and then the editor of *House Beautiful*.

What she had discovered in the process, though, was that a whole generation of women were desperate for guidance in how to make the perfect impression in their homes because, Stewart believed, they needed an anchor in the tumult of modern life. "[W]e have finally become disillusioned with living in a world where the home is not the 'center,' " she wrote in one of her weekly syndicated newspaper columns that advised women on lifestyle. What Stewart now promised was to thrust those women into a modern, high-gloss version of Norman Rockwell.

Of course one could just as easily have concluded that Stewart had by the mid-1990s built a reported two-hundred-million-dollar empire of books, magazines, television programs, radio commentaries and products because women wanted to make their homes a set for their own life movies and not because they were seeking the comfort of family. Stewart herself in fact came awfully close to saying so. "We have come to realize that the creation of a fine family, a lovely lifestyle and a comfortable home is kind of a national art form in itself," she told her readers, fudging the deep emotional need for family with the externalities of homemaking. With her keen appreciation of the aspirations of the middle-class housewife, Stewart's job was to teach her the practical aesthetics of this art form. That she did. For Stewart, there was a right way of doing everything to maximize the visual effect. She even had an instruction for how to shovel the snow from your sidewalk: "Always leave an inch of snow so it looks nice and white. Aesthetics are very important in snow removal."

Along with the aesthetics of living and homemaking, the life movie also gave rise to an aesthetics of the body that made one's own muscle and sinew a form of self-expression. To make themselves healthier and younger-looking, most Americans in one way or another had participated in the exercise and bodybuilding booms that began in the 1970s. But as much as these may have owed to growing concerns about health, they also owed a great deal to the sense that in the life movie one had to look the part to be the part—whether it was bulging biceps and rippling abdominal muscles for the new man or tight buns and a narrow waist for the new woman. As a result, exercise became a kind of sculpture, the means of getting a designer body the way one might buy designer clothes.*

And for the things that exercise couldn't remedy? For those, there was always plastic surgery. As early as the middle of the nineteenth century, when people first became aware of the importance of the stagecraft of life, cosmetic surgery was being performed in America as a form of personal gentrification. Once it was made available to middle-class Americans, more and more of them used it to redesign themselves for their life movies and to expand their choices of roles.

Most individuals who opted for plastic surgery of course simply wanted to improve their appearance. At one extreme, however, a woman named Cindy Jackson underwent twenty plastic surgeries to remake herself in the image of the Barbie doll. At that same extreme, a French performance artist named Orlan, with an apparent understanding that cosmetic surgery was in the service of the life movie, underwent a series of public surgeries as part of a work in progress she called "The Ultimate Masterpiece: The Reincarnation of St. Orlan." The remnants of her "old" self were then sold as reliquaries. Meanwhile, at the other extreme from Cindy Jackson and Orlan, to prove that it wasn't just about improving one's appearance but also about creating one's role, was a dentist who made her living selling sets of crooked, jagged, discol-

---

* Nor was it coincidence that the health clubs themselves came more and more to resemble nightclubs rather than gymnasiums. One aerobics instructor said he lit his studio with fluorescent lights because it made the classes "more like a performance" (Holly Brubach, "Musclebound," New Yorker [January 11, 1993], p.33).

ored dentures for wealthy clients who wanted to appear occasionally as "clodhopping inbreds."

IF CLOTHING, exercise and plastic surgery provided the personal aesthetics for the life movie, then architecture provided the set. As early as the 1920s social critic Lewis Mumford was lamenting what he called "a little architectural hocus pocus" with which we could "transport ourselves to another age, another climate, another social regime. . . ." Mumford was speaking to a tendency at the time for architecture to create bold new artificial spaces, a tendency that was itself a manifestation of the Progressive faith of the early twentieth century in man's ability to control and ultimately perfect his world. It was this tendency, fortified by the materialism of the Gilded Age, that informed the grandiose edifices of architect Stanford White and that inspired the eponymous hero of Steven Millhauser's novel *Martin Dressler*, about a young turn-of-the-century hotelier who keeps building larger and larger complexes, early megamalls or EPCOTs, within which are contained reproductions of Venice, the Amazon jungle, the Tuileries Gardens, a Scottish glen and an Eskimo village, as well as shopping arcades, reading rooms, museums, restaurants and theaters—what Millhauser called the "enclosed eclectic."

For places that had been designed expressly to house entertainment, it was certainly no surprise that there would be some relationship between function and form. The gaudy arcades of the 1910s, the ornate movie palaces of the 1920s, the stylish nightclubs of the 1930s and Disneyland and its progeny from the 1950s through the end of the century all were wrought in high theatricality and emanated an ersatz aura that declared one was leaving the quotidian world and entering a fantastical one. What White had demonstrated, however, was that a space needn't be designed to house entertainment in order to provide entertainment. Virtually every space was a stage for the life movie, and those who entered

White's opulent environments would find themselves experiencing a sense of transport very much like that one experienced watching conventional entertainments, only here the individual was not the audience but the actor. These places had what one critic in Millhauser's novel calls the "provisional air of a theatrical performance."

Over time a great many architects and ordinary citizens alike came to the same realization as White. Space was for entertainment, either providing it for us conventionally, as Disneyland and Disney World did, or furnishing us a stage to let us provide it for ourselves. (Not for nothing were employees at the Disney parks referred to as cast members.) This was now true for stores, stadiums, office buildings, churches and temples, museums, schools, even hospitals. "New York restaurants now have a new thing," Andy Warhol remarked in tribute to this entertainment juggernaut, "they don't sell their food, they sell their atmosphere. . . . They caught on that what people really care about is changing their atmosphere for a couple of hours"—that is, escaping into their own life movies. In the same vein, a senior partner in the hotel design firm of Hirsch/Bedner said of the renovation of the Beverly Hills Hotel in California, "The interior is a stage set, it's theater. . . . Hotel guests are actors and the audience at the same time. It's a people-watching hotel." Another designer on the project admitted that "this isn't architecture but stage decoration."

Nor was the set restricted to individual spaces. Whole areas had become vast back lots, to use the Hollywood term for the studios' old tracts where outdoor scenes were shot—areas like West Fifty-seventh Street and the South Street Seaport in New York or Peachtree Center in Atlanta or Navy Pier in Chicago. Looking at the way America's inner cities were being colonized and commercialized by chain stores, theme restaurants and other tourist attractions, intellectual historian Thomas Bender summoned a new urban vision in which the city was an "entertainment zone—a place to visit, a place to shop; it is no more than a live-in theme park," which he believed was designed to hide a grittier, dirtier, more problematic city from us.

But what Bender said of the city could also have been said of suburbia, small-town America and even rural America, where family farms unable to compete with industrialized megafarms were increasingly turning to what was called agritainment, in which farmers converted their land into agrarian theme parks, installing corn mazes, petting zoos and hay rides. One farmer told the *New York Times*, "Entertainment farming is the wave of the future for small farmers who want to stay on the farm." Indeed, the entire country now seemed to confirm Jean Baudrillard's observation that "Disneyland is presented as imaginary in order to make us believe that the rest is real, when in fact all of Los Angeles and the America surrounding it are no longer real, but of the order of the hyperreal and of simulation"—which critic Robert Hughes rendered in plain English as "[I]t's not that Disneyland is a metaphor of America, but that America is a metaphor of Disneyland."*

If so, the "acknowledged master," as Ada Louise Huxtable called him, of this unreality of reality may have been Jon Jerde, who might also be thought of as the Ralph Lauren of architecture. The California-based Jerde, designer of the Mall of America as well as San Diego's famed Horton Plaza shopping mall, specialized in faux spaces—spaces that looked the way the spaces ought to look if one hadn't had to reinvent them. Perhaps the most vivid example was an indoor mall that Jerde had proposed to build in New York City. He had divided the space into shopping districts for different clientele—a fake Madison Avenue, a fake Fifth Avenue, a fake Third Avenue, a fake Canal Street—even though the originals were obviously still available right outside the mall. ("I am not Madison Avenue but I play one. . . .") The upshot was

---

* Baudrillard couldn't have known just how true this would be. By the 1990s, the Disney Company had planned and built a community in Florida called Celebration that brought the concepts of the theme park to a daily living situation. Essentially the inhabitants of Celebration were cast members on the set of their own life movies.

that as the new urban reclamation projects seemed to confirm Baudrillard's observation, so did Jerde seem to confirm Italian semiotician Umberto Eco's that the "American imagination demands the real thing and, to attain it, must fabricate the absolute fake. . . ."

Where Jerde moved beyond other architects of the artificial like Stanford White or Jerde's contemporary Michael Graves, who had designed fanciful hotels for Disney World and offices for the Disney Company in Burbank, California, was that he perceived the architecture not only as backdrop, though it was certainly that, but as an entertainment of its own not all that different from a movie. Calling his work "experiential placemaking," he meant that the spaces themselves were sensational and that moving through them, even when there was no conventional entertainment offered and even when they weren't functioning as sets, provided entertainment. What kind of entertainment might one enjoy? To cite one example, a pedestrian wandering into Jerde's "Freemont Street Experience" in Las Vegas, which was an imaginative rehabilitation of Las Vegas's original Strip, would find himself in a fourteen-hundred-foot-long walkway with a ninety-foot-high canopy on which ran a glaring light show that included computer-generated jet planes periodically roaring overhead.*

Critics of Jerde, and there were many, decried his facsimiles as yet another offensive in the Disneyfication of America. But with Jerde, at least, the spaces did serve their purpose. There were some reproductions, on the other hand, for which form didn't follow function, but instead overrode it. Veteran film producer Lynda Obst once recounted how executives Peter Guber and Jon Peters upon assuming command of Columbia Pictures embarked on a

---

* The next phase was to add narrative to the sensation. Disney Company head Michael Eisner told *Fortune* magazine: "We ask, 'What is the story we want to tell when people walk into one of our new buildings? What are they going to feel? What is going to happen next? And how will it end?'" ("Imagineer Eisner on Creative Leadership," *Fortune* [December 4, 1989], p. 116).

campaign to renovate Columbia's Culver City studio (once the home of Metro-Goldwyn-Mayer) by slapping new facades over the old ones so that the studio would look more like a studio, even though it obviously was a studio and had been one for years—in short, to Disneyfy Columbia. The problem, as Obst told it, was that so much money had been spent to refurbish the plant that there were now fewer resources to spend on making films there.

But one didn't have to look to public buildings to see how space had been reconceptualized as set. The same thing was happening to private dwellings. For decades so-called shelter magazines—magazines that dealt with interior design—had prepared private residences for photo shoots by dressing the rooms exactly as a set designer might dress a set, with the objective of making the rooms look the way they should look to house the person, usually a celebrity, who lived there, even though, once again, the celebrity actually did live there and the way the living space looked prior to the preparation was the way it really looked.

Odd as that may have seemed on the face of it, odder still was a 1997 photo shoot of fashion model Christie Brinkley's Bridgehampton, Long Island, summer home scheduled for *In Style* magazine. When it turned out that Brinkley had yet to move in, the editor, instead of waiting, quickly dispatched an interior decorator to fill the empty space, meaning that readers who thought they were seeing Brinkley's house were actually seeing an interior decorator's version of her house. Or so it may have seemed. But in yet another plot turn, Brinkley was so taken by the version of the house she was supposed to be already living in that she wound up buying the furnishings.

Finally, whether as a set for our life movie or as a movie of its own, architectural space achieved that ultimate objective of the entertainment society. It became a celebrity. The evidence was in the souvenirs. T-shirts and baseball caps bearing place-names had long been a way of memorializing an experience, reminding one of a great vacation one had enjoyed and telling others where one had been. It was no wonder, then, that more and more architectural spaces, not only theme parks and vacation resorts, had souvenir stands, and at places like the Hard Rock Cafe or Planet Holly-wood, two notable theme restaurants, the merchandise sold there reportedly grossed far more money than the food. But since many visitors apparently bought Hard Rock souvenirs without even eating there, what exactly did the souvenirs memorialize? The answer, one had to assume, is that they memorialized their own purchase. The Hard Rock had been so celebritized that some peo-ple went there to buy a souvenir to commemorate the time they went to the Hard Rock to buy a souvenir which, in turn, broadcast to others that they had been to the Hard Rock to buy a souvenir. Which, needless to say, made for yet another convoluted scene in the life movie.

III

THE SELF OF NO-SELF

ALL THAT REMAINED now for the personal life movie to roll was for the actor to take his place on the set. But this was a more complex proposition than it might have seemed at first blush because it raised the vexing problem of identity. Even conven-tional entertainers, who earned their livings playing roles, were wrestling with this problem. Just as they were forced to experi-ment to find a modus vivendi between their life and their work in a society where lives were increasingly becoming entertainment, so too they were forced to experiment to find a modus vivendi between their own personal identities and their public celebri-tized selves.

Among the first to search for an answer was William F. Cody, widely known in the nineteenth century as Buffalo Bill. Cody was a relatively unknown army scout and Indian fighter in 1869, when dime novelist Ned Buntline, one of the provocateurs in the Astor

Place Riot, decided to make him a protagonist in serial fiction and then, two years later, the starring figure in a stage melodrama. Eventually Buntline convinced Cody to play himself on the stage—with great success, as it turned out, even though Cody admitted he couldn't memorize lines and had to improvise his way through the show.

For all his professed amateurism, when Cody decided to go back West to Wyoming to fight hostile Indians, he demonstrated just how much he had absorbed from his stage experience. In one encounter, reported with relish by his battalion commander in the *New York Herald*, Cody slew a charging Cheyenne and then scalped him. Soon after, the question of how self-consciously Cody had staged this bloody drama was raised when it turned out that he had waded into battle wearing a Mexican vaquero outfit of black velvet with red piping, silver buttons and lace trim, "the sort of costume," wrote historian Richard Slotkin, "that dime-novel illustrations had led the public to suppose was the proper dress of the wild Westerner." In other words, he had dressed for the occasion. Now Cody returned East to the stage wearing the same costume and reenacting his Indian adventure. Thus it could be said that Buffalo Bill wound up playing himself playing himself.

Still, nineteenth-century performers like Cody seemed to retain a sense of their own artfulness and an understanding of the difference between who they really were and who they purported to be, which is to say that they realized the person was not the celebrity. This was what Richard Sennett meant when he talked about the distinction between one's personality and one's identity in society, the first being internal, the second external. It was also what Elizabeth Taylor meant when she described herself as "constricted by shyness" and having to hide herself, that is her real self, "behind somebody else's facade."

But as the twentieth century progressed, Sennett's and Taylor's distinction was becoming more and more difficult to maintain, even for professional actors whose sense of self depended on it. In the first place, actors began to live as if they were in the movies, their own lifies drawing inspiration from their fictional roles. As actress Lana Turner recalled a romantic New Year's Eve with Tyrone Power on location in Mexico, it could have been a scene from one of her melodramas. "In my memory we will always be an especially beautiful couple," she wrote.

> Tyrone, so stunningly handsome, was majestic, and I wanted so to be his equal—I like to think that on that night I succeeded. I wore white satin brocade, cut in the Chinese fashion, with a high mandarin collar and slits up the long, tight skirt. The sides and the sleeves of my gown were heavily beaded with seed pearls and rhinestones that gleamed like the stars in the Mexican skies. I'd even brought jewels with me. I like to think of that Mexican night glittering off the jewels I wore in my hair. Oh, I think we were beautiful.

It was hyperbolic and cinematic, but no more so than Elizabeth Taylor meeting Richard Burton ("There was no point at which Richard and I began. We just loved each other . . .") or Zsa Zsa Gabor seeing George Sanders for the first time on-screen, falling instantly in love and resolving that she would have him as her husband. It was in fact one of the things that was so appealing about stars before our own life movies took hold: They alone seemed to live within their fantasies; they alone seemed able to fuse, as Zsa Zsa Gabor put it, "what is really true and what is enchanting make-believe."

Meanwhile, as stars were making their lives more theatrical, the movies were gradually becoming more realistic, further blurring the lines separating personality from public identity, person from celebrity. This was especially apparent in the change in acting style. The exaggerated, declamatory style of American performance that so enraged William Charles Macready during the Astor Place melee steadily gave way over the next one hundred years to naturalism, and by the 1950s to a whole generation of Method actors who found their characters within themselves rather than impasting them from without. It was, in a way, a metaphor for what was happening to identity generally. "They evidently sort of work themselves into a thing by transplanting themselves out of reality and making the fiction reality," was how Elizabeth Taylor analyzed it, providing a concise description not only of the Method but of the new confusion between person and persona.

Before personality and identity began to merge, Cary Grant could say, "It isn't easy being Cary Grant," meaning that the image had to be tended lest it collapse. "I daren't take any chances with Myrna Loy, for she isn't my property," Myrna Loy once said in the same vein. "I couldn't even go [to the corner drugstore] without looking 'right,' you see. Not because of personal vanity, but because the studio has spent millions of dollars on the personality known as Myrna Loy." And Liz Taylor: "I am disgusted by the amount of myth that is now accepted as fact. The public me, the one named Elizabeth Taylor, has become a lot of hokum and fabrication. . . ." And Zsa Zsa Gabor again: "I have to live up to what the world expects of Zsa Zsa."

While they complained, all these performers assumed that they could still tell the difference between who they were and who they purported to be. That was why Gladys Presley could advise her son, Elvis, "No matter what people say about you, son, you know who you are and that's all that matters." But in the life movie, where even one's daily existence was becoming a performance, this was more easily said than done. As Nicolas Evreinoff quoted Nietzsche from *Menschliches, Allzumenschliches,* "Whenever a man strives long and persistently to appear someone else, he ends up by finding it difficult to be himself again." Pornographic film star Jeff Stryker was a case in point. For years Stryker had assumed the pose of muscle-bound stud, even generating a line of products, and now the pose had assumed him. "They built this person," he told Susan Faludi of *The New Yorker.* "And this person does what it's supposed to do. And I guess that person is me." Playwright Sam Shepard, in a remark about Los Angeles but one applicable now elsewhere in America, put it most succinctly and sharply of all: "people here / have become / the people / they're pretending to be."

Image, then, was a constant hazard of celebrity because it was a constant threat to self. For all the celebrity profiles and autobiographies that had celebrities finding themselves after drifting in the horse latitudes of fame, the fact was that they were *always* in the process of finding themselves, which really meant that they were *always* lost. "I had been divorced by success from any intimate sense of my identity and had a hard time getting half-way back" was how novelist Norman Mailer described it. O. J. Simpson, in his farewell letter before attempting to escape in his Ford Bronco, expressed it more poignantly. "Please think of the real O.J.," he wrote, "and not this lost person."

For these celebrities there had been some kind of disconnect, a fragmentation, an alienation from self. It seemed largely to have been driven by the media's need to abstract them into simple, accessible commodities for readers and viewers and by the celebrities' need to abstract themselves, as Cary Grant and Myrna Loy had, into recognizable products. "What movie-goers wanted," Daniel Boorstin wrote in *The Image,* "was not a strong character, but a definable, publicizable personality; a figure with some physical idiosyncrasy or personal mannerism which could become a nationally advertised trademark." This became even more essential after the studio system broke down in the 1950s and actors were left to fend for themselves. The result for these celebrities was what Marshall McLuhan called "discarnate man," in which the self was cleaved from the corporeal body and rendered in the electronic media as an "image or pattern of information" (even more true now that dead actors can be digitalized into entirely new situations), or what Andy Warhol more prosaically called half-people because they had either been reduced or had reduced themselves to an image.

But *still* implicit in the idea that one could jettison one's self like a booster rocket after liftoff and never recover it was the idea that there had been something to jettison, something basic and rooted that one sacrificed for something transient. There was, however, another possibility. There was the possibility that in the world of celebrity the individual had become so abstracted that there wasn't even a self to lose anymore, a condition the French psychoanalyst Jacques Lacan identified as the "withdrawal of self into the no-self." The image had supplanted the thing itself, and that meant that celebrities had increasingly become, like Jeff Stryker, an image of their own image without the deliberation and perspective that Buffalo Bill had brought to the process.

At what may have seemed its most extreme manifestation, one wasn't even reduced to one's image but to the symbols of that image, making what Boorstin had said of movie stars true of all public figures. The self became synecdoche: a cane and bowler for Charlie Chaplin, a ski-nose profile for Bob Hope, a wild mane of hair for Albert Einstein, a bristle of beard for Ernest Hemingway, the "Air Jordan" logo for Michael Jordan. Every celebrity worth the designation had to have some ready referent, whether a physical characteristic or a signature expression or a distinctive vocal inflection or a style of dress, in order to claim his space in the crowded celebrity universe. Asked why he started wearing round black-framed glasses, the architect Philip Johnson admitted, "I needed a trademark."

In a sense, though, it wasn't the referent that was the trademark; it was the celebrity who was now a human trademark for his own fame. "I want people to be able to recognize me by just looking at a caricature of me that has no name on it," comedian Richard Pryor once told the *Washington Post*. "You see, I want to be great and you can recognize great people like Muhammad Ali and Bob Hope just by looking at a nameless caricature. When everybody can look at my caricature and say, 'That's him, that's Richard Pryor!' then I'll be great." The rock singer formerly known as Prince took Pryor's idea to its logical conclusion. He adopted a glyph as his name, thus literally making himself into an instantly recognizable trademark.

But there was an abstraction even beyond this one. It was a condition in which the celebrity was so minimally connected to anything resembling humanity that he might be considered an alien or a posthuman for the era of postreality. The most prominent example was the singer Michael Jackson. Jackson seemed to relate to himself in ways that no previous celebrity had. While most celebrities were intent on trademarking themselves, Jackson's physical sense of self was plastic. Like the performance artist Orlan, he was constantly resculpting his face, undergoing numerous plastic surgeries and possibly, though he denied it, whitening his skin. When questioned about this during a joint interview on ABC's *Prime Time Live,* his then wife, Lisa Marie Presley, daughter of Elvis, indignantly snapped that Jackson was an artist and whatever he did to his body had to be considered a work of art. It was a strikingly original concept: Jackson had become his very own ongoing, sculptural work-in-progress.

If Jackson didn't look like any other human being, he didn't behave like one either and consequently was never regarded as one by the media. "Is this guy weird, or what?" a *People* cover once asked. It wasn't just that Jackson did peculiar things, like house an animal menagerie on the grounds of his estate or purchase the remains of the so-called Elephant Man, or that he acted like a geisha girl with his feathery falsetto and coquettish eye-batting, or that his sexuality was always at issue, or that he suddenly married Lisa Marie Presley and then just as suddenly divorced her to marry a nurse with whom he quickly had a child, or even that he was charged with molesting young boys who he claimed were only pals of his. It was that underneath it all one had the sense that there was nothing underneath it all: no emotional interconnect, no informing intelligence, no social response mechanism—none of the things that one regards as basic to making a collection of cells a human being. Jackson was more of a Möbius strip than a person, a solipsist folded into himself so that even apparent gestures of humanness—his grabbing his crotch or thrusting out his pelvis—seemed programmed and devoid of sex or menace or spirit or abandon. In a sense he was the final stage in the trade-off between entertainment and self, a stage in which the latter is all but totally sacrificed to the former. Jackson had so thoroughly become an entertainment that he had almost ceased being a person altogether.

THOUGH FEW INDIVIDUALS on this side of the glass could have or would have wanted to have followed where Michael Jackson led, the problems that celebrities encountered with identity nevertheless were the same problems ordinary citizens would encounter in the Republic of Entertainment only writ large. Celebrities had been propelled into their personas by the commercial demands of entertainment. Ordinary people had been encouraged to let their performing selves emerge by the commercial, social and psychological demands of modern culture generally: an industrializing society that loosened the once-secure bonds of kinship and community and forced one to rely on neighbors and strangers for approval; a rapidly expanding service economy that placed a premium on one's selling oneself; a growing sense of dislocation, discontinuity and anxiety that tempted one to find a flexible identity that could adjust to different situations; and, not least of all, the constant inundation of role models provided by the media, especially the movies, that showed one how to act. "That's what show business is for," wrote Andy Warhol, "to prove that it's not what you are that counts, it's what they think you are."

Like Warren Susman, who saw these forces as emphasizing personality at the expense of character, sociologist David Riesman saw them as forging an entirely new kind of social type in America that would pave the way for the personal lifie. In his famous study *The Lonely Crowd*, Riesman described what he called an "inner-directed" character in which the "source of direction for the individual is 'inner' in the sense that it is implanted early in life by the elders and directed toward generalized but nonetheless inescapably destined goals." He believed this was the way Americans had been, by and large, in the nineteenth century, when they internalized values early in their lives and then conducted the rest of their lives accordingly. Contrasted with this, Riesman saw the emergence of an "other-directed" character in the twentieth century in which "contemporaries are the source of direction for the individual—either those known to him or those with whom he is indirectly acquainted through friends and through the mass media" and in which wanting to be liked rather than wanting to fulfill traditional, preordained expectations is the "chief source of direction and chief area of sensitivity."

Riesman was writing about general character types engendered by major social change, but what he had observed would clearly manifest itself in both a new sense of self-awareness among Americans and even in a new kind of behavior by them. To an inner-directed individual—say, a nineteenth-century American farmer—the idea of creating an image for the benefit of others would have had absolutely no meaning. He didn't dress to be a farmer or design his home to look like a farmhouse, and he didn't self-consciously perform in ways that would have signified to others that he was a farmer. He dressed like a farmer and acted like a farmer not for effect but simply because he *was* a farmer.

By definition, other-directed Americans were conscious of performance and of the effect of affect, a self-consciousness that led another sociologist, Erving Goffman, to conclude that in the twentieth century "life itself is a dramatically enacted thing." In Goffman's analysis, every American was engaged in a series of plays and a series of roles, an "exchange of dramatically inflated actions, counteractions, and terminating replies." Sounding very much like a drama coach, Goffman believed that the best actors in life were those who were "taken in by their own performance," though not so much so that they got carried away and ceased to realize that it *was* a performance. Goffman called this being "dramaturgically disciplined." Those who showed little concern for the quality of the illusion they presented he called cynical.*

Regardless of whether one was disciplined or cynical, the public self, as Goffman saw it, was a "product of a scene that comes off, and is not a cause of it"—which is to say that the character didn't really step into the scene full-blown: It was created in the course of performing the scene, be it a conversation at the office or a lovers' quarrel or a shopping spree or a father and daughter heart-to-heart. But these characters, in the movie sense of the word, were just for public consumption. Goffman still believed, as those old movie stars did, that there was a "front stage," where our daily performances took place, and a "back stage," where one could step out of one's public character and presumably be oneself. You simply played the scene when you had to and then left the stage.

What Goffman didn't seem to foresee when he was writing in the late 1950s was how much more complex the life movie would become, how many more scenes and roles there would be to play on a daily basis and how much further the front stage would extend into the back stage until one couldn't be assured of the postperformance decompression that Goffman seemed to promise because sometimes the show never seemed to end. It was this situation that the psychologist Robert Jay Lifton addressed in positing another model for modern identity in the life movie: a

---

* A debate in the mid-1990s about Adolf Hitler revolved around this very dialectic. Historian Hugh Trevor-Roper believed that Hitler was sincere in his hatred of Jews—that he was "dramaturgically disciplined," so to speak. Another historian, Alan Bullock, believed that Hitler used the Jews as a means to gain power (that he was cynical), though Bullock also believed, after Nietzsche, that cynics can come to trust their own power if not the things they say to get it (see Ron Rosenbaum, "Explaining Hitler," *The New Yorker* [May 1, 1995], p. 67).

protean self. As Lifton saw it, in every culture there had been individuals who had been forced to play numerous roles, but the confusions and disorientations of the twentieth century, the sense, as Lifton described it, "that we are losing our psychological moorings" and feel "buffeted about by unmanageable historical forces and social uncertainties," had made everyone a much more flexible and polished actor both because the traditional self was more besieged than ever before and because one had to be a flexible performer in order to survive.

The whole point of a protean self was that it was pliable. In a life movie where one was constantly shuttling from one scene to another, it adjusted to the situation, allowing one to borrow whatever action was appropriate. "My whole person . . . was KOed, you know, taken over by someone else, some other image," was how a young crack addict and thief from the South Bronx of New York described his sense of self to Lifton. "It was like, 'I wanna be this, I wanna be that' . . . I wanted to be like everybody. One day I'm like Johnny over here because I like the way he talks. So I'll try and talk like him. This guy walks pretty cool, I'll walk like this guy. . . . I didn't even know which—you know, Who am I?"

It may have seemed like a frightening prospect—to assemble your identity out of the shards of other people's identities—and the critic Michiko Kakutani, citing novels like Stephen Wright's *Going Native* and Russell Banks's *Rule of the Bone,* in which protagonists shed one identity to assume another, concluded that to "continually assume new identities is to end up having no identity at all." But Lifton himself was not disheartened. Though he recognized that constant role-shifting could lead to fragmentation, he nevertheless saw the protean not as an absence of self but as a testament to the resilience of self and not as an amoral shell but as something integrated that sought "ethical commitment, whatever the difficulty in finding and sustaining it," which made it essentially a moral force.

In effect, what Lifton saw as he surveyed modern America was a life movie in which everyone was a character actor but in which the underlying person of each was still intact. Psychologist Kenneth Gergen, in his book *The Saturated Self: Dilemmas of Identity in Contemporary Life,* basically agreed that the forces of late-twentieth-century society necessitated what he called a "populating of the self" in which one played a variety of ever-shifting roles in order to cope with a variety of ever-shifting relationships. According to Gergen, individuals had even developed a relational sophistication about these roles the way that professional actors might, not just adopting them on a case-by-case basis but actually training themselves for them with aids like adult education courses, career counseling and self-help manuals. The result was a "pastiche personality," a cut-and-paste job of identity virtually identical to Lifton's protean self.

Where Gergen parted company with Lifton was in believing that beyond this pastiche personality there was still another stage of personal development, still another adaptation to the ever-growing demands of the life movie, one that pushed identity across a new frontier and fundamentally changed our sense of self the way fame changed the celebrity's sense of self. In this final stage Gergen—taking a page from the deconstructionists, who thought that everything in life was the result of relationships and that there was no such thing as objective truth—saw the self as a product of relationships too, defined entirely by them and entirely inextricable from them. Thus there was no essence to a person, no core identity, no inner self, no armature, no permanent structure—nothing. To put it in movie terms, in the same way that a movie character has no tangibility outside the movie and exists only as a function of his relationships to other characters in the film, so people's identities in the life movie were only a function of their relationships to other people in the life movie. Without relationships there was no person, or at least no self, which meant that, for Gergen, the life movie was actually the source of identity and not just a showcase for it.

All these theorists were clearly of one mind in viewing one's personal life as a kind of entertainment for an audience of others. The trouble with their analyses was that they didn't seem to account for an obvious countervailing trend—namely, that individuals in the late twentieth century actually appeared to be more narcissistic and more concerned with their inner selves than were previous generations. It was this preoccupation with one's own psychology that Richard Sennett deplored in *The Fall of Public Man* and that Christopher Lasch in *The Culture of Narcissism* charged with undermining the very foundations of public life, and it showed no signs of abating in the decades after they wrote. America was overrun with twelve-step programs, books of popular psychology, courses in how to awaken the giant within, and men's and women's groups helping their members get in touch with their inner selves—the same inner selves that postmodernist theories of identity were denying even existed. So which was it? Were Americans more introspective about themselves or had they lost whatever they might have had to introspect about? *

The answer, which seemed to constitute a new theory of identity in the life movie, was both at the same time—but only because the very nature of the inner self had changed. The ego wasn't an illusion, and individuals didn't lose their sense of identity once they exited the scene, as Gergen and other acolytes of the French psychoanalyst Jacques Lacan seemed to claim. (Though it may seem literal-minded to say so, one can easily test this proposition by asking whether as you read this, presumably alone and silently, you have a sense of who you are or whether you

---

* Not incidentally, narcissism also provided a dramatic context for an individual, complete with its very own narrative: the search for fulfillment. As Tom Wolfe wrote of what he saw as the self-involvement of the women's movement, though just as applicable to the men's movement, its effect was "to elevate an ordinary status—woman, housewife—to the level of drama. One's very existence as a woman . . . as Me . . . becomes something all the world analyzes, agonizes over, draws cosmic conclusions from, or, in any event, takes seriously" (Tom Wolfe, *The Purple Decades: A Reader* [New York: Farrar, Straus & Giroux, 1982], p. 284).

feel totally at sea.) Rather, for all but the most changeable individuals, there was a baseline identity even in off-hours that would be recognizable to one's family, one's friends, one's coworkers.

By the same token, a self-absorbed inner personality hadn't eclipsed a public performing self either, as Sennett had grieved was happening, because this inner personality turned out to be every bit as much a role as those eighteenth-century displays he admired—even if it was only the role of a sensitive individual eagerly showing how much in touch he was with his own feelings. ("The new artificiality is 'I am real, I suffer,' " said the photographer Richard Avedon.) The only difference between this new role and the old one was that the new one purported to be real, an expression of one's soul, whereas the old role never purported to be an expression of anything other than one's social standing. Thus, playacting hadn't really declined; it had simply become more subtle and naturalistic just as conventional acting had. As for the flood of so-called psychobabble that attended this new role and that Sennett so detested, it was to the life movie what Stanislavsky's method was to acting: the way to provide motive and feeling to the life performance.

So it wasn't that the life movie had turned Americans into classical actors constantly digging into their kit bags to find characters to impose on themselves the way a Laurence Olivier had. And it wasn't that it had turned them into improvisational actors discovering themselves in the process of playing their scenes. In the life movie Americans had become Method actors mastering the art of playing themselves by, as Elizabeth Taylor had described it, making their fiction reality. Like those apocryphal cartographers mentioned earlier who used the land as a map of itself, they had learned to reach into themselves to pull out the "sense memories" of their lives in order to use them to make a convincing performance of their own lives, off which they could then launch the protean riffs that Lifton and Gergen described.

If this meant we were always in character even when we were

alone, it also meant that our life movies never ended until the final credits. "As soon as we are given a chance to concentrate," Evreinoff wrote of the life performer offstage and no longer being observed, "we begin to think either of our future or of our past, for, strictly speaking, there is no present." Using the example of a person ruminating alone over his business affairs, Evreinoff described how the individual might visualize a great success or failure and then imagine how his coworkers or his boss might react. From which Evreinoff reasoned: "What is all this, if not the staging of a whole play which we ourselves have invented and in which we act as the leading character?" But one didn't even need to rely on imagination to script his film. When one's own identity was a role, daily living was a show. "A whole day of life is like a whole day of television," Andy Warhol observed, anticipating *The Truman Show*. "TV never goes off the air once it starts for the day, and I don't either. At the end of the day the whole day will be a movie. A movie made for TV."

Though it seemed obvious that Americans had begun learning how to play themselves, one reason that theorists of identity may have missed it is that they had thought of life as a series of scenes, each one requiring some kind of adaption in character. In fact, the personal lifies, like the conventional movies that had served as their model, were not a succession of disparate scenes; each had a plot with a beginning, a provisional middle and a provisional end. And though one necessarily stepped out of character for certain passages, basically one was playing oneself under one's own direction, albeit usually second unit given the number of competing lifies, in a role that one had also scripted for oneself or that one had customized from someone else's script, making all of us what denizens of Hollywood would have termed a triple threat.

As far as personal lifies went, there were as many plots one could use to shape one's life into a dramatic arc as there were people. Some of these were highly original like that of the mad Unabomber Theodore Kaczynski, who seemed to see himself as a modern-day avenging Henry David Thoreau. Most, however, were like the plots of conventional movies: formulaic. One saw a life genre to which one aspired and with which one felt comfortable, and one started easing into the role that fitted the plot. If you wanted to be a young professional on the fast track to success, you began conforming your life to the plot conventions of other successful young professionals as you had seen them in the media and in the life movie itself. If you wanted to be a bohemian artist, you began conforming your life to those conventions. If you wanted to be a Mafioso or drug dealer or man of leisure or an outdoorsman, you conformed your life to the conventions of each. You dressed the way they dressed, acted the way they acted, associated with the kinds of people with whom they associated.

That said, it was nowhere near as simple to live your movie as the pop psychologist Gail Sheehy had implied in her book *New Passages*, where one presumably "mapped" one's life according to one's specifications. Just as Hollywood filmmakers operated within tremendous constraints, the filmmakers of the life movie (we) operated within the limits of their (our) physical appearance, their talent, their financial resources, their ability to gain the cooperation of others and their own sensitivity to the nuances of the role, to name only a few of the myriad of possible impediments. To write the role, then, wasn't necessarily to have the ability or the opportunity to perform it.

To make it easier for aspirants who had to contend with these problems, society had already begun conventionalizing the conventions. "We have tried to discover what it is really like to be a junior executive or a junior executive's wife," Daniel Boorstin commented acidly on the vogue for statistical generalizations, "so we can really be the way we are supposed to be, that is, the way we already are." Others talked of "badging," by which, in the words of one public relations practitioner, "you adopt that element of pop culture like a badge which you wear to say something about you and distinguish yourself from other groups." Still others, like the sociologist Robert Bellah, believed that traditional communities had been replaced in modern America by "lifestyle enclaves" of like-minded, socially compatible people, which, because everyone in an enclave was presumably the same, provided a sense of identity to its members. What Bellah didn't say was that since the enclave itself was subject to certain expectations in terms of its members' career paths, their incomes, their tastes and their mates, anyone entering an enclave was also entering a preplotted movie. All one had to do was do what everyone else was doing.

But what really seemed to illustrate how rapidly personal life was advancing toward theater was the advent of a new profession: self-described "life coaches," reportedly fifteen hundred of them in 1997, who advised clients on how to reorient their lives to reach what one coach called fulfillment but what someone else might have called a happy ending. What the coaches really did, along with routine ego boosting, was replot the client's life. They told him how he should organize his time, how he could improve his social life, how he should deal with business matters, whether or not he should host a party or take a trip. "It's like painting a canvas for a 'life assignment,' " said one coach.

Obviously few people were as overtly self-conscious about their life movies as these clients, but it was a long-accepted psychoanalytic postulate that virtually everyone held in his head a vision of the life he wanted to live, and at some level virtually everyone understood that every aspect of one's life was a plot element in a continuous saga to realize that vision: from the big things, like where you went to school, what profession you decided to pursue, whom you married, who your friends were, where you lived and where you sent your children to school, to the little things, like how you dressed, what car you drove, what books you read, where you vacationed and what you did in your leisure time. Virtually everyone understood too that the movie was a work in progress. If the plot wasn't gelling, you could always try changing the elements. A divorce was a cast change; a move a change of setting; a new job a plot twist.

For the most fortunate and the most admired among us, the narrative of one's life did match the narrative in one's head. During the Wall Street boom of the 1980s, magazines would refer to the beautiful young new spouses of divorced middle-aged millionaires as "trophy wives" who had been cast for the credit they reflected back on their husbands. By the 1990s, with the deliberation that people were bringing to their entire existence, one could talk in the same way about "trophy lives," like Donald Trump's, which were designed as vehicles big enough and brilliant enough for the magnitude of stardom that the successful and wealthy had achieved.

But even as it aggrandized its stars, the idea of a blockbuster life also served to signal to the rest of us how much our own concept of life had changed under the influence of the movies and other media. "At one point in cultural history we asked whether movies furnished an adequate likeness of real life," Kenneth Gergen observed. "The good movies were the more realistic. Now we ask of reality that it accommodate itself to film. The good person, like the good party, should be more 'movieistic.' " Or to put it another way, where we had once measured the movies by life, we now measured life by how well it satisfied the narrative expectations created by the movies.

DURING ONE EPISODE of the television program *America's Funniest Home Videos,* in which people sent in videos of what purported to be entertaining and usually spontaneous moments in their lives, the host Bob Saget asked the week's winning entrant when he realized that he was going to submit his tape. "Right away," said the man. To which Saget quipped, "The new consciousness." Of course Saget was right. People increasingly had come to regard their own lives as entertainment, and this consciousness would only be encouraged and abetted by new technologies that did for ordinary individuals what the mass media did for celebrities.

No doubt one of the appeals of the video camera, if not its chief appeal, was that it put ordinary people on the other side of the glass, making everyone in its purview a star. While home videos had been preceded by home movies, these had provided rather shapeless experiences, loose and unstructured, with people waving or smiling at the camera in nervous embarrassment which only underscored how unlike stars they were. Videos were different. The ease of use of the video camera and its sound capability coupled with Americans' rising self-consciousness of performance rapidly made videos an entertainment medium, not just a medium for preserving memories. People didn't wave or smile nervously at the video camera or bury their faces in their hands to hide from it, as they had done when confronted by the movie camera. People acted for it: They sang; they danced; they told jokes; they did tricks. Afterward they could add titles and effects to professionalize the show. Some even edited the tapes to tighten them.

Occasionally the performances were more studied. Criminals especially seemed to appreciate the star-making capabilities of the video camera and enjoyed acting out for it; that is why one often heard reports of miscreants who were apprehended because they videotaped their transgressions and then posed triumphantly over their victims like movie heroes. Other individuals, with less malign intent, deliberately staged events for the camera exactly as film directors did. One young man whose parents had divorced even asked them to reenact scenes from their marriage on video so that their granddaughter might see how they looked when they were happy.

But more than perform for the camera, people also began tailoring the major events of their lives to its demands, which were the demands of entertainment. Weddings, baby showers, bar mitz-

vahs, anniversary parties, even surgeries, all of which had traditionally been undramatic, if occasionally unruly, affairs, were
now frequently reconfigured as shows for the video camera complete with narratives and entertaining set pieces throughout.
Sometimes a hastily edited version of the tape, with a musical
sound track and effects added to boost its entertainment value
higher still, would be shown at the climax of the occasion as if the
entire purpose of the celebration had really been to tape it.

If anything, the Internet was even more accommodating to life
movie performers. A few exhibitionists converted their lives into
entertainment and placed themselves on the other side of the glass
by mounting television cameras in their dwellings that, like security surveillance equipment, recorded their every move. Anyone
who logged onto the site could then view the ongoing drama or
lack thereof of the individual's daily existence: Life the TV Show.

The more modest had another option. In chat rooms, where
one could communicate from the safe anonymity of the computer
keyboard with others who had logged on, or in Multi-User
Domains, where one could role-play in interactive games, users
constructed their identities and wrote their plots from whole
cloth, with none of the obstacles that the life movie itself threw in
one's way. By one report, in the mid-1990s hundreds of thousands
of users were spending anywhere from a few hours a day to nearly
all their waking hours at their consoles collaborating with fellow
users to write virtual movies with virtual dinner dates, virtual sex
(and virtual rape), virtual marriage, virtual children, virtual pets,
virtual friends, virtual houses, virtual jobs, virtual success, virtual
fame, even virtual emotions. All you had to do was type out your
fantasies. "You can be whoever you want to be," one participant
told the psychologist Sherry Turkle. "You can completely redefine
yourself if you want. . . . All they see is your words."

Whether this was just a form of playacting or a new variant of
the life movie was open to interpretation. One could certainly
think of this as a kind of game for one's own entertainment.

Devout users, however, argued, legitimately, that if they spend more time on the Internet than in so-called real life, if they interact with more people on the Internet than in real life, if they engage in more activities on the Internet than in real life, if they feel more fully themselves on the Internet than in real life, who is to say that this virtual life of theirs isn't as real as, if not more real than, the physical existence outside it? Which may have made the computer, in this function at least, yet another ingenious technological instrument of the large, implacable force of entertainment, yet another tool of *Homo scaenicus,* and the Internet itself not an information superhighway but an entertainment superhighway.

IV

INFINITE JEST

DESPITE THE ADMONITIONS in the introduction, as this book draws to a close, many readers will expect some grand conclusion about entertainment as the engine of our lives, some firmly staked-out position that applauds or condemns it. They will be disappointed. This isn't to say that value judgments on the life movie aren't valid. Though entertainment may be an ineluctable force, value judgments are both valid and necessary, and the judgments one makes will certainly have consequences for how one lives one's life. Those value judgments, however, will have to be made *by* each reader rather than *for* him, especially since the verdict may not be as self-evident as he might assume.

One can understand why many people—especially those who read and who take ideas seriously—reflexively recoil at the idea that life is a movie and all of us performers in it. Even as these critics participate in the spectacle, they assume that the transmutation of character into personality, of the life unself-consciously lived into the life calculatedly constructed, is a horrible thing. It is essentially the same argument as the one leveled against conventional entertainment with different terms, though one can see where it would have more force when the issue isn't a movie but a *life* movie in which so much is at stake.

As these critics see it, life is not a lark, and its end is not pleasure alone. Life is a difficult and complicated enterprise. It entails joy but also suffering, gain but also loss, hope but also despair. Yet, whatever pain these might inflict, one shouldn't wish away the suffering, loss and despair even if one could. One needs them in order to be annealed, to be fully and feelingly alive. To deny them would be to deny the process of one's humanization as well as the full range of human experience. To deny them would be to deny life itself.

It is certainly a tenable position, one that resonates in the greatest works of art. In fact, it seems irrefutable. Nevertheless, there is weight on the other side of the argument too, and it warrants more extended treatment because it is seldom discussed and when it is, is casually dismissed. Even if personal lifies serve only as a way to bring excitement to the otherwise dull routines and patterns of our own lives, as movies temporarily do, they may perform an invaluable psychological service. Montaigne, believing in a kind of ontological unhappiness that afflicts us all, also believed that nature equipped man to relieve it "by supplying our imagination with other and still other matters" we could use as distraction. Creating an imaginative life for ourselves, a movie of our own devising into which we can jump the way Buster Keaton jumps into the screen in *Sherlock, Jr.,* may be the best way yet to relieve that unhappiness. "If we make any kind of decent, useful life for ourselves we have less need to run from it to those diminishing pleasures of the movies," critic Pauline Kael once wrote, without realizing that many Americans were learning how to make a decent life for themselves out of the conventions the movies had provided.

While this transport both by and into one's own life was no small thing, it was far from the only value of the personal lifies, just as escapism was far from the only value of the movies. In their first decades of existence the movies had offered many forms of guidance to confused Americans who saw the small-town verities of the nineteenth century succumbing to the awful truths of the twentieth century; for immigrants they had been a veritable primer of acculturation. But one of the most important and subtle services the movies offered was to provide a model of narrative coherence in a world of seeming anarchy.

Religion had once performed this function by providing what one critic called a "sacred masterplot that organizes and explains the world." Ideology had performed it too by letting us believe in some eschaton, or finale, toward which life was supposedly progressing. "For the truth is," wrote José Ortega y Gasset on the uses of ideology, "that life on the face of it is a chaos in which one finds oneself lost. The individual suspects as much, but is terrified to encounter this frightening reality face to face, and so attempts to conceal it by drawing a curtain of fantasy over it, behind which he can make believe that everything is clear."

So long as religion and ideology prevailed, there was little need for other plots. But as both religious and ideological dogma withered under the onslaught of modern life, the burden of drawing the curtain of fantasy fell to popular culture and especially to the movies. If life was overwhelming, one could always carve it into a story, as the movies did. One could bend life to the familiar and comforting formulas one saw on the screen and thus domesticate its terrors. "All sorrows can be borne," said the writer Isak Dinesen, "if you put them into a story or tell a story about them." Stories gave solace. Robert Jay Lifton, interviewing a successful lawyer and former judge who was raised in poverty by a brutal father who threw the mother out of the house, asked how the man had survived. "I told myself stories," he said. And Lifton quoted Saul Bellow's Herzog to the same effect on a larger scale: "The dream of man's heart, however much we may distrust and resent it, is that life may complete itself in significant pattern. Some incomprehensible way. Before death. Not irrationally but incomprehensibly fulfilled."

What seemed to rile some traditionalists was the fact that the stories into which people often shaped their lives and the roles into which they often slipped their selves were not real; they were mediations of the way things really were. There had always been this hard, pragmatic strain in American life along with the more fanciful one—the premium on taking life as it came, on seeing things the way they really were rather than on how one wished them to be. Realism was even regarded as the foundation of mental health. The healthy individual was one who saw things clearly and accurately, the unhealthy individual one who distorted reality.

But the psychologist Shelley E. Taylor, after conducting a study of individuals who had successfully adapted to some traumatic event in their lives, and after surveying the general public, came to exactly the opposite conclusion. Those who exhibited the most robust mental health—those who were most successful, most creative, most in control of their lives, most well adjusted, above all, happiest—were those who had learned to operate within what Taylor called "positive illusions." These were not, Taylor hastened to add, delusions, which she defined as being directly contradicted by one's experience, and they were not a form of repression or denial, which failed to acknowledge anything that did not gibe with one's lifie. Rather, positive illusions were more like embellishments or exaggerations. They were the best spin one could put on the plot one hoped to play: that one was better at things, more in control of his life, more hopeful about the outcome of his efforts than the facts, if strictly interpreted, might warrant.

In lifie terms, what Taylor was saying was that the movies we created for ourselves, including a bit of self-puffery, gave us the same sort of pleasure that conventional movies did, only here it wasn't through some vicarious identification with the heroes, it was through a vicarious identification with ourselves. This suggested something terribly important. It suggested that the mind had begun processing life the way it processed the movies and consequently that if the movies were a metaphor for the condition of modern existence, the moviegoer was a metaphor for how one could cope with that existence.

On the one hand, at the movies the moviegoer responded to the stimulus on-screen as if it were happening at that moment. That was why we sometimes had to restrain ourselves from yelling to the characters on-screen. On the other hand, however powerful the spell, one was always conscious in some recess of one's mind that what one saw was not happening at that moment. That was why we didn't yell at the characters on-screen. Movies took the elements of sensation that were the very basis of entertainment—among them, feeling pain, experiencing tragedy, enjoying romance, facing terror—and re-created them in the safe context of narrative closure so that one could suffer anxiety with the characters on-screen while at the same time relaxing in the security that it was only a movie one was watching and that nothing in it could breach the space that separated their story from ours. This dual consciousness was integral to the pleasure we felt. We could be frightened without being threatened, feel romance without the pangs, mourn without an actual loss.

The mind, it seems, did something very similar with one's daily reality even as that reality was already distorted by the theatricalization of life. As Shelley Taylor described it, "At one level, it constructs beneficent interpretations of threatening events that raise self-esteem and promote motivation; yet at another level, it recognizes the threat or challenge that is posed by these events." Of course the difference was that no matter how we responded to the movies, they remained movies—ribbons of celluloid. When life is treated like a movie to disarm its threats and anxieties, it obviously remains life, but because life is interactive, as conventional movies are not, it is also transformed. Our fictions can impregnate the facts, and that is why Taylor's subjects who had suffered some loss or shock not only rebounded but rebounded to lives that were, in her view, "at least as happy and satisfying as they were before these disastrous events." They had learned to accept their own gloss on reality. In the words of the political scientist Michael Paul Rogin, who was describing mental processing in the other-directed individual, "Since he replaces reality by fantasy, his pleasure and the reality principles do not collide. Freed from the reproaches of either the conscience or the unconscious, he gains a reassuring serenity."

More, this seemed to be a general adaptive behavior that enabled people to deal with the stresses of modern life. As Taylor found her positive-illusionists to be in better mental health than so-called realists, a study by University of Minnesota psychologist Mark Snyder found that "self-monitoring" individuals—that is, individuals who were keenly aware of their image and self-presentation were more positive, outgoing, stable, expressive and influential than another group that was less interested in public display. It may have even been an evolutionary adjustment. One could argue that at least in America, where the basic necessities of life had been satisfied, man's next adaptation was in satisfying the need for pleasure and that both generating entertainments and making one's own life into an entertainment were the Darwinian answers. As Taylor's and Snyder's studies indicated, the best entertainers, the ones who put on the best shows for others and the ones who wrote the best scripts for themselves, were among the happiest members of society and perhaps the ones most likely to survive and flourish.

Not surprisingly, realists found this unacceptable because it seemed to avoid the engagement with life that they felt gives life its meaning. Stating their position in *Civilization and Its Discontents,* Sigmund Freud had written, "One can try to re-create the world, to build up in its stead another world in which its most unbearable features are eliminated and replaced by others that are in conformity with one's own wishes. But whoever, in desperate defiance, sets out upon this path to happiness will, as a rule, attain nothing. Reality is too strong for him. He becomes a madman, who for the most part finds no one to help him in carrying through his delusion." In short, he would be living within a fraud.

The fact that all of society now conspired to help him carry out his delusion and that reality itself was replacing its most unbearable features with entertainment, only exacerbated the problem as realists saw it. It made the issue not one of personal pathology but of social pathology—an epidemic of entertaining escapism. "When a population becomes distracted by trivia," wrote Neil Postman, "when cultural life is redefined as a perpetual round of entertainments, when serious public conversation becomes a form of baby-talk, when, in short, a people becomes an audience and their public business a vaudeville act, then a nation finds itself at risk: culture-death is a clear possibility."

To these critics, Americans, and everyone else who lived within the orbit of American popular culture, lived on Pinocchio's Pleasure Island, where people sated themselves only to be turned into asses later on—a situation that subordinated reality to pleasure. This triumph of pleasure, so closely connected to the triumph of entertainment, also drove the realists to distraction as it had driven the elitists to distraction a century earlier. Though she was talking primarily about how academic poststructuralists insisted on denying the romantic, sensuous, accessible pleasures of literature that previous generations of readers had counted among their greatest joys, the literary critic Wendy Steiner saw a host of forces, everyone from deconstructionists to feminists to right-wing conservatives to left-wing anticapitalists, mounting an attack on pleasure and finding their own pleasure in driving pleasure out of the canon of values. And no wonder. Pleasure was a threat this time not only to high art but to reality itself.

On the other side of the argument were those who saw life not as Pleasure Island but as John Lennon's Strawberry Fields, where

"nothing was real and nothing to get hung about." For them, pleasure and entertainment and ultimately the happiness these could
bring were the primary objectives of life, and they saw no benefit
in reality, as traditionalists defined it, if it didn't contribute to
the larger cause. Instead, like the characters in David Foster
Wallace's novel *Infinite Jest,* who are searching for a film of that
title that allegedly provides the most powerful bliss imaginable,
they wanted the grail of total gratification and asked why they
shouldn't have it.

The great cultural debate that loomed at the end of the twentieth century and promised to dominate the twenty-first, then, was
one between the realists who believed that a clear eyed appreciation of the human condition was necessary to *be* human, and the
postrealists who believed that glossing reality and even transforming it into a movie were perfectly acceptable strategies if these
made us happier—a debate, one might say, between humanness
and happiness. In a sense, the controversy over Prozac and other
antidepressants—was a happiness induced by pharmacology better than a less euphoric state that was natural or *real?*—was an
early skirmish in the war, and a template for it. Now so many other
deep cultural tensions in America—between art and conventional
entertainment, between traditional journalism and the new news,
between old-fashioned ward politics and the new politics of "feel-
good," between heroes and celebrities, between functional architecture and expressive architecture, between biological naturalists
and genetic engineers, between Luddites and computer hack-
ers—resolved themselves into a similar question: Is reality, as it
was traditionally construed, morally, aesthetically and epistemo-
logically preferable to postreality? Or: Is life, as traditionally construed, preferable to the movie version of life?

There were and are no simple answers, only vitally important
issues with the most profound implications. To the realists, this
shadow life so many were opting for edged us closer to Philip
Roth's dark, prophetic vision of a world where entertainment was

the purpose of existence and everything else would either conform or cease to matter. To the postrealists, a life in which entertainment was the governing cosmology and all of existence an endless movie edged us closer to the possibility that we need never suffer life's hurts again. Either we stood on a precipice or we stood in a bright new dawn. Which it was to be, the end of traditional human values or the beginning of a brave new world, would be the new question of the epoch.

Notes

Introduction

PAGE 3 **the "American writer in the middle of the 20th century . . ."** "Writing American Fiction," in Philip Roth, *Reading Myself and Others* (New York: Farrar, Straus & Giroux, 1975), p. 120.

4 **a "world where fantasy . . ."** Daniel J. Boorstin, *The Image: A Guide to Pseudo-Events in America* (New York: Atheneum, 1987 [1961]), p. 37.

"We risk being . . ." Ibid., p. 240.

Stéphane Mallarmé's aphorism. Marshall McLuhan, *Understanding Media: The Extensions of Man*, 2nd ed. (New York: McGraw-Hill, 1964), p. 66.

5 **"visible, interactive suicide."** Edward Rothstein, "Technology," *New York Times*, April 29, 1996, p. D23.

D.C. teenagers. Tracy Thompson, "Tolerance or Survival? Video Case Reveals Street Reality," *Washington Post*, June 16, 1991, pp. C1, C9. The purpose of the video, apparently, was to show New York City gangs how tough District of Columbia gangs could be.

6 **Nazi-themed resort and Communist theme park.** Gary Krist, "Tragedyland," *New York Times*, November 27, 1993, p. A17.

245

6 **"rearrangement of our problems . . ."** Michael Wood, *America in the Movies: or "Santa Maria, It Had Slipped My Mind!"* (New York: Delta, 1976), p. 18.

Lewis Carroll's cartographers. McLuhan, p. 60. A similar parable was told by Jorge Luis Borges. For an elaboration, see Jean Baudrillard, *Selected Writings,* ed. Mark Poster (Stanford, Calif.: Stanford University Press, 1988), p. 166.

9 **"We had fed the heart on fantasies."** W[illiam] B[utler] Yeats, *The Collected Poems of W.B. Yeats* (New York: Macmillan Company, 1933), p. 202.

10 **"This is a large subject . . ."** Boorstin, p. ix.

"We have to start again . . ." Umberto Eco, *Travels in Hyperreality,* tr. William Weaver (New York: Harcourt Brace Jovanovich, 1987), p. 150.

Chapter One / The Republic of Entertainment

11 **"One man in the pit . . ."** Frances Trollope, *Domestic Manners of the Americans,* ed. John Lauritz Larson (St. James, N.Y.: Brandywine Press, 1993), p. 121.

11–12 **"in what concerns the higher civilization . . ."** Matthew Arnold, *Civilization in the United States: First and Last Impressions of America* (Boston: Cupples and Hurd, 1888), p. 189.

12 **"a kind of divine service . . ."** Leo Lowenthal, *Literature, Popular Culture, and Society* (Palo Alto, Calif.: Pacific Books, 1968 [1961]), p. 42.

13 **Crime pamphlets.** David S. Reynolds, *Beneath the American Renaissance: The Subversive Imagination in the Age of Emerson and Melville* (New York: Alfred A. Knopf, 1988), pp. 176–79, 209.

13–14 **Nineteenth-century theater.** David Grimsted, *Melodrama Unveiled: American Theater and Culture, 1800–1850* (Chicago: University of Chicago Press, 1968), pp. 99, 104, 117–18.

14 **Practical uses of music.** Constance Rourke, *The Roots of American Culture and Other Essays,* ed. Van Wyck Brooks (New York: Harcourt, Brace & Co., 1942), p. 168.

"entertainment is of more real value . . ." John Philip Sousa, *Marching Along* (Boston: 1928), pp. 274–75, quoted in Neil Harris, *Cultural Excursions: Marketing Appetites and Cultural Tastes in Modern America* (Chicago: University of Chicago Press, 1990), p. 204.

Wide, Wide World. Henry Nash Smith, *Democracy and the Novel: Popular Resistance to Classic American Writers* (New York: Oxford University Press, 1978), p. 7; Carl Bode, *The Anatomy of American Popular Culture, 1840–1861* (Berkeley: University of California Press, 1960), p. 173.

14 **"I should have no chance . . ."** Quoted in Smith, pp. 7–8.

14–15 **Eighty thousand copies.** Frank L. Schick, *The Paperbound Book in America* (New York: R. R. Bowker, 1958), p. 51.

15 **"greatest literary movement . . ."** W. H. Bishop, "Story-Paper Literature," *Atlantic Monthly* 44 (September 1879), p. 389, quoted in Michael Denning, *Mechanic Accents: Dime Novels and Working-Class Culture in America* (London: Verso, 1987), p. 2.

"highest pleasure." Frank Kermode, "The Pleasure of the Text," *New York Review of Books* (September 19, 1996), p. 32.

"centering in small upper-class communities . . ." Dwight Macdonald, *Against the American Grain: Essays on the Effects of Mass Culture* (New York: Random House, 1962), p. 56.

16 **"to present images of beauty . . ."** Smith, pp. 13–14.

"spurious gratification . . ." Lowenthal, p. 6.

"Nonsense placed before the eyes . . ." Goethe to Schiller, August 9, 1797, quoted ibid., p. 24.

17 **"stimulus or opiate."** Rev. Jonathan Baxter Harrison, *Certain Dangerous Tendencies in American Life, and Other Papers* (Boston: Houghton, Osgood & Co., 1880), p. 167, quoted in Denning, p. 54.

"gross and violent stimulants . . ." William Wordsworth and Samuel Taylor Coleridge, Preface to *Second Edition of Lyrical Ballads,* ed. W. J. B. Owen (Copenhagen: Rosenkilde and Bagger, 1957), quoted in Lowenthal, p. 29.

"the sensual side of the art . . ." Theodore Thomas, *A Musical Autobiography,* ed. George P. Upton (Chicago: 1905), p. 3, quoted in Lawrence W. Levine, *Highbrow/Lowbrow: The Emergence of Cultural Hierarchy in America* (Cambridge, Mass.: Harvard University Press, 1988), p. 136.

"Most of those who frequent . . ." Alexis de Tocqueville, *Democracy in America* (New York: Everyman's Library, 1994), vol. 2, p. 82.

"the body of history . . ." Edwin Percy Whipple, *Lectures on Subjects Connected with Literature and Life* (Boston: Ticknor, Reed and Fields, 1849), p. 8, quoted in Reynolds, p. 209.

"increasingly jangled and incoherent . . ." David Denby, "Buried Alive," *New Yorker* (July 15, 1996), p. 53.

prefer graphic entertainments. Rourke, p. 73.

18 **"entertainment."** *The Compact Edition of the Oxford English Dictionary* (Oxford: Oxford University at the Clarendon Press, 1971 [1933]), vol. 1, p. 876.

19 **"non-man."** Macdonald, pp. 10–11.

19 **"predigests art . . ."** Clement Greenberg, *Art and Culture: Critical Essays* (Boston: Beacon Press, 1965 [1961]), p. 15.

20 **"to overturn all morality . . ."** *Confessions and Experience of a Novel Reader* (Chicago: William Stacy, 1855), p. 77, quoted in Reynolds, p. 210.

Fun. Johan Huizinga, *Homo Ludens: A Study of the Play-Element in Culture* (Boston: Beacon Press, 1950), paperback ed., p. 3.

"[S]how business is amusement . . ." Umberto Eco, *Travels in Hyperreality,* tr. William Weaver (New York: Harcourt Brace Jovanovich, 1987), p. 152.

21 ***"The characteristic note of our time . . ."*** José Ortega y Gasset, *The Revolt of the Masses,* tr. Anthony Kerrigan (South Bend, Ind.: University of Notre Dame Press, 1985), p. 10. His italics.

22–3 **European elites and popular culture.** See Peter Burke, *Popular Culture in Early Modern Europe* (New York: New York University Press, 1978), pp. 270–81.

23 **European middle class.** John Brewer, *The Pleasures of the Imagination: English Culture in the Eighteenth Century* (New York: Farrar, Straus & Giroux, 1997). Though Brewer's is an analysis of English culture and though the middle class gained cultural power there somewhat earlier than in most other European countries, the basic fact obtains that the middle class wanted to seem like the nobility even though in practice it wound up making slightly different demands on artists—in part, that they be more entertaining.

"the Christian religion . . ." Quoted in Bernard A. Weisberger, *They Gathered at the River: The Story of the Great Revivalists and Their Impact upon Religion in America* (Boston: Little, Brown & Co., 1958), p. 12.

Number of church members. Richard Hofstadter, *Anti-Intellectualism in American Life* (New York: Alfred A. Knopf, 1963), p. 89.

24 **"the sinner had to *feel* . . ."** Weisberger, p. 39.

25 **"our amusements."** Walt Whitman, *Uncollected Poetry and Prose of Walt Whitman,* ed. Emory Holloway (Gloucester, Mass.: Peter Smith, 1972), vol. II, pp. 255, 293, quoted in Reynolds, p. 25.

a **"stranger from the continent of Europe . . ."** Trollope, p. 43.

"We have seen it . . ." Moncure D. Conway, *A Discourse, Delivered in the Unitarian Church, Cincinnati, Ohio* (Cincinnati: 1857), quoted in Grimsted, p. 48.

Sermons. Reynolds, pp. 15–16.

"Execution sermons." Karen Halttunen, "Early American Murder Narratives: The Birth of Horror," in *The Power of Culture: Critical*

Essays in American History, ed. T. J. Jackson Lears and Richard Wightman Fox (Chicago: University of Chicago Press, 1993), pp. 67–101.

25 **"Nothing gives me more pain . . ."** *Christian Palladium* (March 10, 1837), quoted in Weisberger, p. 145.

26 **"The 'star' system . . ."** Hofstadter, p. 86.

"[I]f at the present day . . ." Tocqueville, vol. 1, p. 52.

"Of all the countries . . ." Quoted in Robert V. Remini, ed., *The Age of Jackson* (Columbia: University of South Carolina Press, 1972), p. 95.

27 **"indescribably bitter . . ."** Reverend J. B. Harrison, *Certain Dangerous Tendencies,* p. 198, quoted in Denning, pp. 54–55.

Theater's attitude toward aristocrats. Rourke, p. 128.

Daniel Webster. Hofstadter, pp. 164–65.

Callithumpians. Paul A. Gilje, *The Road to Mobocracy: Popular Disorder in New York City, 1763–1834* (Chapel Hill: University of North Carolina Press, 1987), pp. 257–58.

Thirty-five major riots. Michael Feldberg, *The Turbulent Era: Riot and Disorder in Jacksonian America* (New York: Oxford University Press, 1980), p. 5.

28 **"great contest between . . ."** Edward P. Gaines to Andrew Jackson (1826), Jackson Papers, quoted in Robert V. Remini, *The Life of Andrew Jackson* (New York: Penguin, 1988), pp. 159–60.

"John Quincy Adams who can write . . ." Ibid., p. 159.

Balance of cultural power. See Arthur Schlesinger, Jr., "The Ages of Jackson," *New York Review of Books* (December 7, 1989), pp. 48–51.

Attitudes toward culture. See Larzer Ziff, *Literary Democracy: The Declaration of Cultural Independence in America* (New York: Viking, 1981 [Penguin ed., 1982]), p. 54.

"this rank rabble party . . ." Ralph Waldo Emerson, *The Heart of Emerson's Journals,* ed. Perry Bliss (Boston: Houghton Mifflin, 1926), p. 85, quoted in Carl Russell Fish, *The Rise of the Common Man, 1830–1850* (New York: Macmillan, 1927), p. xvii.

29 **Literacy.** Stow Persons, *The Decline of American Gentility* (New York: Columbia University Press, 1973), p. 53.

Increase of newspaper circulation between 1870 and 1900. Edwin Emery, *The Press in America* (Englewood Cliffs, N.J.: Prentice-Hall, 1962), p. 346.

30 **Wealth.** Edward Pessen, *Jacksonian America: Society, Personality, Politics,* rev. ed. (Urbana: University of Illinois Press, 1985), pp. 81–82.

Social mobility. Ibid., p. 86. This study was based on three-quarters of the interurban rich and the figures extrapolated from that group.

Government. Ibid., pp. 97–99, 299.

30 **"the common man appears . . ."** Ibid., p. 304.

a **"dynamic, revolutionary force . . ."** Macdonald, pp. 11–12.

31 **carnivals.** Burke, pp. 178–204.

"Perhaps the single most intense pleasure . . ." Pauline Kael, "Trash, Art and the Movies," *Going Steady* (New York: Bantam paperback ed., 1971), pp. 126–27.

32 **"music of cracking peanuts."** *New York Mirror*, April 5, 1934, quoted in Grimsted, p. 59.

"their entire contempt . . ." *American Athenaeum* (June 28, 1825), p. 119, quoted ibid., p. 54.

the **"whole crowded auditorium . . ."** Walt Whitman quoted in Richard Moody, *The Astor Place Riot* (Bloomington: Indiana University Press, 1958), pp. 29–30.

33 **Opening of the Astor Place Opera House.** Robert Lacour-Gayet, *Everyday Life in the United States Before the Civil War, 1830–1860*, tr. Mary Ilford (New York: Frederick Ungar, 1969), pp. 101–02.

A **"generally diffused air . . ."** Quoted in Moody, p. 103.

Curiosity-seekers. Lacour-Gayet, p. 102.

Macready as actor. Grimsted, p. 70.

34 **"vehemence and rude force."** Quoted in Moody, p. 29.

"A more wanton . . ." *New York Tribune*, May 9, 1849, quoted ibid., pp. 119–20.

Accusation of hissing. Ibid., p. 99.

35 **"Shall Americans or English . . ."** Ibid., pp. 130–32.

"[T]he police rushed in . . ." Ibid., pp. 4–5.

The Astor Place Riot. Ibid., pp. 4–12.

"two actors had quarreled!" Ibid., p. 205.

36 **"[O]ur citizens have a perfect . . ."** Ibid., pp. 188–89.

"Was it done for the sake of justice?" Captain Rynders quoted ibid., p. 190.

"[T]he 'White and the Red Roses of York and Lancaster' . . ." *Home Journal* (May 12, 1849), quoted ibid., p. 228.

"It leaves behind a feeling . . ." *Philadelphia Public Ledger*, May 14, 1849, quoted ibid., pp. 228–29.

37 **Differentiation.** David Nasaw, *Going Out: The Rise and Fall of Public Amusements* (New York: Basic Books, 1993), pp. 12–14.

The same bourgeois transformation. Richard Sennett, *The Fall of Public Man: The Forces Eroding Public Life and Burdening the Modern Psyche with Roles It Cannot Perform* (New York: Alfred A. Knopf, 1977), p. 75. Sennett also describes an eighteenth-century theatrical experience in London that was very similar to the early nineteenth-century American one where different forms of entertainment freely mingled, but the rise of the middle class ended it there as here.

37–8 **According to one study of New York City.** Larry May, *Screening Out the Past: The Birth of Mass Culture and the Motion Picture Industry* (New York: Oxford University Press, 1980), p. 18.

38 **Columbian Exposition.** See Harris, p. 123.

Segregation of forms. Levine, pp. 76–77.

Sacralization. Ibid., p. 33, 134.

39 **"horse-play, belly laughter . . ."** George Jean Nathan, *The Popular Theatre* (New York: 1923), pp. 227–33, quoted in Nasaw, p. 37.

"pleasure clubs." Kathy Peiss, *Cheap Amusements: Working Women and Leisure in Turn-of-the-Century New York* (Philadelphia: Temple University Press, 1986), p. 60.

"The trouble is that these high people . . ." Agnes M., "The True Story of a Nurse Girl," in *Workers Speak*; ed. Leon Stein and Philip Taft (New York: Arno Press, 1971), pp. 103–04, quoted ibid., p. 116.

40 **Middle class.** See Gilje, p. 176.

"a mercantilist republic . . ." Michael Schudson, *Discovering the News: A Social History of American Newspapers* (New York: Basic Books, 1978), p. 44.

40–1 **"on the one hand a quite unclouded . . ."** Van Wyck Brooks, *America's Coming-of-Age* (New York: B.W. Huebsch, 1915), pp. 6–7.

41 **"it pretends to respect . . ."** Macdonald, p. 37.

41–2 **"dull and unsensual."** Richard Sennett, *Families Against the City: Middle-Class Homes of Industrial Chicago, 1872–1890* (Cambridge, Mass.: Harvard University Press, 1970), pp. 52–53.

42 **Dime novel into moralistic novel.** Denning, pp. 60–61.

"not likely to be distinguished from audiences . . ." Charles R Sherlock, "Where Vaudeville Holds the Boards," *Cosmopolitan* 32 (February 1902), p. 413, quoted in Gunther Barth, *City People: The Rise of Modern City Culture in Nineteenth-Century America* (New York: Oxford University Press, 1980), pp. 214–15.

43 **Reconvergence of American culture.** See Nasaw, pp. 1–2.

44 **Eleven million immigrants.** Paul Boyer, *Urban Masses and Moral Order in America, 1820–1920* (Cambridge, Mass.: Harvard University Press, 1978), p. 123.

44–5 **Magazines "aimed at entertainment alone . . ."** Mark Sullivan, *Our Times: America at the Birth of the Twentieth Century*, ed. Dan Rather (New York: Scribner's, 1995 [orig. ed., 1926–1932]), p. 254.

45 **The average manufacturing worker.** Nasaw, p. 4.

45 **"spiritual reaction."** John Higham, "The Reorientation of American Culture in the 1890s," in *The Origins of Modern Consciousness,* ed. John Weiss (Detroit: Wayne State University Press, 1965), pp. 26–27.

"It was quite wonderful . . ." "Making Ends Meet on the Minimum Wage," *Life and Labor* 3 (October 1913), p. 302, quoted in Peiss, pp. 43–44.

Women. See ibid., pp. 4–5, 41–44.

46 **"It has come then, this new weapon . . ."** Vachel Lindsay, *The Art of the Moving Picture* (New York: Liveright, 1970 [1922]), p. 317.

"any ultramarine, full-dress formulas . . ." Walt Whitman, "Democratic Vistas," *Complete Poetry and Collected Prose* (New York: Library of America, 1982), pp. 968–69. "Above all previous lands, a great original literature is surely to become the justification and reliance, (in some respects the sole reliance,) of American democracy" [pp. 932–33].

47 **Seventy-two percent of the audience.** Michael M. Davis, *The Exploitation of Pleasure: A Study of Commercial Recreation in New York* (New York: Russell Sage Foundation, 1911), table 8, p. 30.

60 percent of the working class. "People's Institute Motion Picture Show Report," Riis Neighborhood Settlement Records (n.d.), in Peiss, pp. 146, 150.

"that in the larger towns, where the higher-priced drama . . ." Walter Prichard Eaton, "Class-Consciousness and the 'Movies,'" *Atlantic Monthly* (January 1915), p. 50.

"emancipated the gallery." Stephan Bush, "The Triumph of the Gallery," *Motion Picture World* (December 13, 1913), in May, p. 152.

"He will sit on the ground floor . . ." Eaton, p. 51.

48 **"democratic art."** "A Democratic Art," *Nation* (August 28, 1913), p. 193.

"I especially liked the reduction of authority . . ." Quoted in Edward Wagenknecht, *The Movies in the Age of Innocence* (Norman: University of Oklahoma Press, 1962), p. 41.

LOW GRADE PERSONS ONLY LIKE CHARLIE CHAPLIN . . . *Detroit News,* April 13, 1916, quoted in Charles J. Maland, *Chaplin and American Culture: The Evolution of a Star Image* (Princeton, N.J.: Princeton University Press, 1989), p. 16.

"the change from Victorian to modern life . . ." May, p. xii.

49 **Reformers' complaints.** See ibid., pp. 74–101.

Shuttering of theaters in New York City. Robert Sklar, *Movie-Made America: A Cultural History of American Movies* (New York: Random House, 1975), pp. 30–31.

49 **Number of movie theaters.** Daniel J. Czitrom, *Media and the American Mind: From Morse to McLuhan* (Chapel Hill: University of North Carolina Press, 1982), p. 42.

Theaters in New York City. Davis, p. 21.

Boston survey. "The Amusement Situation in the City of Boston," Drama Committee, Twentieth Century Club, Boston, 1910, in Garth Jowett, *Film: The Democratic Art* (Boston: Little, Brown, 1976), p.37.

50 **"sensory hallucinations and illusions . . ."** Hugo Munsterberg, *The Photoplay: A Psychological Study* (New York: Dover, 1970 [1915]), p. 95.

"Should you ever seek the source of the moving pictures . . ." "How the Cinematographer Works and Some of His Difficulties," *Moving Picture World* (May 18, 1907), p. 165, quoted in Richard deCordova, *Picture Personalities: The Emergence of the Star System in America* (Urbana: University of Illinois Press, 1990), p. 30.

"veritable house of dreams." Jane Addams, *The Spirit of Youth and City Streets* (New York: Macmillan, 1909), pp. 75–76, 103.

51 **"appearances as signs of personal character . . ."** Sennett, *Fall of Public Man,* p. 146.

"[t]ransformation seemed to be what . . ." Warren I. Susman, *Culture as History: The Transformation of American Society in the Twentieth Century* (New York: Pantheon, 1984), p. xxvii.

Chapter Two / The Two-Dimensional Society

53 **"Over-illustration."** "Over-Illustration," *Harper's Weekly* 55 (July 29, 1911), p. 6, in Neil Harris, *Cultural Excursions: Marketing Appetites and Cultural Tastes in Modern America* (Chicago: University of Chicago Press, 1990), p. 312.

Number of daguerreotype studios in New York City. Leo Braudy, *The Frenzy of Renown: Fame and Its History* (New York: Oxford University Press, 1986), p. 493.

54 **Shakespeare's decline.** Lawrence W. Levine, *Highbrow/Lowbrow: The Emergence of Cultural Hierarchy in America* (Cambridge, Mass.: Harvard University Press, 1988), 46.

"Chromo-civilization." E. L. Godkin, *Reflections and Comments, 1865–1895* (New York: Scribner's, 1895), pp. 201–05.

Images would replace words. "A Growl for the Unpicturesque," *Atlantic Monthly* 98 (July 1906), pp. 141–42, in Harris, pp. 312–13.

Image-thinking and ideal-thinking. Daniel J. Boorstin, *The Image: A Guide to Pseudo-Events in America* (New York: Atheneum, 1987 [1961]), pp. 197–98.

55 **"unique mode of discourse."** Neil Postman, *Amusing Ourselves to Death: Public Discourse in the Age of Show Business* (New York: Viking Press, 1985), p. 10.

"To engage the written word . . ." Ibid., p. 50.

"No matter what is depicted . . ." Ibid., p. 87.

"[A]ny technology gradually creates . . ." Marshall McLuhan, *Understanding Media: The Extensions of Man,* 2d ed. (New York: McGraw-Hill, 1964), p. viii.

56 **"command center of the new epistemology."** Postman, p. 78.

57 **"increased devotion to pleasure . . ."** Quoted in *Vanity Fair: A Cavalcade of the 1920s and 1930s,* ed. Cleveland Amory and Frederic Bradlee (New York: Viking Press, 1960), p. 13.

"Everybody could go into the same dark room . . ." Geoffrey O'Brien, *The Phantom Empire* (New York: W. W. Norton & Co., 1993), p. 116.

"An analyst tells me . . ." Pauline Kael, "Trash, Art and the Movies," *Going Steady* (New York: Bantam Books, 1971), p. 153.

58 **"Movies were not 'out there' . . ."** O'Brien, p. 107.

Myth of total cinema. André Bazin, *What Is Cinema?,* tr. and ed. Hugh Gray (Berkeley: University of California Press, 1967), vol. 1, pp. 9, 17–22.

59 **"[T]he reason we have newspapers at all . . ."** Robert E. Park, "The Yellow Press," *Sociology and Social Research* 12:1 (September–October 1927), pp. 3–11.

Hawk & Buzzard. James L. Crouthamel, *Bennett's New York Herald and the Rise of the Popular Press* (Syracuse, N.Y.: Syracuse University Press, 1989), p. 19.

"an open and coarse appeal . . ." Alexis de Tocqueville, *Democracy in America* (New York: Everyman's Library, 1994), vol. 1, p. 187.

"mechanics and the masses generally." Quoted in Park, p. 7.

Circulation of typical newspaper. John D. Stevens, *Sensationalism and the New York Press* (New York: Columbia University Press, 1991), p. 15.

Total circulation. Michael Schudson, *Discovering the News: A Social History of American Newspapers* (New York: Basic Books, 1978), p. 18.

60 **Combined circulation of penny papers.** Ibid., p. 18.

"human interest story." Ibid., pp. 26–27.

61 ***Invented* the concept of news.** Ibid., p. 22.

"dull business air . . ." Crouthamel, p. 23.

In the *Herald*'s first two weeks. Ibid., p. 25.

61 **Helen Jewett murder case.** See Andie Tucher, *Froth & Scum: Truth, Beauty, Goodness, and the Ax Murder in America's First Mass Medium* (Chapel Hill: University of North Carolina Press, 1994), pp. 21–25.

62 **Bennett's coverage.** Ibid., pp. 31–39.

63 **"while the newspaper press of America . . ."** Charles Dickens, *American Notes,* intro. Christopher Lasch (Gloucester, Mass.: Peter Smith, 1968), p. 280.

Moral War. Crouthamel, pp. 35–36.

Moral War pressure. Schudson, pp. 55–57.

"affected prudery." [Isaac C. Pray,] *Memoirs of James Gordon Bennett and His Times* by a Journalist (New York: Stringer & Townsend, 1855), p. 266.

"entered the hearts of people . . ." *New York Herald,* December 4, 1836, quoted in Stevens, pp. 38–39. Note that he doesn't say he has entered their *minds.*

Circulation of 20,000. Ibid., p. 37.

Circulation of 51,000. Crouthamel, p. 36.

"were more ready to seek . . ." Quoted in Pray, p. 255.

64 **Bennett sold 135,000 copies.** David S. Reynolds, *Walt Whitman's America: A Cultural Biography* (New York: Alfred A. Knopf, 1995), p. 422.

"A week passed without reports . . ." Charles Royster, *The Destructive War: William Tecumseh Sherman, Stonewall Jackson, and the Americans* (New York: Alfred A. Knopf, 1991), p. 240.

"When it was feared . . ." T. L. Nichols, *Forty Years of American Life,* vol. I, p. 275, in Reynolds, *Walt Whitman's America,* p. 422.

"He made the newspaper powerful . . ." *New York Tribune,* June 3, 1872, quoted in Crouthamel, p. 156.

65 **"the interests of the country at large . . ."** Edgar Allan Poe, "The Literati of New York City" (1846), in Poe, *Essays and Reviews* (New York: Library of America, 1984), p. 1214.

Pulitzer's editorial campaigns. Stevens, p. 74.

a "public whose only literature was the family story paper . . ." Park, p. 9.

Circulation of the *World*. Richard Kluger, *The Paper: The Life and Death of the* New York Herald Tribune (New York: Alfred A. Knopf, 1986), p. 148.

***New York World* headlines.** *New York World,* May 11, 1883, in Stevens, pp. 69–70.

Examples of headlines. Kluger, p. 146.

66 **Pulitzer's comparing headlines to store windows.** Stevens, p. 77.

66 **"In the final stages . . ."** Gunther Barth, *City People: The Rise of Modern City Culture in Nineteenth-Century America* (New York: Oxford University Press, 1980), p. 105.

"The public is even more fond of entertainment . . ." *New York Journal,* November 8, 1896, quoted in Helen MacGill Hughes, *News and the Human Interest Story* (New York: Greenwood Press, 1968 [1940]), p. 21.

66–7 **MLLE. ANNA HELD RECEIVES ALAN DALE.** Frank Luther Mott, *American Journalism: A History, 1690–1960,* 3d ed. (New York: Macmillan, 1962), p. 522.

67 **Story function.** Kluger, p. 163.

"The news that actually happened . . ." W. A. Swanberg, *Citizen Hearst* (New York: Charles Scribner's Sons, 1961), p. 60.

"News Novelettes from Real Life . . ." Hughes, p. 21.

Another Hearst biographer saw this. John K. Winkler, *William Randolph Hearst: An American Phenomenon* (New York: Simon & Schuster, 1928), p. 111, quoted ibid., p. 21.

Guldensuppe case. Joyce Milton, *The Yellow Kids: Foreign Correspondents in the Heyday of Yellow Journalism* (New York: Harper & Row, 1989), p. 196; Stevens, pp. 91–93.

"The *Journal,* as Usual, ACTS . . ." *New York Journal,* July 7, 1897, quoted in Stevens, p. 93.

Evangelina Cosio y Cisneros. Milton, pp. 196–202; Mott, p. 530.

68 **"You furnish the pictures . . ."** Swanberg, p. 108. The line is also used in *Citizen Kane* (RKO), written by Orson Welles and Herman Mankiewicz, 1941.

Hearst and Spanish-American War. Edward Robb Ellis, *The Epic of New York City: A Narrative History from 1524 to the Present* (New York: Coward-McCann, 1966), pp. 442–44.

"I rather like the idea of war . . ." Ibid., p. 442.

69 **Richard Harding Davis.** See Arthur Lubow, *The Reporter Who Would Be King: A Biography of Richard Harding Davis* (New York: Charles Scribner's Sons, 1992).

"to provide fresh new abattoirs . . ." *Journalist* (August 5, 1893), quoted in Stevens, p. 78.

"The condition of excitement . . ." E. L. Godkin, "Journalistic Dementia," *Nation* 60: 1550 (March 14, 1895), pp. 195–96.

"All the World's News . . ." Schudson, p. 112.

70 **"Information is a genre of self-denial . . ."** Ibid., p. 119.

Increase in circulation from 1880 to 1890. Park, p. 11.

Ratio of readers to papers. William S. Rossiter, "Printing and Publishing," in U.S. Department of the Interior, Bureau of the Census,

Twelfth Census (Washington, D.C.: Government Printing Office, 1902), vol. IX, p. 1048, in Barth, p. 64.

70 **One-third of the papers.** Mott, p. 539; Stevens, p. 100.

70–1 **"Papers of highest news . . ."** Swanberg, p. 162.

71 **Readers thinking of newspaper as entertainment.** Louise Bolard More, *Wage-Earner's Budgets* (New York: Arno Press, 1971 [1907]), p. 133, in Kathy Peiss, *Cheap Amusements: Working Women and Leisure in Turn-of-the-Century New York* (Philadelphia: Temple University Press, 1986), pp. 22–23.

"there is too much moral sense . . ." *New York Evening Post,* March 20, 1832, quoted in Barth, p. 79.

"If bad institutions . . ." *New York Journal,* April 10, 1901, quoted in Mott, p. 540.

Pulitzer's change of heart. W. A. Swanberg, *Pulitzer* (New York: Charles Scribner's Sons, 1967), p. 255.

Spanish-American War and film. David Nasaw, *Going Out: The Rise and Fall of Public Amusements* (New York: Basic Books, 1993), pp. 136–37.

72 **"The story that is told by a picture . . ."** *Illustrated Daily News,* June 26, 1919.

the "very essence of tabloidism." *Editor & Publisher* (July 26, 1924), p. 7.

73 **Two-thirds of its nonadvertising space.** Stevens, p. 133.

Tabloid circulation. Mott, pp. 667–69.

"Everything it reports . . ." Richard Schickel, *Intimate Strangers: The Culture of Celebrity* (Garden City, N.Y.: Doubleday & Co., 1985), p. 51.

74 **"news story" and "fiction story."** Park, p. 4.

58 percent more columns devoted to crime. Wiggins DuBois, "Recent Newspaper Tendencies in New York City," M.A. thesis, Columbia University (1924), p. 79.

Increase in column inches. Survey by Joseph L. Holmes, cited in John R. Brazil, "Murder Trials, Murder and Twenties America," *American Quarterly* 33: 2 (Summer 1981), p. 165.

Hall-Mills case. See William Kunstler, *The Minister and the Choir Singer: The Hall-Mills Murder Case* (New York: William Morrow & Co., 1964).

75 **Reopening the case.** Ibid., pp. 115–18.

Comic strip on the case. Stevens, p. 148.

"injustice done to me . . ." Quoted in Kunstler, p. 180.

When the trial opened. Ibid., pp. 181–82.

76 **Number of reporters.** Stevens, p. 148.

76 **Charlotte Mills covered the trial.** Kunstler, pp. 188, 191, 203.

"The yellows see such stories . . ." Quoted ibid., p. viii.

Pig Woman. Ibid., pp. 242–43.

77 **"Never had a more theatrical day . . ."** *New York World,* November 18, 1926, quoted in Stevens, p. 148.

Snyder-Gray. Brazil, p. 164.

"[V]irtually every sizable paper . . ." Ibid., p. 164.

"nationally famous trial for homicide . . ." Charles Merz, "Bigger and Better Murders," *Harper's Magazine* 155 (August 1927), p. 341, quoted ibid., p. 163.

Gauvreau's idea. Hughes, p. 240.

Edward Browning. Ibid., pp. 240–42. See also Stanley Walker, *Mrs. Astor's Horse* (New York: Frederick A. Stokes, 1935).

78 **"The philosophy which inspires . . ."** Walter Lippmann, "Blazing Publicity," in *Vanity Fair: A Cavalcade of the 1920s and 1930s,* ed. Cleveland Amory and Frederic Bradlee (New York: Viking Press, 1960), p. 122.

79 **"There was a time when the reader . . ."** Boorstin, p. 7.

"be more interesting." Dwight Macdonald, *Against the American Grain: Essays on the Effects of Mass Culture* (New York: Random House, 1962), p. 399.

"share your commute." *New York Times,* November 17, 1991, Sec. 1, p. 64.

82 **"In Los Angeles, we've got a movie . . ."** Don Hewitt, "Pencils, Yes; Camera, No," *New York Times,* June 20, 1995, p. A15.

Coverage of Simpson verdict. *New York Times,* October 3, 1995, p. A16.

83 **"General Sherman had it all wrong . . ."** "The Video War Comes Home," *Nation* (July 1, 1991), p. 1.

Negotiation on TV. Michael Specter, "See Hostage-Takers Go Free! Live, on TV!," *New York Times,* June 20, 1995, p. A10.

84 **Connie Chung.** Bill Carter, "The Empty Chair," *New York Times,* May 22, 1995, p. A10.

"[T]he anchors win a degree of fame . . ." Walter Goodman, "Twinkle, Twinkle, Network News Stars," *New York Times,* May 28, 1995, sec. 2, p. 28.

85 **"It's show business."** Quoted in Allen R. Myerson, "The Best Little Sideshow in Texas," *New York Times,* March 9, 1994, p. C10.

87 **"There was the voyeuristic interest . . ."** Robert Hughes, "Why Watch It, Anyway?," *New York Review of Books* (February 16, 1995), p. 40.

87 **"If you're running a magazine show . . ."** Quoted in Eric Mink, "PBS' 'Tabloid Truth': Anatomy of a Scandal," *New York Post,* January 7, 1994, p. 100.

"new news." Bill Moyers, "Old News and the New Civil War," *New York Times,* March 22, 1992, sec. 4, p. 15.

88 **"[W]e should all be ashamed . . ."** Quoted in Elizabeth Kolbert, "Dan Rather Scolds TV News," *New York Times,* October 1, 1993, p. A12.

"an overwhelming desire to please . . ." David Remnick, "Good News Is No News," *Esquire* (October 1987), p. 158, quoted in Ian I. Mitroff and Warren Bennis, *The Unreality Industry: The Deliberate Manufacturing of Falsehood and What It Is Doing to Our Lives* (New York: Birch Lane Press, 1989), p. 17.

89 FIRE ON ICE. William Glaberson, "Newsday Imagines an Event and Sets Off a Debate," *New York Times,* February 17, 1994, p. D22.

New York Times openings. *New York Times,* May 8, 1994, p. 1. That this was a Sunday paper no doubt skewed the stories toward the novelistic, but the technique has become common in every edition.

"I want the traditional, first-paragraph lead . . ." Jacques Barzun, *The Press and the Prose,* Occasional Paper no. 10, March 1992 (New York: Freedom Forum Media Studies Center), p. 6.

90 **The fall of the Czech Communist Party.** Janos Horvat with Andras Szanto, *The Crucial Facts: Misleading Cues in the News of Central and Eastern Europe During Communism's Collapse* (New York: Freedom Forum, Media Studies Center, 1993), pp. 15–16.

Fall of Berlin Wall. Ibid., pp. 11–12.

91 **"I realized that the time had come . . ."** Peter Maass, *Love Thy Neighbor: A Story of War* (New York: Alfred A. Knopf, 1996), p. 247. Some journalists became so enthralled by the possibilities of fiction that they dispensed with fact altogether in the service of better entertainment. A columnist for the *Boston Globe* was dismissed for fabricating conversations and characters. (*New York Times,* June 19, 1998, p. A18.) Similarly, a young free-lance reporter whose work had appeared in *The New Republic, Rolling Stone* and *George,* among other publications, was discovered to have freely imagined conversations, situations and sources. An oblivious editor remarked on the young man's ability to find an "extraordinarily vivid anecdote." (*New York Times,* June 12, 1998, pp. A1, A18.) One might say they were victims of "entertainment-itis."

92 **"He in the end taught them . . ."** Melville Stone, *New York Times,* September 19, 1926, quoted in Schudson, p. 107.

Loss of supermarket tabloid circulation. Iver Peterson, *New York Times,* September 9, 1996, p. D7.

94 **Newsweek's doubts on Lewinsky's credibility.** Elisabeth Bumiller, "Man with Clinton Scoop Is Scooped Again," *New York Times*, January 23, 1998, p. B2.

Chapter Three / The Secondary Effect

96 **Pseudo-events.** Daniel J. Boorstin, *The Image: A Guide to Pseudo-Events in America* (New York: Atheneum, 1987 [1961]), pp. 38–39.

98 **"ricochet effect."** Neil Postman, *Amusing Ourselves to Death: Public Discourse in the Age of Show Business* (New York: Viking Press, 1985), p. 112.

99 **Cicero.** Leo Braudy, *The Frenzy of Renown: Fame and Its History* (New York: Oxford University Press, 1986), p. 73.

Napoleon. Ibid., p. 403.

Antebellum oration. Constance Rourke, *The Roots of American Culture and Other Essays,* ed. Van Wyck Brooks (New York: Harcourt, Brace & Co., 1942), pp. 83–84, 156.

Theodore Roosevelt. Braudy, p. 552.

"[T]he reality of politics . . ." Richard Sennett, *The Fall of Public Man: The Forces Eroding Public Life and Burdening the Modern Psyche with Roles It Cannot Perform* (New York: Alfred A. Knopf, 1977), pp. 284–85.

"wherever we see glamor . . ." David Riesman, *The Lonely Crowd: A Study of the Changing American Character,* with Nathan Glazer and Reuel Denney, abr. ed. (New Haven, Conn.: Yale University Press, 1969 [1961]), p. 191.

100 **"What we are dealing with here . . ."** Richard Schickel, *Intimate Strangers: The Culture of Celebrity* (Garden City, N.Y.: Doubleday & Co., 1985), p. 135.

"America's politics would now . . ." Norman Mailer, *The Presidential Papers* (New York: G. P. Putnam's Sons, 1963), p. 44.

101 **Length of sound bites.** Kiku Adatto, *Sound Bite Democracy: Network Evening News Presidential Campaign Coverage, 1968 and 1988,* Research Paper R-2, June 1990 (Cambridge, Mass.: The Joan Shorenstein Barone Center, Harvard University), p. 4.

"boiled down to speculation . . ." James Fallows, "Why Americans Hate the Media," *Atlantic Monthly* (February 1996), pp. 52, 55.

"provide a manageably small cast . . ." Russell Baker, "Mired in Stardom," *New York Times*, March 15, 1994, p. A23.

102 **"Entertainer-in-Chief."** Kurt Andersen, "Entertainer-in-Chief," *New Yorker* (February 16, 1998), p. 34.

"politainment." Jamie Malanowski, "Generals Fighting the Last War," *WJR* (December 1992), p. 25.

102 **Enumerating flaws and correctives.** Joe McGinniss, *The Selling of the President 1968* (New York: Trident Press, 1969), p. 36.

"**The whole day was built . . .**" Ibid., p. 62.

103 "**[T]he sophisticated candidate . . .**" Ibid., p. 31.

"**Voters are basically lazy . . .**" Ibid., p. 38.

"**incredible pap.**" Jim Sage, assistant on campaign advertising, quoted ibid., p. 114.

"**The words are given meaning . . .**" Ibid., p. 114.

104 "**a set . . .**" Joan Didion, "Insider Baseball," *New York Review of Books* (October 27, 1988), p. 20.

"**What we had in the tarmac arrival . . .**" Ibid., p. 24.

104–5 **North campaign.** *A Perfect Candidate.* Dir. by David Van Taylor and R.J. Cutler, Seventh Arts, 1996.

105 "**We spent more time . . .**" Adatto, p. 11.

"**dress extras.**" Didion, p. 26.

106 "**The language of political reporting . . .**" Adatto, pp. 4–5.

107 **Dukakis's tank episode.** Ibid., p. 13.

108 "**began to frame policy . . .**" Jonathan Schell, *The Time of Illusion* (New York: Alfred A. Knopf, 1976), p. 223.

109 "**What he wanted to be . . .**" Lou Cannon, *President Reagan: The Role of a Lifetime* (New York: Simon & Schuster, 1991), pp. 50–51.

"**There have been times . . .**" Ibid., p. 51.

110 "**I don't know . . .**" Ibid., p. 37.

everything was scripted. Ibid., pp. 54, 35.

Hollywood terminology. Ibid., p. 54.

White House compared with acting. Didion, p. 21.

Criticism of Nixon's line-readings. Cannon, p. 76.

111 **B-17 story.** Ibid., p. 59.

"**Where do we find such men?**" Michael Paul Rogin, *Ronald Reagan, the Movie and Other Episodes in Political Demonology* (Berkeley: University of California Press, 1987), p. 7.

solutions from movies. Cannon, pp. 57–58.

"**There are not two Ronald Reagans.**" Quoted in Rogin, p. 7.

"**has cast a kind of golden glow . . .**" Quoted in James Fallows, "The New Celebrities of Washington," *New York Review of Books* (June 12, 1986), p. 45.

112 "**You believed it . . .**" Cannon, pp. 38–39.

113 "**They can run . . .**" Maureen Dowd, "Book Review: *Under Fire* by Oliver North," *New York Times Book Review,* November 17, 1991, p. 12. The quote shows the unholy alliance between one entertainment

medium, the presidency, and another, the tabloids. A *New York Post* editor had phoned Reagan communications aide Pat Buchanan and asked him to use the line because it would make a good headline. Buchanan—and Reagan—obliged.

115 **"We know how to govern."** Quoted in Maureen Dowd, "Grand Funk Railroad," *New York Times*, September 28, 1995, p. A27.

"We've got to get this . . ." Michael Wines, "Bush's Responses Come from Script," *New York Times*, November 27, 1991, p. B9.

116 **Show business for ugly people.** Quoted in James Wolcott, "Hear Me Purr," *New Yorker* (May 20, 1996), p. 55.

Albert Gore on *The Late Show*. Elizabeth Kolbert, "My Next Guest's Policy Opens Today!," *New York Times*, September 10, 1993, p. A17.

"You like the audience." Cannon, p. 117.

"We refer to Washington . . ." Dick Belsky, quoted in Zane J. Peder, "Liz's Love Life! Oprah's Diet! Dole's Foreign Policy!," *New York Times*, September 29, 1996, sec. 4, p. 2.

117 **"We want to make politics sort of entertaining."** Quoted in Deirdre Carmody, "Politics as Entertainment," *New York Times*, February 20, 1995, p. C5.

"another aspect of cultural life . . ." Deirdre Carmody, "Early Signs Are Promising for George Magazine," *New York Times*, January 29, 1996, p. D5.

Chorus girls at 1924 World Series. John D. Stevens, *Sensationalism and the New York Press* (New York: Columbia University Press, 1991), p. 108.

118 **Mighty Ducks and California Angels.** Steve Rushin, "Who Stole the Show?," *Sports Illustrated* (June 3, 1996), pp. 26–27.

"Just remember . . ." Fred Speck, quoted in *Baseball Weekly* (February 9, 1994), p. 2.

"Story." David Remnick, "Inside-Out Olympics," *New Yorker* (August 5, 1996), p. 26.

119 **Deion Sanders calling himself entertainer.** Dave Anderson, "The Super Key," *New York Times*, September 3, 1995, p. C4.

121 **Best rock music in town.** Chris Seay, quoted in Charles Trueheart, "Welcome to the Next Church," *Atlantic Monthly* (August 1996), p. 50.

Megachurch movement. Ibid., pp. 42, 39, 53.

"He did not wave . . ." Colm Tobin, "The Paradoxical Pope," *New Yorker* (October 9, 1995), p. 36.

122 **"The contents of the book . . ."** Allen Lane, Penguin Books, quoted in James Twitchell, *Carnival Culture: The Trashing of Taste in America* (New York: Columbia University Press, 1992), p. 89.

122 **serialization.** Mark Sullivan, *Our Times: America at the Birth of the Twentieth Century,* ed. Dan Rather (New York: Charles Scribner's Sons, 1995 [1925–1933]), pp. 356–57.

Brad Leithauser. Doreen Carvajal, "Triumph of the Bottom Line," *New York Times,* April 1, 1996, p. D1.

124 **"excitement about the excitement."** Frank Bruni, "The Grunge American Novel," *New York Times Magazine,* March 24, 1996, p. 40. The same term was used by Walter Lippmann. See "Blazing Publicity," in *Vanity Fair: A Cavalcade of the 1920s and 1930s,* ed. Cleveland Amory and Frederic Bradlee (New York: Viking Press, 1960), p. 122.

"Byron's reputation was different . . ." Dwight Macdonald, *Against the American Grain: Essays on the Effects of Mass Culture* (New York: Random House, 1962), p. 23.

"poseur of truly colossal proportions . . ." David S. Reynolds, *Walt Whitman's America. A Cultural Biography* (New York: Alfred A. Knopf, 1995), p. 161.

"If I am an unknown man . . ." George Gissing, *New Grub Street* (1891), quoted in Schickel, p. 211.

Hemingway compared to Byron. John Raeburn, *Fame Became of Him: Hemingway as Public Writer* (Bloomington: Indiana University Press, 1984), p. 156.

125 **"the Hemingway of the handsome photographs . . ."** Edmund Wilson, *Atlantic Monthly* (July 1939), pp. 148–49, quoted ibid., p. 55.

"the prime case . . ." Braudy, p. 547.

Hemingway's immunity from criticism. Raeburn, p. 142.

"The way to save your work . . ." Norman Mailer, *Advertisements for Myself* (New York: Perigee, 1976), p. 5.

126 **"When we expressed anxiety . . ."** Michael Korda, "Wasn't She Great," *New Yorker* (August 14, 1995), p. 67.

"oversee the book's production." "Book Venture for Clancy," *New York Times,* November 20, 1995, p. D7.

127 **"very primitive . . ."** Jan Hoffman, "A Page-Turner of a Courtroom Drama," *New York Times,* February 7, 1996, p. B3.

128 **"*fatwa* chic."** Frank Rich, "Magical Rushdie Tour," *New York Times,* January 20, 1996, p. A23.

"Her story seems to be the story . . ." Doreen Carvajal, "Suddenly a Success in Poetry, and Not Everyone Applauds," *New York Times,* August 7, 1996, pp. C11, C15.

"I think part of it . . ." Ibid., p. C15.

Dr. Michael Palmer. Clyde Haberman, "From Despair to Best Seller," *New York Times,* July 11, 1996, pp. C1, C8.

129 **Authors' appearances.** Sarah Lyall, "Book Notes," *New York Times,* May 4, 1994, p. C22.

129–30 **Music and books.** Neil Straus, "The Pop Life," *New York Times,* June 27, 1996, p. C12; *New York Observer,* August 14, 1995.

130 **"What is offered for everybody . . ."** Jack Miles, "A Study in Scarlett," *Los Angeles Times Book Review,* October 13, 1991, p. 15.

132 **"*in* the painting."** Quoted in Robert Hughes, *American Visions: The Epic Story of Art in America* (New York: Alfred A. Knopf, 1997), p. 486.

133 **"liquidated the century-old tension . . ."** Harold Rosenberg, *Art on the Edge: Creators and Situations* (New York: Macmillan Publishing Co., 1975), pp. 105–06.

"I want to have an impact . . ." Dodie Kazanjian, "Koons Crazy," *Vogue* (August 1990), p. 341.

"visual and physical entertainment." Keith Haring, *Keith Haring Journals* (New York: Penguin Books, 1996), p. 95.

134 **Kostabi Worlds.** Anthony Haden-Guest, "The Art of the Hype," *Vanity Fair* (June 1989), p. 186.

135 **Warhol's Village Voice ad.** Tom Wolfe, *The Painted Word* (New York: Farrar, Straus & Giroux, 1975), p. 88.

"reinvented the idea of the life of the artist . . ." Haring, p. 117.

Ed Ruscha. Paul Taylor, "The Art of P.R., and Vice Versa," *New York Times,* October 27, 1991, sec. 2, p. 1.

136 **"some of the greatest art . . ."** Kazanjian, p. 385.

Koons's movie preparations. Ibid., pp. 343, 384.

"something to do for gain." Rosenberg, p. 106.

137 **"to project cultural authority."** Neil Harris, *Cultural Excursions: Marketing Appetites and Cultural Tastes in Modern America* (Chicago: University of Chicago Press, 1990), p. 137.

"Its role is not that of a custodian . . ." Lee Simonson, "Skyscrapers for Art Museums," *American Mercury* 10 (August 1927), p. 401, ibid., p. 75.

"It has become a low-rating mass medium . . ." Robert Hughes, *Nothing if Not Critical: Selected Essays on Art and Artists* (New York: Alfred A. Knopf, 1990), p. 389.

"the art museum as indoor theme park." Hilton Kramer, "The Whitney's New 'Ambition,'" *Arts & Antiques* (October 1996), p. 116.

138 **"That usually meant creating . . ."** Mark Edmundson, "As Lite Entertainment for Bored College Students," *Harper's Magazine* (September 1997), p. 44.

140 **"academostars."** Professor Jeffrey Williams, quoted in Janny Scott, "Scholars Fear 'Star' System May Undercut Their Mission," *New York Times,* December 20, 1997, p. A1.

"the bomp back into the bomp-de-domp." Camille Paglia, *Vamps and Tramps: New Essays* (New York: Vintage, 1994), p. 358.

141 **"something snappy."** Laura Mansnerus, "Timothy Leary, Pied Piper of Psychedelic 60s, Dies at 75," *New York Times,* June 1, 1996, pp. A1, A12.

Chapter Four / The Human Entertainment

143 **"Forty years ago, when I was growing up . . ."** Richard Schickel, *Intimate Strangers: The Culture of Celebrity* (Garden City, N.Y.: Doubleday & Co., 1985), p. 23.

Fame and America. Leo Braudy, *The Frenzy of Renown: Fame and Its History* (New York: Oxford Univ. Press, 1986), p. 393.

144 **"love of fame . . ."** Quoted in Douglass Adair, "Fame and the Founding Fathers," in *Fame and the Founding Fathers,* ed. Trevor Colbourn (New York: W. W. Norton, 1974), p. 8.

"where new kinds of men . . ." Braudy, p. 394.

"The celebrity is a person . . ." Daniel Boorstin, *The Image: A Guide to Pseudo-Events in America* (New York: Atheneum, 1987 [1961]), p. 57.

145 **"fascinating blend . . ."** Braudy, p. 509.

Survey of magazine biographical stories. Leo Lowenthal, *Literature, Popular Culture, and Society* (Palo Alto, Calif.: Pacific Books, 1968 [1961]), pp. 111–13.

The rise of movie stars in the media. Richard deCordova, *Picture Personalities: The Emergence of the Star System in America* (Urbana: University of Illinois Press, 1990), pp. 54–58.

"[S]tories about the stars . . ." Louis Menand, "That's Entertainment," *New Yorker* (November 22, 1993), p. 125.

"[T]he individual buried in the mass audience . . ." Dwight Macdonald, *Against the American Grain: Essays on the Effects of Mass Culture* (New York: Random House, 1962), p. 25.

147 **"That blast of notoriety . . ."** Evelyn Nesbit, *Prodigal Days: The Untold Story* (New York: Julien Messner, Inc., 1934), pp. 16–17.

"Newspapers the country over . . ." Ibid., p. 184.

"dementia Americana." Ibid., p. 207.

"I became public property . . ." Ibid., p. 209.

148 **"Presenting personalities . . ."** Quoted in Tom Matthews, "High Gloss News," *Newsweek* (May 1, 1989), p. 54.

***People* magazine's circulation.** Judy Kessler, *Inside People: The Stories Behind the Stories* (New York: Villard Books, 1994), p. 15.

148–9 **Appearances on *People* covers and formula.** Ibid., pp. xx, 11.

149 **"an ongoing cultural enterprise."** Richard Locke, quoted in Matthews, p. 56.

149 **"sort of an intellectual MTV."** Quoted in "Tina: Talk of the Town," *Newsweek* (July 13, 1992), pp. 64–65.

150 *Vanity Fair's* **circulation.** Ibid, pp. 64–65.

Vanity Fair's **turning a profit.** Elizabeth Kolbert, "How Tina Brown Moves Magazines," *New York Times Magazine,* December 5, 1993, p. 66.

"Tina almost created . . ." Ibid., p. 66.

superlatives. *Vanity Fair* (June 1990, July 1990, August 1990, August 1990).

153 **"journalist as good-tempered diva."** Caryn James, "When Lucy Dissed Desi," *New York Times,* May 1, 1996, p. C15.

154 **"No one expects a commercial TV network . . ."** Frank Rich, *New York Times,* June 22, 1995, p. A27.

155 **"as journalists . . ."** Quoted in Bill Carter, "Simpson Deal Causing Angst Inside NBC and Out," *New York Times,* October 11, 1995, pp. A1, A20.

Times **interview with Simpson.** Ibid., pp. A1, B7.

156 **Doris Lilly.** *Avenue* (April 1991), p. 30.

157 **"props for the show."** Quoted in Mark Singer, "Trump Solo," *New Yorker* (May 19, 1997), p. 65.

158 **"I'm not an actress."** George Dullea, "Thinner, Blonder, Wiser," *New York Times,* April 5, 1995, pp. C1, C14.

Kato Kaelin. Dominick Dunne, "Letter from Los Angeles," *Vanity Fair* (August 1995), p. 70.

Scheck and Neufeld development deal. Timothy Egan, "After Simpson Trial, Inquiries and Deals," *New York Times,* October 6, 1995, p. A18.

"power" florist. Jennet Conant, "The Flower and the Glory," *Vanity Fair* (December 1995), pp. 266–70, 296.

159 **"Murder of a Model."** "In a Shallow Grave," *People* (December 11, 1995), pp. 56–61.

underground celebrities. See Rene Chun, "K Shows Fashion World His 'X' Factor," *New York Times,* July 23, 1995, p. 33. The subject of this piece is a twenty-three-year-old singer/songwriter/model named K who skulked about art openings and fashion shows and thus took the scepter from the preceding year's celebrity who functioned to make the people who knew him feel knowing—another young singer without an album named Donovan Leitch, son of the 1960s folksinger Donovan.

159–60 **60 percent of physicians in Los Angeles.** Elisabeth Rosenthal, "Medicine Promotes Itself with Professional Help," *New York Times,* December 11, 1991, p. C1.

160 **Paying to become a celebrity.** William Henry III, "Pssst . . . Did You Hear About?" *Time* (March 5, 1990), p. 48.

In the future. David Suter to author.

superstar. Andy Warhol, *The Philosophy of Andy Warhol (From A to B and Back Again)* (New York: Harcourt Brace Jovanovich, 1975), p. 26.

161 **"Metaphor has left art . . ."** Joan Juliet Buck, "Live Mike," *Vanity Fair* (June 1994), p. 81.

162 **"everyday life a stage . . ."** Zsa Zsa Gabor with Gerold Frank, *Zsa Zsa Gabor: My Story* (New York: New World, 1960), p. 21.

Zsa Zsa's name. Ibid., p. 20.

"the press liked to write about me." Ibid., p.83.

"In time I was to discover . . ." Ibid., p. 177.

Bachelor's Haven. Ibid., pp. 200–03.

"I realized that my fame . . ." Ibid., p. 219.

163 **"I liked playing the role . . ."** Donald Spoto, *A Passion for Life: The Biography of Elizabeth Taylor* (New York: HarperCollins, 1995), p. 67.

164 **One of her biographers theorized.** Ibid., p. 93.

"And they were sitting on tombstones . . ." Elizabeth Taylor, *Elizabeth Taylor: An Informal Memoir* (New York: Harper & Row, 1965), p. 83.

"Once you're up there . . ." Ibid., p. 128.

Tragedy of celebrity. Braudy, p. 408.

"The very agency . . ." Boorstin, p. 63.

165 **"I am my own commodity."** Quoted by Mark Crispin Miller in "Gossiping About Gossip," *Harper's Magazine* (January 1986), p. 44.

"One can only enjoy oneself . . ." Quoted in Lowenthal, p. 20.

People **test cover.** Kessler, p. xvi.

166–7 **Boorstin on Barnum.** Boorstin, p. 209.

168 **"our fictional characters."** Randall Jarrell, "A Sad Heart at the Supermarket," in *Culture for the Millions?*, ed. Norman Jacobs (Boston: Beacon Press, 1964), p. 106.

"easy transcendence." Mark Edmundson, *Nightmare on Main Street: Angels, Sadomasochism, and the Culture of Gothic* (Cambridge, Mass.: Harvard University Press, 1997), p. xv.

"The public seems to revel . . ." Taylor, p. 175.

"powerless elite." Francesco Alberoni, "The Powerless 'Elite': Theory and Sociological Research on the Phenomenon of Stars," in *Sociology of Mass Communications,* ed. Denis McQuail (Harmondsworth, U.K.: Penguin Books, 1972), p. 75, quoted in Joshua Gamson, *Claims to Fame: Celebrity in Contemporary America* (Berkeley: University of California Press), p. 184.

169–70 **"It has always been the prime function . . ."** Joseph Campbell, *The Hero with a Thousand Faces*, 2d ed. (Princeton, N.J.: Princeton University Press, 1968), p. 11.

170 **"A hero ventures forth . . ."** Ibid., p. 30.

"There's only four basic stories . . ." Jay McInerney, "Bruce Willis in the Hot Zone," *Esquire* (May 1995), p. 70.

"world of secondary effects." Campbell, p. 17.

"with extraordinary powers . . ." Ibid., p. 319.

"road of trials," "woman as temptress." Ibid., p. 36.

171 **"The essence of oneself . . ."** Ibid., p. 383.

"I became famous . . ." Kevin Sessums, "Cruise Speed," *Vanity Fair* (October 1994), p. 270.

Sylvester Stallone. Zoe Heller, "Sly's Body Electric," *Vanity Fair* (November 1993), pp. 144, 184, 188.

172 **Julia Roberts.** Kevin Sessums, "The Crown Julia," *Vanity Fair* (October 1993), pp. 234, 294.

"rock bottom." Ingrid Sischy, "Madonna and Child," *Vanity Fair* (March 1998), p. 212.

"I think people are turning . . ." Ibid., p. 206.

173 **"carries within himself the all . . ."** Campbell, p. 385.

"There was a time . . ." Quoted in James Wolcott, "The Video Library," *New Yorker* (December 11, 1995), p. 111.

174 **"internalized them . . ."** Schickel, p. 4.

"I MUST achieve . . ." quoted in Kessler, p. 198.

175 **"I play a game of basketball . . ."** Steve Rushin, "World Domination," *Sports Illustrated* (October 27, 1997), p. 69.

Church of Kurt Cobain. "Your God Is Too Hairy," *New York Times Magazine*, June 30, 1996, p. 13.

"a fusion of our longing for spirituality . . ." Ron Rosenbaum, "Among the Believers," *New York Times Magazine*, September 24, 1995, p. 51.

176 **Entertainment as standard of individual worth.** See Meg Greenfield, "Celebrity Communion," *Newsweek* (May 19, 1997), p. 94, for just one example of how this concept has entered our discourse.

"[T]here are no rules for celebrities." Quoted in *New York Times*, September 28, 1995, p. B9.

"I am famous." *New York Times*, May 29, 1995, p. A9.

177 **"Far be it from me . . ."** Winston Churchill, *The Celebrity: An Episode* (New York: Macmillan, 1898), p. 2.

"crowning result of the star system . . ." C. Wright Mills, *The Power Elite* (London: Oxford University Press, 1956), pp. 71, 74.

177 **Charles Saatchi.** Stephen Schiff, "Master of Illusion," *New Yorker* (May 15, 1995), pp. 52–69.

178 **Julian Schnabel.** "Why Schnabel's Feeling Insecure," *New Yorker* (June 5, 1995), pp. 33–34.

179 **Alex J. Mandl.** Mark Landler, "Why America Pays to Play Top Executives," *New York Times,* August 25, 1996, sec. 4, p. 4.

"[E]ntertainment pushed to an extreme . . ." Marshall McLuhan, *Understanding Media: The Extensions of Man,* 2d ed. (New York: McGraw-Hill, 1964), p. 243.

Celebrity theory of value. Philip J. Cook and Robert H. Frank, *The Winner-Take-All Society: Why the Few at the Top Get So Much More than the Rest of Us* (New York: Penguin Books, 1996).

180 **Koons's Nike posters.** Paul Taylor, "The Hot Four," *New York* magazine (October 27, 1986), pp. 50–56.

Run on Versace clothes. "Death Sparks Demand for Merchandise," *New York Times,* July 18, 1997, p. A18. "Is 'bizarre' too hideous a word to use?" the fashion director of Bloomingdale's department store was quoted as asking.

Onassis auction: James Barron, "Camelot Trophies' Cost Is Nothing Compared with Plans for Pedestals," *New York Times,* April 27, 1996, pp. 25–26; James Barron, "The Auction Aftermath," *New York Times,* April 28, 1996, p. 35.

"Look at what Camelot brought." Thomas Jacobson, quoted in Dirk Johnson, "Bid to Auction Killer's Tools Provokes Disgust," *New York Times,* May 20, 1996, p. A10. In the event, the auction was canceled.

181 **Mark David Chapman.** Kessler, pp. 160–62.

Timothy McVeigh and *Newsweek*. David Hackworth and Peter Annin, "The Suspect Speaks Out," *Newsweek* (July 3, 1995), pp. 23–28.

182 **"present our client to the public . . ."** Stephen Jones, quoted in Pam Belluck, "McVeigh Says He'll Plead Not Guilty," *New York Times,* June 26, 1995, p. A8.

McVeigh's media requests. Jo Thomas, "U.S. Opposes Interviews for Oklahoma Suspect," *New York Times,* August 30, 1996, p. A16.

"Nowadays if you're a crook . . ." Warhol, p. 85.

183 **John Salvi's demand.** Mimi Swartz, "Family Secret," *New Yorker* (November 17, 1997), p. 99.

Unabomber's image. "Kaczynski Worried About 'Sick' Label," *New York Times,* November 20, 1997, p. A18.

"regain his position as . . ." *New York Times,* April 13, 1996, p. A10.

McVeigh renting *Blown Away*. Kit Roane, "In Arizona Desert Town, Suspicion Stalks the Streets," *New York Times,* June 18, 1995, p. A16.

184 **Mark David Chapman's arrangement.** Kessler, p. 162.

Chapman losing weight. Ibid., p. 164.

"Mr. Bundy is the producer of a play . . ." Quoted in Schickel, p. 8.

"overly concerned with my appearance . . ." Arthur H. Bremer, *An Assassin's Diary,* intro. Harding Lemay (New York: Harper Magazine Press, 1973), pp. 76–77.

"A penny for your thoughts." Ibid., p. 137.

185 **"SHIT! I won't even rate . . ."** Ibid., p. 105.

"FAILURES." Ibid., pp. 98, 116.

"I'm as important as the start . . ." Ibid., p. 98.

"Hollywood (I KNOW IT SOUNDS INSANE . . .)" Ibid., pp. 109–10.

186 **"Celebrities have an intimate life . . ."** George W. S. Trow, *Within the Context of No Context* (Boston: Little, Brown & Co., 1981), p. 9.

"I know I'm nothing." Susan Faludi, "The Money Shot," *New Yorker* (October 30, 1995), p. 79.

"Unfortunately in America . . ." Quoted in Schickel, p. 251.

"Everybody wants to be famous." McInerney, p. 65.

"the 'star' provided . . ." Stuart Ewen, *All Consuming Images: The Politics of Style in Contemporary Culture* (New York: Basic Books, 1988), pp. 92–93.

187 **"mystic community of other famous people . . ."** Braudy, p. 7.

The "Center." Tom Wolfe, *The Painted Word* (New York: Farrar, Straus & Giroux, 1975), p. 17.

"best reason to be famous." Warhol, p. 78.

"I know who they are . . ." Quoted in Michael Korda, "Wasn't She Great?," *New Yorker* (August 14, 1995), p. 68.

188 **The King of Comedy.** Directed by Martin Scorsese. Written by Paul D. Zimmerman. Twentieth Century-Fox. 1982.

To Die For. Directed by Gus Van Sant. Written by Buck Henry. Columbia Pictures. 1995.

189 **drunken fan.** *The Late Show with David Letterman.* September 13, 1995, CBS Network.

189–90 **Number of daytime talk show guests.** Elizabeth Kolbert, "Wages of Deceit." *New York Times,* June 11, 1995, sec. 2, p. 29.

190 **Thousands waiting in the foyer.** Talk show host Jerry Springer said he received thousands of requests each week to appear on his show. *Vibe.* January 30, 1998, WB Network.

"For a show on rape . . ." *Geraldo* executive producer Martin Berman, quoted in Kolbert, "Wages of Deceit," p. 29.

190 **"as a way of becoming immortal."** Mrs. Tony Orlando, quoted in Kessler, p. 53.

"I wonder if Savannah . . ." Faludi, p. 87.

"How many times do I have to kill . . ." Associated Press, February 12, 1978, quoted in Braudy, p. 3.

191 **"It was the greatest moment . . ."** Lisa Belkin, "Death on the CNN Curve," *New York Times Magazine,* July 23, 1995, p. 19.

"a man so changed . . ." Ibid., p. 19.

Chapter Five / The Mediated Self

193 **Theatrical instinct.** Nicolas Evreinoff, *The Theatre in Life,* ed. and tr. Alexander I. Nazaroff (New York: Brentano's, 1927), pp. 107–08.

"The birth of a child . . ." Ibid., p. 27.

Sennett on appearance and self-presentation. Richard Sennett, *The Fall of Public Man: The Forces Eroding Public Life and Burdening the Modern Psyche with Roles It Cannot Perform* (New York: Alfred A. Knopf, 1977).

194 **"These men of the back country . . ."** Constance Rourke, *The Roots of American Culture and Other Essays,* ed. Van Wyck Brooks (New York: Harcourt, Brace & Co., 1942), pp. 130–31.

"terrible doubt of appearances." Quoted in Jackson Lears, *Fables of Abundance: A Cultural History of Advertising in America* (New York: Basic Books, 1994), p. 55.

195 **"unmistakable signs . . ."** Ira Steward, Massachusetts labor leader, quoted in Stuart Ewen, *All Consuming Images: The Politics of Style in Contemporary Culture* (New York: Basic Books, 1988), p. 67.

"[t]o be stunningly attired . . ." Kathy Peiss, *Cheap Amusements: Working Women and Leisure in Turn-of-the-Century New York* (Philadelphia: Temple University Press, 1986), p. 65.

"modes of externalization." Nathaniel Southgate Shaler, *The Individual* (1900), quoted in Warren I. Susman, *Culture as History: The Transformation of American Society in the Twentieth Century* (New York: Pantheon, 1984), p. 281.

Delsarte Speaker. Mark Sullivan, *Our Times: America at the Birth of the Twentieth Century,* ed. Dan Rather (New York: Scribner, 1996 [1925–1933]), pp. 153–54.

195–6 **"a development of self-consciousness . . ."** Marshall McLuhan, *Understanding Media: The Extensions of Man,* 2d ed. (New York: McGraw-Hill, 1964), pp. 176–77.

196 **"My life was going to the movies."** "The Serious Business of Being Funny," *New Yorker* (August 21 and 28, 1995), p. 56.

"You know how to brood . . ." Louis Menand, "That's Entertainment," *New Yorker* (November 22, 1993), p. 121.

196 **"end up adopting a whole life."** Geoffrey O'Brien, *The Phantom Empire* (New York: W. W. Norton & Co., 1993), pp. 45–46.

197 **Character vs. personality.** Susman, p. xxi.

"The social role demanded . . ." Ibid., p. 280.

"The truth was that Jay Gatsby . . ." F. Scott Fitzgerald, *The Great Gatsby* (New York: Charles Scribner's Sons, 1925), p. 89.

198 **"There's a regular customer . . ."** Abigail Witherspoon, "This Pen for Hire," *Harper's Magazine* (June 1995), p. 57.

199 **"their inheritance into phonographs . . ."** George Jean Nathan and H. L. Mencken, *The American Credo: A Contribution Toward the Interpretation of the National Mind* (New York: Alfred A. Knopf, 1921), pp. 25, 28, quoted in Neil Harris, *Cultural Excursions: Marketing Appetites and Cultural Tastes in Modern America* (Chicago: University of Chicago Press, 1990), pp. 189–90.

"needs" culture to "desires" culture. Quoted in William Leach, *Land of Desire: Merchants, Power, and the Rise of a New American Culture* (New York: Pantheon, 1993), p. 290.

a "stage on which the play is enacted." Quoted ibid., p. 147.

200 **"People who come to shop . . ."** Quoted in Michael Gross, "Ralph's World," *New York* magazine (September 20, 1993), p. 47.

"just the right balance . . ." Paul Goldberger, "25 Years of Unabashed Elitism," *New York Times*, February 2, 1992, sec. 2, p.34.

Niketown. Marshall Sella, "Jock Citadel," *New York Times*, July 19, 1992, sec. 10, p. 3.

Artificial rock and oversized video screens. Paul Goldberger, "The Store Strikes Back," *New York Times Magazine*, April 6, 1997, p. 46.

200–1 **Megamalls.** Ada Louise Huxtable, *The Unreal America: Architecture and Illusion* (New York: New Press, 1997), pp. 101–02.

201 **Sony Retail Entertainment.** Goldberger, "The Store Strikes Back," p. 48.

Lindbergh's endorsements. Leo Braudy, *The Frenzy of Renown: Fame and Its History* (New York: Oxford University Press, 1986), p. 21.

201–2 **"The nationally advertised product . . ."** Daniel J. Boorstin, *The Image: A Guide to Pseudo-Events in America* (New York: Atheneum, 1987 [1961]), p. 221.

202 **"As long as people dislike the anonymity . . ."** J. Gordon Lippincott, *Design for Business* (Chicago: 1947), p. 62, quoted in Ewen, p. 106.

Windows 95 madness. Carey Goldberg, "Midnight Sales Frenzy Ushers in Windows 95," *New York Times*, August 28, 1995, pp. A1, D3.

Ralph Lauren Sport Paint Collection. Advertisement, *New York Times Magazine*, Feb. 4, 1996.

203 **"to rank high . . ."** Thorstein Veblen, *The Theory of the Leisure Class* (New York: Penguin Books, 1979 [1899]), p. 31.

"[i]n order to gain and to hold . . ." Ibid., p. 36.

"norm of reputability . . ." Ibid., p. 84.

204 **"desire for a magical transfiguration . . ."** Lears, p. 43.

"The television commercial has oriented business . . ." Neil Postman, *Amusing Ourselves to Death: Public Discourse in the Age of Show Business* (New York: Viking Press, 1985), p. 128.

205 **"product now in demand . . ."** David Riesman, *The Lonely Crowd: A Study of the Changing American Character,* with Nathan Glazer and Reuel Denney, abr. ed. (New Haven, Conn.: Yale University Press, 1969 [1961]), p. 46.

"The chief business of the American people . . ." Calvin Coolidge, Speech to the American Society of Newspaper Editors, January 17, 1925, in John Bartlett, *Familiar Quotations,* 15th ed., ed. Emily Morrison Beck (Boston: Little, Brown & Co., 1980), p. 736.

206 **"[O]ne stepped into clothes . . ."** Sennett, pp. 67–68.

"code language of status." Tom Wolfe, "Introduction," in René König, *A la Mode: On the Social Psychology of Fashion,* tr. F. Bradley (New York: Seabury Press, 1973), p. 27.

"To choose clothes . . ." Alison Lurie, *The Language of Clothes* (New York: Random House, 1981), p. 5.

207 **Ralph Lauren's background.** Holly Brubach, "Ralph Lauren's Achievement," *Atlantic Monthly* (August 1987), p. 70.

"Whether that world exists or not . . ." Quoted in Stephen Koepp, "Selling a Dream of Elegance and the Good Life," *Time* (September 1, 1986), p. 54.

"represent living, not fashion." Quoted in Gross, p. 50.

the **"whole atmosphere of the good life."** Brubach, p. 72.

image manager. Gross, p. 47.

207–8 **"America is a mix . . ."** Michael Gross, "The American Dream," *New York* magazine (December 21 and 28, 1992), pp. 71–72.

208 **Practical liberation.** Jean Baudrillard. *America,* tr. Chris Turner (New York: Verso, 1988), p. 96.

"To father on the occasion . . ." Brubach, p. 73.

"His chuck wagon holds . . ." Gross, "Ralph's World," p. 46.

208–9 **Martha Stewart's background.** Martha Stewart, "Ask Martha," syndicated newspaper column, November 25, 1995.

209 **"[W]e have finally become disillusioned . . ."** Ibid.

Two-hundred-million-dollar empire. *Web Guide to Martha Stewart.* Internet.

"We have come to realize that the creation . . ." Ibid.

209 **"Always leave an inch . . ."** *USA Today,* Life Section, January 17, 1996.

210 **Cindy Jackson.** Charles Siebert, "The Cuts that Go Deeper," *New York Times Magazine,* July 7, 1996, p. 25.

Orlan. Ibid., p. 25.

211 **"clodhopping inbreds."** "Look Ma, All Cavities," *New York Times Magazine,* July 23, 1995, p. 6.

"a little architectural hocus pocus." Lewis Mumford, "The Architecture of Escape," *New Republic* 63 (August 12, 1925), pp. 321–22.

Martin Dressler. Steven Millhauser, *Martin Dressler: The Tale of an American Dreamer* (New York: Vintage, 1997 [1996]), pp. 194–97, 238–39.

212 **"provisional air . . ."** Ibid., p. 240.

"New York restaurants now have a new thing . . ." Warhol, p. 159.

"The interior is a stage set . . ." Howard Hirsch, quoted in Bernard Weinraub, "A Grand Hotel, Still Pink, Still Posh," *New York Times,* June 1, 1995, p. C6.

212–13 **"entertainment zone . . ."** Thomas Bender, "City Lite," *Los Angeles Times,* December 22, 1996, p. M1.

213 **agritainment.** Julie V. Iovine, "A New Cash Crop: The Farm as Theme Park," *New York Times,* November 2, 1997, pp. 1, 30.

"Disneyland is presented as imaginary . . ." Jean Baudrillard, *Selected Writings,* ed. Mark Poster (Stanford, Calif.: Stanford University Press, 1988), p. 172.

"[I]t's not that Disneyland is a metaphor . . ." Robert Hughes, *Nothing if Not Critical: Selected Essays on Art and Artists* (New York: Alfred A. Knopf, 1990), p. 380.

"acknowledged master." Huxtable, p. 98.

New York shopping mall. Ibid., p. 102.

214 the **"American imagination demands the real thing . . ."** Umberto Eco, *Travels in Hyperreality,* tr. William Weaver (New York: Harcourt Brace Jovanovich, 1987), p. 8.

"experiential placemaking." Quoted in Huxtable, p. 98.

"Freemont Street Experience." Ibid., p. 76; Jon Jerde lecture, International Design Conference at Aspen, June 7, 1997.

214–15 **Columbia studio.** Lynda Obst, International Design Conference at Aspen, June 7, 1997.

215 **Christie Brinkley's house.** Julie V. Iovine, "Making the Imperfect Picture Perfect," *New York Times,* July 17, 1997, p. C1.

216 **Buffalo Bill Cody.** W. F. Cody, *Story of the Wild West and Campfire Tales* (Freeport, N.Y.: Books for Libraries Press, 1970 [1888]), pp.

633–89; Richard Slotkin, *Gunfighter Nation: The Myth of the Frontier in Twentieth-Century America* (New York: Atheneum, 1992), pp. 70–72.

217 **"the sort of costume . . ."** Slotkin, p. 72.

"constricted by shyness." Elizabeth Taylor, *Elizabeth Taylor: An Informal Memoir* (New York: Harper & Row, 1965), p. 5.

218 **"In my memory we will always be . . ."** Lana Turner, *Lana—the Lady, the Legend, the Truth* (New York: E. P. Dutton, 1982), pp. 112–13.

"There was no point . . ." Taylor, p. 105.

"what is really true . . ." Zsa Zsa Gabor with Gerold Frank, *Zsa Zsa Gabor: My Story* (New York: New World, 1960), p. 18.

219 **"They evidently sort of work . . ."** Taylor, p. 49.

"I daren't take any chances with Myrna Loy . . ." Quoted in Frank Service, "So You'd Like to Be a Star: Myrna Loy Shows You What Is Back of Hollywood's Glamor [*sic*] Front," in *Hollywood and the Great Fan Magazine,* ed. Martin Levin (New York: Arbor House, 1970), p. 142, quoted in Joshua Gamson, *Claims to Fame: Celebrity in Contemporary America* (Berkeley: University of California Press, 1994), p. 35.

"I am disgusted . . ." Taylor, p. 2.

"I have to live up to . . ." Zsa Zsa Gabor with Wendy Leigh, *One Lifetime Is Not Enough* (New York: Delacorte Press, 1991), p. 310.

"No matter what people say about you . . ." Peter Guralnick, *Last Train to Memphis: The Rise of Elvis Presley* (Boston: Little, Brown and Co., 1994), p. 235.

"Whenever a man strives . . ." Evreinoff, p. 50.

219–20 **"They built this person."** Susan Faludi, "The Money Shot," *New Yorker* (October 30, 1995), p. 76.

220 **"people here / have become . . ."** Sam Shepard, *Motel Chronicles* (San Francisco: City Lights, 1982), p. 42.

"I had been divorced by success . . ." Norman Mailer, *Advertisements for Myself* (New York: Perigee, 1976), pp. v–vi.

"Please think of the real O.J. . . ." *New York Times,* June 18, 1994, p. A10.

"What movie-goers wanted . . ." Boorstin, p. 156.

Breakdown of studio system. Gamson, p. 45.

"discarnate man." Philip Marchand, *Marshall McLuhan: The Medium and the Messenger* (New York: Ticknor & Fields, 1989), p. 238.

220–1 **half-people.** Andy Warhol, *America* (New York: Harper & Row, 1985), p. 30.

221 **"withdrawal of self into the no-self."** Quoted in C. Fred Alford, *The Psychoanalytic Theory of Greek Tragedy* (New Haven, Conn.: Yale University Press, 1992), p. 119.

synecdoche. John Raeburn, *Fame Became of Him: Hemingway as Public Writer* (Bloomington: Indiana University Press, 1984), p. 1. Raeburn cites a *Look* magazine photo quiz in which the reader was asked to identify famous people from their trademarks.

"I needed a trademark." "Built to Last," *New Yorker* (June 3, 1996), p. 30.

"I want people to be able to recognize me by just looking . . ." *Washington Post*, April 15, 1976, quoted in Braudy, p. 548.

222 **Lisa Marie Presley's response.** *Prime Time Live*, ABC network, June 14, 1995.

"Is this guy weird . . ." Judy Kessler, *Inside People: The Stories Behind the Stories* (New York: Villard Books, 1994), p. 193.

223 **"That's what show business is for . . ."** Warhol, *America*, p. 179.

224 **"inner-directed."** Riesman, p. 15.

"other-directed." Ibid., p. 21.

"chief source of direction . . ." Ibid., p. 22.

"life itself is a dramatically enacted thing." Erving Goffman, *The Presentation of Self in Everyday Life* (Woodstock, N.Y.: Overlook Press, 1973 [1959]), p. 72.

224–5 **"exchange of dramatically inflated actions . . ."** Ibid., p. 72.

225 **"dramaturgically disciplined."** Ibid., p. 216.

"product of a scene that comes off . . ." Ibid., pp. 252–53.

"front stage" and "back stage." Ibid., p. 112.

226 **"that we are losing our psychological moorings."** Robert Jay Lifton, *The Protean Self: Human Resilience in an Age of Fragmentation* (New York: Basic Books, 1993), p. 1.

"My whole person . . ." Ibid., pp. 198–99.

"continually assume new identities . . ." Michiko Kakutani, "When Fluidity Replaces Maturity," *New York Times*, March 20, 1995, p. C11.

"ethical commitment . . ." Lifton, p. 127.

227 **"populating of the self."** Kenneth J. Gergen, *The Saturated Self: Dilemmas of Identity in Contemporary Life* (New York: Basic Books, 1991), p. 69.

relational sophistication. Ibid., p. 184.

"pastiche personality." Ibid., pp. 150–51.

Self as relational. Ibid., pp. 156–57.

228 **The Culture of Narcissism.** Christopher Lasch, *The Culture of Narcissism: American Life in an Age of Diminishing Expectations* (New York: W. W. Norton, 1979).

229 **"The new artificiality . . ."** Quoted in John Lahr, "The Voodoo of Glamour," *New Yorker* (March 21, 1994), p. 121.

230 **"As soon as we are given a chance . . ."** Evreinoff, pp. 52–53.

"A whole day of life . . ." Warhol, *Philosophy,* p. 5.

231 **"We have tried to discover . . ."** Boorstin, p. 202.

"badging." Jane Newman, Merekly Newman Harty, quoted in *The Inside Take on American Popular Culture* (*People* magazine publication, 1994), p. 15.

232 **"lifestyle enclaves."** Robert Bellah et al., *Habits of the Heart: Individualism and Commitment in American Life* (Berkeley: University of California Press, 1985), p. 72.

"life coaches." *Impact,* Cable News Network, December 21, 1997.

233 **"At one point in cultural history . . ."** Gergen, p. 122.

"Right away." *America's Funniest Home Videos,* ABC network, October 20, 1991.

234 **Taping divorced parents.** George Dullea, "Camcorder! Action! Lives Become Roles," *New York Times,* August 15, 1991, pp. A1, C10.

235 **"You can be whoever you want to be."** Sherry Turkle, *Life on the Screen: Identity in the Age of the Internet* (New York: Simon & Schuster, 1997), p. 184.

237 **"by supplying our imagination . . ."** Quoted in Leo Lowenthal, *Literature, Popular Culture, and Society* (Palo Alto, Calif.: Pacific Books, 1968 [1961]), p. 16.

"If we make any kind of decent, useful life . . ." Pauline Kael, "Trash, Art and the Movies," *Going Steady* (New York: Bantam, 1971), p. 158.

238 **"sacred masterplot . . ."** Peter Brooks, *Reading for the Plot: Design and Intention in Narrative* (New York: Alfred A. Knopf, 1985), p. 6.

"For the truth is that life on the face of it . . ." José Ortega y Gasset, *The Revolt of the Masses,* tr. Anthony Kerrigan (Notre Dame, Ind.: Univ. of Notre Dame Press, 1985), p. 142.

"All sorrows can be borne . . ." Quoted in Suzanne Ruta, "Book Review: *Paula* by Isabel Allende," *New York Times Book Review,* May 21, 1995, p. 11.

"I told myself stories." Lifton, p. 137.

"The dream of man's heart . . ." Saul Bellow, *Herzog* (New York: Viking, 1964), p. 303, quoted in Lifton, p. 87.

239 **"positive illusions."** Shelley E. Taylor, *Positive Illusions: Creative Self-Deception and the Healthy Mind* (New York: Basic Books, 1989).

240 **"At one level, it constructs beneficent . . ."** Ibid., p. xi.

241 **"at least as happy . . ."** Ibid., p. vii.

"Since he replaces reality . . ." Michael Paul Rogin, *Ronald Reagan, the Movie and Other Episodes in Political Demonology* (Berkeley: University of California Press, 1987), p. 9.

study by Mark Snyder. Mark L. Snyder, "Self-Monitoring Processes," in *Advances in Experimental Social Psychology*, vol. 12, ed. Leonard Berkowitz (New York: Academic Press, 1979), quoted in Gergen, p. 151.

"One can try to re-create the world . . ." Sigmund Freud, *Civilization and Its Discontents*, tr. and ed. James Strachey (New York: W. W. Norton & Co., 1961 [1930]), p. 30.

242 **"When a population becomes distracted by trivia . . ."** Postman, pp. 155–56.

Denial of pleasure. Wendy Steiner, *The Scandal of Pleasure* (Chicago: University of Chicago Press, 1995).

A Select Bibliography

THE LIST THAT FOLLOWS is a highly select bibliography of books that should enable one to explore further the issues raised in this volume. The reader is advised that not all the books consulted or all those referred to in the text or notes are listed here and that the relevant details about the newspaper and magazine articles drawn upon may be found in the notes section.

Ahlstrom, Sydney E. *A Religious History of the American People*. New Haven: Yale University Press, 1972.

Amory, Cleveland, and Frederic Bradlee, eds. *Vanity Fair: A Cavalcade of the 1920s and 1930s*. New York: Viking Press, 1960.

Barth, Gunther. *City People: The Rise of Modern City Culture in Nineteenth-Century America*. New York: Oxford University Press, 1980.

Baudrillard, Jean. *America*. Translated by Chris Turner. New York: Verso, 1988.

———. *Selected Writings*. Edited by Mark Poster. Stanford, Calif.: Stanford University Press, 1988.

Bazin, André. *What Is Cinema?* Vol. 1. Translated and edited by Hugh Gray. Berkeley: University of California Press, 1967.

Bellah, Robert N., Richard Madsen, William M. Sullivan, Ann Swidler, and Steven M. Tipton. *Habits of the Heart: Individualism and Commitment in American Life*. Berkeley: University of California Press, 1985.

Bode, Carl. *The Anatomy of American Popular Culture, 1840–1861.* Berkeley: University of California Press, 1960.

Boorstin, Daniel J. *The Americans: The National Experience.* New York: Random House, 1965.

———. *The Image: A Guide to Pseudo-Events in America.* 1961. Reprint. New York: Atheneum, 1987.

Boyer, Paul. *Urban Masses and Moral Order in America, 1820–1920.* Cambridge, Mass.: Harvard University Press, 1978.

Braudy, Leo. *The Frenzy of Renown: Fame and Its History.* New York: Oxford University Press, 1986.

Bremer, Arthur. *An Assassin's Diary.* New York: Harper Magazine Press, 1973.

Brewer, John. *The Pleasures of the Imagination: English Culture in the Eighteenth Century.* New York: Farrar, Straus & Giroux, 1997.

Brooks, Peter. *Reading for the Plot: Design and Intention in Narrative.* New York: Alfred A. Knopf, 1984.

Brooks, Van Wyck. *America's Coming-of-Age.* New York: B. W. Huebsch, 1915.

Burke, Peter. *Popular Culture in Early Modern Europe.* New York: New York University Press, 1978.

Burns, James MacGregor. *The Vineyard of Liberty.* New York: Random House, 1982.

Campbell, Joseph. *The Hero with a Thousand Faces.* 2d edition. Princeton, N.J.: Princeton University Press, 1968.

Cannon, Lou. *President Reagan: The Role of a Lifetime.* New York: Simon & Schuster, 1991.

Cody, W. F. *Story of the Wild West and Campfire Tales.* 1888. Reprint. Freeport, N.Y.: Books for Libraries Press, 1970.

Cook, Philip J., and Robert H. Frank. *The Winner-Take-All Society: Why the Few at the Top Get So Much More than the Rest of Us.* New York: Viking, 1995; Penguin Books, 1996.

Crouthamel, James L. *Bennett's* New York Herald *and the Rise of the Popular Press.* Syracuse, N.Y.: Syracuse University Press, 1989.

Czitrom, Daniel J. *Media and the American Mind: From Morse to McLuhan.* Chapel Hill: University of North Carolina Press, 1982.

deCordova, Richard. *Picture Personalities: The Emergence of the Star System in America.* Urbana: University of Illinois Press, 1990.

Denning, Michael. *Mechanic Accents: Dime Novels and Working-Class Culture in America.* London: Verso, 1987.

Dickens, Charles. *American Notes.* Introduction by Christopher Lasch. Gloucester, Mass.: Peter Smith, 1968.

Douglas, Ann. *Terrible Honesty: Mongrel Manhattan in the 1920s.* New York: Farrar, Straus & Giroux, 1995.

Dyer, Richard. *Only Entertainment*. London: Routledge, 1992.

Eco, Umberto. *The Open Work*. Translated by Anna Cancogni. Cambridge, Mass.: Harvard University Press, 1989.

————. *Travels in Hyperreality*. Translated by William Weaver. New York: Harcourt Brace Jovanovich, 1987.

Edmundson, Mark. *Nightmare on Main Street: Angels, Sadomasochism, and the Culture of Gothic*. Cambridge, Mass.: Harvard University Press, 1997.

Emery, Edward. *The Press in America*. Englewood Cliffs, N.J.: Prentice-Hall, 1962.

Evreinoff, Nicolas. *The Theatre in Life*. Edited and translated by Alexander I. Nazaroff. New York: Brentano's, 1927.

Evreinov, Nikolai. *Life as Theater*. Edited and translated by Christopher Collins. Ann Arbor, Mich.: Ardis, 1973.

Ewen, Stuart. *All Consuming Images: The Politics of Style in Contemporary Culture*. New York: Basic Books, 1988.

Ewen, Stuart and Elizabeth. *Channels of Desire: Mass Images and the Shaping of American Consciousness*. 2d edition. Minneapolis: University of Minnesota Press, 1992.

Feldberg, Michael. *The Turbulent Era: Riot and Disorder in Jacksonian America*. New York: Oxford University Press, 1980.

Fiedler, Leslie. *What Was Literature? Class, Culture and Mass Society*. New York: Simon & Schuster, 1982.

Fish, Carl Russell. *The Rise of the Common Man, 1830–1850*. New York: Macmillan, 1927.

Gabor, Zsa Zsa, with Wendy Leigh. *One Lifetime Is Not Enough*. New York: Delacorte Press, 1991.

————, with Gerold Frank. *Zsa Zsa Gabor: My Story*. New York: New World, 1960.

Gamson, Joshua. *Claims to Fame: Celebrity in Contemporary America*. Berkeley: University of California Press, 1994.

Gergen, Kenneth J. *The Saturated Self: Dilemmas of Identity in Contemporary Life*. New York: Basic Books, 1991.

Gilje, Paul A. *The Road to Mobocracy: Popular Disorder in New York City, 1763–1834*. Chapel Hill: University of North Carolina Press, 1987.

Ginger, Ray. *The Age of Excess: The United States from 1877 to 1914*. New York: Macmillan, 1965.

Godkin, E[dwin] L[awrence]. *Problems of Modern Democracy*. Edited by Morton Keller. Cambridge, Mass.: Belknap Press of Harvard University Press, 1966.

————. *Reflections and Comments, 1865–1895*. New York: Charles Scribner's Sons, 1895.

Goffman, Erving. *The Presentation of Self in Everyday Life.* 1959. Reprint. Woodstock, N.Y.: Overlook Press, 1973.

Greenberg, Clement. *Art and Culture: Critical Essays.* 1961. Reprint. Boston: Beacon Press, 1965.

Grimsted, David. *Melodrama Unveiled: American Theater and Culture, 1800–1850.* Chicago: University of Chicago Press, 1968.

Haring, Keith. *Keith Haring Journals.* New York: Penguin Books, 1996.

Harris, Neil. *Cultural Excursions: Marketing Appetites and Cultural Tastes in Modern America.* Chicago: University of Chicago Press, 1990.

Hofstadter, Richard. *Anti-Intellectualism in American Life.* New York: Alfred A. Knopf, 1963.

Hollander, Anne. *Moving Pictures.* New York: Alfred A. Knopf, 1989.

Hughes, Helen MacGill. *News and the Human Interest Story.* 1940. Reprint. New York: Greenwood Press, 1968.

Hughes, Robert. *American Visions: The Epic Story of Art in America.* New York: Alfred A. Knopf, 1997.

———. *Nothing if Not Critical: Selected Essays on Art and Artists.* New York: Alfred A. Knopf, 1990.

Huizinga, Johan. *Homo Ludens: A Study of the Play-Element in Culture.* 1950. Reprint. Boston: Beacon Press, 1955.

Huxtable, Ada Louise. *The Unreal America: Architecture and Illusion.* New York: New Press, 1997.

Jowett, Garth. *Film: The Democratic Art.* Boston: Little, Brown and Co., 1976.

Kael, Pauline. *Going Steady.* Boston: Little, Brown and Co., 1970; New York: Bantam, 1971.

Kernan, Alvin B., Peter Brooks, and J. Michael Holquist. *Man and His Fictions: An Introduction to Fiction-Making, Its Forms and Uses.* New York: Harcourt Brace Jovanovich, 1973.

Kessler, Judy. *Inside People: The Stories Behind the Stories.* New York: Villard Books, 1994.

Kluger, Richard. *The Paper: The Life and Death of the New York Herald Tribune.* New York: Alfred A. Knopf, 1986.

König, René. *A la Mode: On the Social Psychology of Fashion.* Translated by F. Bradley. New York: Seabury Press, 1973.

Kunstler, William. *The Minister and the Choir Singer: The Hall-Mills Murder Case.* New York: William Morrow and Co., 1964.

Lacour-Gayet, Robert. *Everyday Life in the United States Before the Civil War, 1830–1860.* Translated by Mary Ilford. New York: Frederick Ungar, 1969.

Lasch, Christopher. *The Culture of Narcissism: American Life in an Age of Diminishing Expectations.* New York: W. W. Norton, 1979.

Leach, William. *Land of Desire: Merchants, Power, and the Rise of a New American Culture.* New York: Pantheon, 1993.

Lears, Jackson. *Fables of Abundance: A Cultural History of Advertising in America*. New York: Basic Books, 1994.

Lears, T. J. Jackson, and Richard Wightman Fox, eds. *The Culture of Consumption: Critical Essays in American History, 1880–1980*. New York: Pantheon, 1983.

———. *The Power of Culture: Critical Essays in American History*. Chicago: University of Chicago Press, 1993.

Lessard, Suzannah. *The Architect of Desire: Beauty and Danger in the Stanford White Family*. New York: Dial Press, 1996.

Levine, Lawrence W. *Highbrow/Lowbrow: The Emergence of Cultural Hierarchy in America*. Cambridge, Mass.: Harvard University Press, 1988.

Lifton, Robert Jay. *The Protean Self: Human Resilience in an Age of Fragmentation*. New York: Basic Books, 1993.

Linderman, Gerald. *The Mirror of War: American Society and the Spanish American War*. Ann Arbor: University of Michigan Press, 1974.

Lindsay, Vachel. *The Art of the Moving Picture*. 1922. Reprint. New York: Liveright, 1970.

Lofaro, Michael A. *The Tall Tales of Davy Crockett: The Second Nashville Series of Crockett Almanacs, 1839–1841*. Knoxville: University of Tennessee Press, 1987.

Lowenthal, Leo. *Literature, Popular Culture, and Society*. 1961. Reprint. Palo Alto, Calif.: Pacific Books, 1968.

Lubow, Arthur. *The Reporter Who Would Be King: A Biography of Richard Harding Davis*. New York: Charles Scribner's Sons, 1992.

Lurie, Alison. *The Language of Clothes*. New York: Random House, 1981.

Macdonald, Dwight. *Against the American Grain: Essays on the Effects of Mass Culture*. New York: Random House, 1962.

Mailer, Norman. *Advertisements for Myself*. New York: Perigee, 1976.

———. *The Presidential Papers*. New York: G. P. Putnam's Sons, 1963.

Maland, Charles J. *Chaplin and American Culture: The Evolution of a Star Image*. Princeton, N.J.: Princeton University Press, 1989.

May, Larry. *Screening Out the Past: The Birth of Mass Culture and the Motion Picture Industry*. New York: Oxford University Press, 1980.

McGinniss, Joe. *The Selling of the President 1968*. New York: Trident Press, 1969.

McLuhan, Marshall. *Understanding Media: The Extensions of Man*. 2d edition. New York: McGraw-Hill, 1964.

Mills, C. Wright. *The Power Elite*. London: Oxford University Press, 1956.

———. *Power, Politics and People: The Collected Essays of C. Wright Mills*. Edited by Irving Louis Horowitz. New York: Oxford University Press, 1963.

Milton, Joyce. *The Yellow Kids: Foreign Correspondents in the Heyday of Yellow Journalism*. New York: Harper & Row, 1989.

Mitroff, Ian I., and Warren Bennis. *The Unreality Industry: The Deliberate Manufacturing of Falsehood and What It Is Doing to Our Lives.* New York: Birch Lane Press, 1989.

Moody, Richard. *The Astor Place Riot.* Bloomington: Indiana University Press, 1958.

Mott, Frank Luther. *American Journalism: A History, 1690–1960.* 3d edition. New York: Macmillan, 1962.

Munsterberg, Hugo. *The Photoplay: A Psychology Study.* 1915. Reprint. New York: Dover Publications, 1970.

Nasaw, David. *Going Out: The Rise and Fall of Public Amusements.* New York: Basic Books, 1993.

Nesbit, Evelyn. *Prodigal Days: The Untold Story.* New York: Julien Messner, Inc., 1934.

O'Brien, Geoffrey. *The Phantom Empire.* New York: W. W. Norton and Co., 1993.

Ortega y Gasset, José. *The Revolt of the Masses.* Translated and annotated by Anthony Kerrigan. Notre Dame, Ind.: University of Notre Dame Press, 1985.

Paglia, Camille. *Vamps and Tramps: New Essays.* New York: Vintage Books, 1994.

Parenti, Michael. *Make-Believe Media: The Politics of Entertainment.* New York: St. Martin's Press, 1992.

Peiss, Kathy. *Cheap Amusements: Working Women and Leisure in Turn-of-the-Century New York.* Philadelphia: Temple University Press, 1986.

Persons, Stow. *The Decline of American Gentility.* New York: Columbia University Press, 1973.

Pessen, Edward. *Jacksonian America: Society, Personality, Politics.* Revised edition. Urbana: University of Illinois Press, 1985.

———. *Riches, Class and Power Before the Civil War.* Lexington, Mass.: D. C. Heath and Co., 1973.

Poe, Edgar Allan. *Essays and Reviews.* New York: Library of America, 1984.

Postman, Neil. *Amusing Ourselves to Death: Public Discourse in the Age of Show Business.* New York: Viking Press, 1985.

Raeburn, John. *Fame Became of Him: Hemingway as Public Writer.* Bloomington: Indiana University Press, 1984.

Remini, Robert V. *The Life of Andrew Jackson.* New York: Penguin Books, 1988.

Remini, Robert V., ed. *The Age of Jackson.* Columbia: University of South Carolina Press, 1972.

Reynolds, David S. *Beneath the American Renaissance: The Subversive Imagination in the Age of Emerson and Melville.* New York: Alfred A. Knopf, 1988; Cambridge, Mass.: Harvard University Press, 1988.

———. *Walt Whitman's America: A Cultural Biography.* New York: Alfred A. Knopf, 1995.

Riesman, David, with Nathan Glazer and Reuel Denney. *The Lonely Crowd: A Study of the Changing American Character.* Abridged edition. New Haven, Conn.: Yale University Press, 1969.

Rogin, Michael Paul. *Ronald Reagan, the Movie and Other Episodes in Political Demonology.* Berkeley: University of California Press, 1987.

Rosenberg, Harold. *Art on the Edge: Creators and Situations.* New York: Macmillan Publishing Co., 1975.

Rourke, Constance. *The Roots of American Culture and Other Essays.* Edited by Van Wyck Brooks. New York: Harcourt, Brace and Co., 1942.

Royster, Charles. *The Destructive War: William Tecumseh Sherman, Stonewall Jackson, and the Americans.* New York: Alfred A. Knopf, 1991.

Ruland, Richard, and Malcolm Bradbury. *From Puritanism to Postmodernism: A History of American Literature.* New York: Viking Penguin, 1991.

Schell, Jonathan. *The Time of Illusion.* New York: Alfred A. Knopf, 1976.

Schick, Frank L. *The Paperbound Book in America.* New York: R. R. Bowker, 1958.

Schickel, Richard. *Intimate Strangers: The Culture of Celebrity.* Garden City, N.Y.: Doubleday and Co., 1985.

Schudson, Michael. *Discovering the News: A Social History of American Newspapers.* New York: Basic Books, 1978.

Sennett, Richard. *The Fall of Public Man: The Forces Eroding Public Life and Burdening the Modern Psyche with Roles It Cannot Perform.* New York: Alfred A. Knopf, 1977.

———. *Families Against the City: Middle-Class Homes of Industrial Chicago, 1872–1890.* Cambridge, Mass.: Harvard University Press, 1970.

Slotkin, Richard. *The Fatal Environment: The Myth of the Frontier in the Age of Industrialization, 1800–1890.* New York: Atheneum, 1985.

———. *Gunfighter Nation: The Myth of the Frontier in Twentieth-Century America.* New York: Atheneum, 1992.

———. *Regeneration Through Violence: The Mythology of the American Frontier, 1600–1860.* New York: Atheneum, 1973.

Smith, Henry Nash. *Democracy and the Novel: Popular Resistance to Classic American Writers.* New York: Oxford University Press, 1978.

Spoto, Donald. *A Passion for Life: The Biography of Elizabeth Taylor.* New York: HarperCollins, 1995.

Steiner, Wendy. *The Scandal of Pleasure.* Chicago: University of Chicago Press, 1995.

Stephens, Mitchell. *A History of the News: From the Drum to the Satellite.* New York: Viking Press, 1988.

Stevens, John D. *Sensationalism and the New York Press.* New York: Columbia University Press, 1991.

Sullivan, Mark. *Our Times: America at the Birth of the Twentieth Century.* Edited by Dan Rather. New York: Charles Scribner's Sons, 1995.

Susman, Warren I. *Culture as History: The Transformation of American Society in the Twentieth Century.* New York: Pantheon, 1984.

Swanberg, W. A. *Citizen Hearst.* New York: Charles Scribner's Sons, 1961.

———. *Pulitzer.* New York: Charles Scribner's Sons, 1967.

Taylor, Elizabeth. *Elizabeth Taylor: An Informal Memoir.* New York: Harper & Row, 1965.

Taylor, Shelley E. *Positive Illusions: Creative Self-Deception and the Healthy Mind.* New York: Basic Books, 1989.

Tocqueville, Alexis de. *Democracy in America.* New York: Everyman's Library, 1994.

Trollope, Frances. *Domestic Manners of the Americans.* 1832. Reprint. Edited by John Lauritz Larson. St. James, N.Y.: Brandywine Press, 1993.

Trow, George W. S. *Within the Context of No Context.* Boston: Little, Brown and Co., 1981.

Tucher, Andie. *Froth & Scum: Truth, Beauty, Goodness, and the Ax Murder in America's First Mass Medium.* Chapel Hill: University of North Carolina Press, 1994.

Turkle, Sherry. *Life on the Screen: Identity in the Age of the Internet.* New York: Simon & Schuster, 1995.

Twitchell, James B. *Carnival Culture: The Trashing of Taste in America.* New York: Columbia University Press, 1992.

Veblen, Thorstein. *The Theory of the Leisure Class.* 1899. Reprint, New York: Penguin Books, 1979.

Ward, John William. *Andrew Jackson: Symbol for an Age.* New York: Oxford University Press, 1955.

Warhol, Andy. *America.* New York: Harper & Row, 1985.

———. *The Philosophy of Andy Warhol (From A to B and Back Again).* New York: Harcourt Brace Jovanovich, 1975.

Weisberger, Bernard A. *They Gathered at the River: The Story of the Great Revivalists and Their Impact upon Religion in America.* Boston: Little, Brown and Co., 1958.

Weiss, John, ed. *The Origins of the Modern Consciousness.* Detroit: Wayne State University Press, 1965.

Whitman, Walt. *Complete Poetry and Collected Prose.* New York: Library of America, 1982.

Wolfe, Tom. *The Painted Word.* New York: Farrar, Straus & Giroux, 1975.

———. *The Purple Decades: A Reader.* New York: Farrar, Straus & Giroux, 1982.

Wood, Michael. *America in the Movies or "Santa Maria, It Had Slipped My Mind!"* New York: Basic Books, 1975; New York: Delta, 1975.

Zha Jianying. *China Pop: How Soap Operas, Tabloids, and Bestsellers Are Transforming a Culture.* New York: New Press, 1995.

Ziff, Larzer. *Literary Democracy: The Declaration of Cultural Independence in America.* New York: Viking Press, 1981.

Zurcher, Louis A., Jr. *The Mutable Self: A Self-Concept for Social Change.* Beverly Hills, Calif.: Sage Publications, 1977.

Acknowledgments

THIS BOOK BEGAN life as an idea formulated during a fellowship at the Freedom Forum Media Studies Center in New York, then under the directorship of Everette Dennis, to whom I owe the first of many debts of gratitude. It would have never evolved into an essay for the Sunday *New York Times* Arts and Leisure section were it not for the encouragement and generosity of Constance Rosenblum, then the section's editor. Its themes would not have been explored and amplified were it not for the opportunities provided over the years by the brilliant editor of the *Los Angeles Times* Opinion section, Allison Silver. And it would have never become a book were it not for the faith, the support, the enthusiasm and the nurture of my agent, Elaine Markson, for whom all superlatives are insufficient and any expression of gratitude inadequate.

Nor would this book have reached completion without the pioneers whose work energized and informed my own. Though I know all but one of them exclusively through their work, I owe them an enormous intellectual debt which I can only hope the book itself will partially repay: Daniel J. Boorstin, whose *The Image* remains a seminal work in the study of contemporary culture; Leo Braudy, whose *The Frenzy of Renown* is a dazzlingly encyclopedic tour through the history of fame; David Grimsted, whose *Melodrama Unveiled* explicates the themes of nineteenth-century cultural tension as well as any volume I know; Neil Postman, whose *Amusing Ourselves to Death* provocatively clarifies the effects of television on American society with great intelligence and wit; David S. Reynolds, whose *Beneath the American Renaissance* and *Walt Whitman's America* provide pathbreaking perspectives on American popular culture in the nineteenth century; and Richard Schickel, whose *Intimate Strangers* is simply, in my estimation, the single most important book on the subject of celebrity.

When I embarked on this project, I intended it as an interstitial book between doorstop-sized biographies of Walter Winchell and Walt Disney. After more than three years, it seems to have grown from interstitial to interminable. During this period, as I investigated and attempted to synthesize the materials, several dear friends of mine not only listened to me expatiate long beyond the point that politeness required of them but constantly contributed fresh insights. I shall always be grateful to them for their patience and for their interest: Elizabeth Bassine, Randye Lordon, Annemarie McCoy and David Suter. I am grateful too to Elizabeth, David and my old friend Charles Maland, at the University of Tennessee, for reading the manuscript and making thoughtful suggestions.

At the Amagansett Free Library, in the community in which I live and which I love, librarians Carleton Kelsey and Judith Wolfe filled my hundreds of requests for books with good humor and unflagging helpfulness above and beyond the call of duty. At Alfred A. Knopf, I am indebted to my editor, Jonathan Segal, for his keen scrutiny of the manuscript and for his championing of the book; to his assistant, Ida Giragossian, both for her assistance in things large and small and for caring so much; to Melvin Rosenthal for his loving attention to detail as production editor; to Cassandra Pappas for her elegant design; to Barbara de Wilde for the cover; and to Sonny Mehta, once again, for his belief in the value of this project. Finally, I owe my greatest debt to my wife, Christina, and to my children, who make all things worthwhile.

The book would not exist were it not for all these people, but to those readers who find it too entertaining to be taken seriously and to those who find it too serious to be entertaining, the fault is solely mine.

Index

Abdul, Paula, 166
academia, 139–42
Access Hollywood (television show), 98
Ace in the Hole (film), 81
Achille Lauro hijacking, 113
action painters, 132
Adair, Virginia Hamilton, 128
Adams, Eddie, 181
Adams, John Quincy, 28
Adatto, Kiku, 101, 106–7
Addams, Jane, 50–1, 57
Advertisements for Myself (Mailer), 125
Aesop, 99
aesthetics, personal, 206–11
Agassi, Andre, 206
"agritainment," 213
Ailes, Roger, 102, 107
Alberoni, Francesco, 168
Alexander, Jason, 176
Ah, Muhammad, 221
America in the Movies (Wood), 6
American Broadcasting Company
    (ABC), 82, 86, 94, 153, 154, 182, 222
American Committee, 35

American Renaissance, 13
American Telephone & Telegraph, 179
American Tragedy, An (Dreiser), 197
America's Funniest Home Videos
    (television show), 233
Amusing Ourselves to Death (Postman),
    55
Andersen, Kurt, 102
Anderson, Loni, 173
Angels in the Outfield (film), 118
Angelyne, 163n
Ants on the Melon (Adair), 128
archetypes, celebrities as, 169–73
architecture, 211–16
aristocracy, 41
    American antipathy to, 26–8, 40
    European, 22–3
Arnett, Peter, 83
Arnold, Matthew, 11–12
art, 16–20, 122–38
    nineteenth-century notions of, 15–16
    and rise of middle class, 23, 41–2
    sacralization of, 38–9
Art of the Comeback, The (Trump), 157

assassinations, 181, 182, 184–5
Association of Christian Schools
    International, 115
Astor Place Riot (1847), 33–7, 216–18
Atlantic Monthly, 15, 47, 54
audience
    behavior of, 32, 37
    class segregation of, 33–8
    for movies, 47–50
    nature of, 19
    for television newsmagazines, 87
Avedon, Richard, 229

Babilonia Tai, 166
Bachelor's Haven (television show), 162
Baker, Russell, 101–2
Banks, Russell, 226
Barbie doll, 210
Barbieri, Paula, 158
Barkley, Charles, 120
Barney's department store, 135
Barnum, P. T., 166–7
Barr, Roseanne, 166
Barrymore, Drew, 166
Barrymore, John, 146
Barth, Gunther, 66
Barzun, Jacques, 89
Basayev, Shamil, 83
baseball, 117–19
basketball, 117–20, 174–5
Basquiat, Jean-Michel, 135
Baudrillard, Jean, 208, 213, 214
Bazin, André, 58
Beatles, 133
Beatty, Warren, 167
Beecher, Henry Ward, 25
beer gardens, 37, 38, 42
Belkin, Lisa, 191
Bellah, Robert, 232
Bellow, Saul, 238
Ben & Jerry's ice cream, 202
Bender, Thomas, 212–13
Bennett, James Gordon, 62–7
Bennett, Michael, 186
Bennett, Tony, 131, 178
Bentsen, Lloyd, 105
Berle, Milton, 180
Berlin, Irving, 42
Berlin Wall, 84, 90–1
Berriz, Col., 67
Beuys, Joseph, 136

Beverly Hills Hotel, 212
Bierstadt, Albert, 14
Birthday Letters (Hughes), 128
black music, transmutation of, 42–3
Blown Away (film), 183
Bobbitt, Lorena and John Wayne, 161
body, aesthetics of, 209–11
bodybuilding, 210
Body of Evidence (film), 172
Book-of-the-Month Club, 122
book publishing, 122–31
Boorstin, Daniel, 3–5, 10, 53–5, 79, 96,
    136, 144, 146, 151, 160, 162, 164–6,
    202, 220, 221, 231
Bosnian civil war, 91
Boston University School for the Arts,
    176
Bowie, David, 136
boxing, 120
Boys Town (film), 113
Bradbury, Ray, 85
Braudy, Leo, 99, 125, 145, 164, 187
Bremer, Arthur, 181, 184–5
Bridges at Toko-Ri, The (film), 111
Bridges of Madison County, The
    (Waller), 129
Brinkley, Christie, 215
Brinkley, David, 109
Britain, nineteenth-century, 12
Broder, David, 104
Brokaw, Tom, 155, 182
Brooks, Van Wyck, 40
Brother Rat (film), 112
Brown, James, 121–2
Brown, Tina, 149–52, 156
Browning, Edward West, 77–8
Bryant, William Cullen, 71
Buchanan, Pat, 105
Buckley, William F., Jr., 139
Buddha, 174
Bullock, Alan, 225n
Bundy, Theodore, 184
Buntline, Ned, 35, 216–17
burlesque shows, 37, 42
Burnett, Carol, 196
Burton, Richard, 164, 165, 218
Bush, George, 104, 113–15
businessmen, celebrity, 156–8, 178–9
Buttafuoco, Joey, 159
Buttafuoco, Mary Jo, 5
Byron, George Gordon, Lord, 124

Cable News Network (CNN), 82, 83, 104, 191
Calhoun, John C., 99
California Angels baseball team, 118
Callithumpians, 27
Calvinism, 22
campaigns, presidential, 99–100, 102–8
Campbell, Joseph, 170, 171, 173
Cannon, Lou, 109, 110
Canon cameras, 206
Capra, Frank, 7
caricatures, celebrity, 221–2
Carmichael, Stokely, 139
Carnegie, Andrew, 156
Carnegie, Dale, 197
carnival culture, 9
Carroll, Lewis, 6
Carson, Johnny, 181, 188
Carter, Bill, 155
Castle, Vernon and Irene, 42
Catcher in the Rye, The (Salinger), 184
Catholic Church, 121–2
Ceauçescu, Nicolai, 150
celebrities, 7–8, 143–91
  academic, 140–2
  as authors, 126–7
  biographies of, 130–1
  criminals as, 180–5
  desire of ordinary Americans to become, 186–91
  in magazines, 147–51
  as mythic figures, 169–74
  newspaper coverage of, 89
  paintings by, 131
  personal identities of, 216–23
  product endorsements by, 201
  profusion of, 156–60
  self-created, 160–8
  television interviews with, 151–6
  value bestowed on, 176–81
  Warhol's paintings of, 134
  worship of, 173–6
  see also stars
Celebrity, The (Churchill), 177
Celestine Prophecy, The (Redfield), 130
Chaplin, Charlie, 48, 221
Chapman, Mark David, 181, 184
Chaucer, Geoffrey, 124
Chayefsky, Paddy, 83

Chechnya, 83
Cher, 148
Chernomyrdin, Viktor 5., 83, 115n
Chicago Cubs baseball team, 118
Chicago Tribune, 72, 118
China, 30n
  Nixon in, 109
Chopra, Deepak, 130
Christianity, 23
Chrysler Corporation, 156
Chung, Connie, 84, 153
Church, Frederic, 12, 14, 29
Churchill, Winston, 177
Cicero, Marcus Tullius, 99
Civil War, 64
Civilization and Its Discontents (Freud), 241–2
Clancy, Tom, 128
Clark, Marcia, 158
classical music, 14
Clay, Andrew Dice, 150
Clay, Henry, 99
Cleopatra (film), 164
Clinton, Bill, 5, 92–4, 102, 115, 166n
Cobain, Kurt, 175
Coca-Cola Corporation, 202
Cochran, Johnnie, 158
Cody, William F. "Buffalo Bill," 13, 216–17, 221
Cole, Thomas, 14, 29
Collier's magazine, 145
Collins, Joan, 127
Columbia Broadcasting System (CBS), 82, 84, 88, 152, 158, 182
Columbia Pictures, 214–15
Columbian Exposition (1893), 38
commercials, 198, 204, 206
  political, 103–4
communism, collapse of, 84, 90
conspicuous consumption, 203–4
consumption, interaction of entertainment and, 199–205
Cook, Philip J., 179
Cook, Robin, 128
Coolidge, Calvin, 205
Cops (television show), 85
Cosio y Cisneros, Evangelina, 67–8
Coupland, Douglas, 129
Couric, Katie, 155
Court-TV, 85

crime pamphlets, 13
crime reporting
  in penny press, 61–3
  in tabloids, 74–7
criminals
  celebrity of, 180–5, 190–1
  videotapes of, 234
Crossfire (television show), 139
Crowninshield, Frank, 56–7, 149
Cruise, Tom, 169, 171, 172
Culture of Narcissism, The (Lasch),
  228

Dahmer, Jeffrey, 180
Dale, Alan, 66
Darden, Christopher, 158, 176
Dateline (television show), 155
Davis, Richard Harding, 69, 84 Day,
  Benjamin, 59, 62
debates, televised, 105–6
deconstructionism, 10, 227
Delsarte System, 195, 196
democracy, cultural, 28–31
  movies and, 47–8
  newspapers and, 63
  theatricality and, 194
Democratic Party, 63, 91, 104, 105, 107,
  166
DeNiro, Robert, 188
department stores, 199–200
designer publishing, 126
Detroit News, 48
Diana, Princess, 5, 7, 85, 148, 153n, 169,
  174, 175
Dickens, Charles, 63
Dickinson, Emily, 12
Didion, Joan, 104, 105
Diebenkorn, Richard, 12
dime novels, 13–15, 17, 35, 42
Dinesen, Isak, 238
Disney Company, 118, 213n, 214
Disneyland and Disney World, 201,
  211–14
Donahue, Phil, 190n
Douglas, Kirk, 81
Dreiser, Theodore, 197
Dryden, John, 124
Du Bois, W. E. B., 198–9
Dukakis, Kitty, 166
Dukakis, Michael, 104, 107, 166
Dunaway, Faye, 83

E! cable channel, 98
East, Nick, 186
Eastwood, Clint, 113
Eco, Umberto, 10, 20–1, 214
economics of celebrity, 179
Edison, Thomas Alva, 49, 156
Edmundson, Mark, 138–9, 168
education, 138–9
Einstein, Albert, 221
Eisenhower, Dwight D., 99
Eisner, Michael, 214n
elocution, 195
Emerson, Ralph Waldo, 12
empowerment, popular culture as
  instrument of, 46, 56, 168
endorsements, celebrity, 201
Entertainment Revolution, 56
Entertainment Tonight (television
  show), 98
Era of the Common Man, 30
Ernani (Verdi), 33
Erotica (album), 172
ESPN, 82
Esquire magazine, 170, 186
evangelicalism, 24–5, 120
Evreinoff, Nicolas, 193, 219, 230
Ewen, Stuart, 186
exercise, 210
externalization, modes of, 195–7

Fahrenheit 451 (Bradbury), 85
Fall of Public Man, The (Sennett), 99,
  193, 228
Fallows, James, 101
Faludi, Susan, 186, 220
fame, 143–4
  see also celebrities
farms, "agritainment" 213
fashion industry, 206–8
Ferguson, Sarah, 148
fiction, challenge of reality to, 3
films, *see* movies
Finch, Peter, 83
Fish, Stanley, 140
Fisher, Eddie, 164, 165
Fitzgerald, F. Scott, 197
Flowers, Gennifer, 91–4
football, 117–20
Forbes, Malcolm, 156
Ford, Harrison, 150
Ford, Henry, 156

Forrest, Edwin, 33–6, 37n
Fortune magazine, 214n
Founding Fathers, 143–4
France, nineteenth-century, 12
Frank, Robert H., 179
French Revolution, 26
Frenzy of Renown, The (Braudy),
  164
Freud, Sigmund, 241–2
Fuhrman, Mark, 158
Fukuyama, Francis, 141

Gabor, Zsa Zsa, 161–3, 167, 198, 218,
  219
Gamson, Joshua, 163n
Gap, The, 135–6
Garland, Judy, 184
Gates, Henry Louis, Jr., 140
Gates, William, 156
Gauvreau, Emile, 77–8
George (magazine), 117
Gergen, Kenneth, 227–9, 233
Germany, nineteenth-century, 12
Gibson, Jane, 76–77
Gilded Age, 211
Gingrich, Newt, 113
glamour, political, 99–100
globalization of markets, 179
Globe (tabloid), 92
Godiva chocolates, 202
Godkin, E. L., 54, 69
Goethe, Johann Wolfgang von, 16,
  165
Goffman, Erving, 224–5
Going Native (Wright), 226
Goldberger, Paul, 199
Goldhagen, Daniel Jonah, 141
Goodman, Walter, 84
Gorbachev, Mikhail, 110
Gore, Albert, 116n
Grandma Moses, 131
Grant, Cary, 219, 220
Grant, Hugh, 168
Graphic Revolution, 53–6
Graves, Michael, 214
Gray, Judd, 77
Great Gatsby, The (Fitzgerald), 197–8
Greeley, Horace, 64
Greenberg, Clement, 19
Gretsky, Wayne, 120
Guber, Peter, 214–15

Guldensuppe, Willie, 67
Gulf War, 7, 82, 85, 113–14

Hall-Mills murder case, 74–7
Hamilton, Alexander, 144
Hammer, Armand, 156
Hard Rock Cafe, 216
Harding, Tonya, 84, 89, 95, 161
Haring, Keith, 133–5
Harper's Magazine, 77, 198
Harris, Neil, 137
Harrison, Jonathan Baxter, 17
Hart, Gary, 91, 92
Hawk & Buzzard (newspaper), 59
Hawke, Ethan, 129, 178
Hawthorne, Nathaniel, 13, 14
Hearst, William Randolph, 66–9, 71, 72,
  74, 94
Heat (film), 184n
Heenan, Frances "Peaches," 78
Hefner, Hugh, 139
Held, Ann, 66
Hemingway, Ernest, 124–6, 171n, 197,
  221
Hemingway, Margaux, 171n
Hero with a Thousand Faces, The
  (Campbell), 170
Hewitt, Don, 82
Hilton, Conrad, 162, 163
Hilton, Nicky, 163
Hirsch/Bedner hotel design firm, 212
Hirst, Damien, 136
Hitchcock, Alfred, 100
Hitler, Adolf, 109n, 225n
hockey, 118, 120
Hoffman, Abbie, 139
Hofstadter, Richard, 26
Hoizer, Jenny, 178
Home Journal, 36
homemaking, aesthetics of, 208–9
Homo Ludens (Huizinga), 20, 193
Hope, Bob, 221
Horton Plaza (San Diego), 213
Horvat, Janos, 90
House Beautiful, 209
*How to Win Friends and Influence
  People* (Carnegie), 197
Hughes, Robert, 86–7, 137, 213
Hughes, Ted, 128
Huizinga, Johan, 20, 193
human interest stories, 60

Hurrell (photographer), 181
Huston, Anjelica, 150
Huxtable, Ada Louise, 213

Iacocca, Lee, 156
ideas, entertainment value of, 138–42
identity, theories of, 223–30
illusions, positive, 239
Illustrated Daily News, 72–3, 76, 77
Image, The (Boorstin), 3, 10, 79, 96,
    164–5, 202, 220
immigration, 44
In Style magazine, 215
Infinite Jest (Wallace), 123, 243
inner-directed individuals, 224
intellectuals, 20–1, 139–42
interior design, 215
International House (film), 161
Internet, 94, 235–6
interviews, celebrity, 151–6
Intimate Strangers (Schickel), 174
Iraq, *see* Gulf War
Isabell, Robert, 158–9

Jackson, Andrew, 28–30, 40
Jackson, Cindy, 210
Jackson, Michael, 116, 154, 161, 169, 174,
    222–3
Jacksonianism, 32, 46, 48, 59
James, Caryn, 153
James, Henry, 58
Jammer, Cal, 190
Jarrell, Randall, 168
Jerde, Jon, 213–14
Jesus, 174
Jewett, Helen, 61–3, 76
John, Elton, 175
John Paul II, Pope, 121–2
Johnson, Philip, 221
Jones, Samuel Porter, 25
Jordan, Michael, 120, 174–5, 200, 221
journalism, *see* newspapers
Joyce, Peggy Hopkins, 161
Judson, E. Z. C., *see* Buntline, Ned

Kaczynski, Theodore, 183, 230–1
Kael, Pauline, 31, 57, 237
Kaelin, Kato, 77, 158
Kakutani, Michiko, 226
Kant, Immanuel, 58
Keaton, Buster, 237

Kelley, Kitty, 130–1
Kennedy, John F., 91, 100, 105, 108, 110,
    180, 182
Kennedy, John F., Jr., 116–17
Kennedy, Joseph P., 100
Kent, Arthur, 83
Kerrigan, Nancy, 84, 89, 95, 161
Khomeini, Ayatollah Rhuhollah, 127
Kiam, Victor, 156
Kidman, Nicole, 171, 188–9
King, Larry, 153, 155
King, Martin Luther, Jr., 12
King of Comedy, The (film), 188
Klein, Joe, 104
Knapp brothers, 13
Kondracke, Morton, 111
Koons, Ciccolina, 136
Koons, Jeff, 133, 135, 136, 180
Korda, Michael, 126
Kostabi, Mark, 134
Kramer, Hilton, 137
Kramer, Michael, 104
Kravis, Henry, 156
Kuwait, *see* Gulf War

labor conditions, change in, 45
Lacan, Jacques, 221, 228
Lack, Andrew, 155
Lady of the Orchids, The (play), 161
Lane, Kenneth Jay, 180
Lang, Fritz, 167
Language of Clothes, The (Lurie), 206
Lasch, Christopher, 228
Late Show with David Letterman, The,
    116, 189
Lauren, Ralph, 199, 202, 207–8
Lawrence, Florence, 144
Lazar, Irving "Swifty," 127
Lears, Jackson, 204
Leary, Timothy, 5, 139, 141
Lee, Robert E., 64
Leggett, William, 26–7
Leithauser, Brad, 122
Lennon, John, 181, 184, 242
Lennon, Thomas, 87
Leno, Jay, 115–16
Lentricchia, Frank, 140
Levine, Lawrence W., 38
Lewinsky, Monica S., 94
Lewis, Jerry, 166, 188
Lieberman, Alexander, 148

life coaches, 232
Life magazine, 148, 162
lifestyle enclaves, 232
Lifton, Robert Jay, 225–7, 229, 238
Lilly, Doris, 156
Lincoln, Abraham, 12
Lindbergh, Charles, 201
Lindbergh kidnapping, 6
Lindsay, Vachel, 46
Lippard, George, 13, 14, 17
Lippincott, J. Gordon, 202
Lippmann, Walter, 78–9
literacy, 29
literature, *see* novels
Lonely Crowd, The (Riesman), 224
Longo, Robert, 136n
Los Angeles Police Department, 158
Los Angeles Times, 90
Lowe, Rob, 166
Lowell, Robert, 12
Loy, Myrna, 219, 220
Luddites, 243
Lurie, Alison, 206
Lyrical Ballads (Wordsworth), 17

Maass, Peter, 91
Macbeth (Shakespeare), 33
Macdonald, Dwight, 15, 19, 30, 41, 42, 124, 145
macguffins, 100, 119, 123
Macready, William Charles, 33–6, 218
Mademoiselle magazine, 129
Madonna, 116, 148, 166–7, 172
magazines
    celebrities and, 147–51, 155–6
    illustrated, 53, 54
    shelter, 215
    see also specific publications
Mailer, Norman, 100, 125–6, 139, 178, 220
Maine (battleship), 68
Mall of America (Minnesota), 201, 213
Mallarmé, Stephane, 4
Mandi, Alex J., 179
Mann, Michael, 184n
Mansfield, Irving, 126
Mantle, Mickey, 166
manufactured reality, theory of, 10
Marden, Orison Swett, 197
markets, globalization of, 179
Martin Dressler (Millhauser), 211

Marx, Karl, 9, 17
Masterful Personality (Marden), 197
Maynard, Joyce, 129–30
Mazur, Paul, 199
McCarthy, Mary, 139
McCartney, Paul, 181
Mcclatchy, J. D., 128
McClure, Jessica, 191
McGinniss, Joe, 102
McInerney, Jay, 170, 186
McKinley, William, 68, 71
McLaughlin Group, The (television show), 139
McLuhan, Marshall, 10, 55–6, 141, 179, 195–6, 220
McNichol, Kristy, 166
Mcveigh, Timothy, 181–4
media determinism, 10
megamalls, 200–1, 213
Melville, Herman, 13
Menand, Louis, 145, 196
Mencken, H. L., 199
Mephisto shoes, 202
Method acting, 111, 219, 229
Metro-Goldwyn-Mayer (MGM), 111, 163, 215
Metropolis (film), 167
Miami Herald, 92
Microsoft, 156
    Windows 95, 202
Midcult, 41–6, 52
middle class
    emergence of, 23, 26, 33, 37, 38, 40–3
    movies and, 47–9, 51
    reformism in, 43–4, 49
    self-presentation of, 194–5
Mighty Ducks, The (film), 118
Mike Douglas Show, The, 102
Miles, Jack, 130
Milken, Michael, 156
Millhauser, Steven, 211, 212
Milli Vanilli, 198
Mills, C. Wright, 177
Milton, John, 124
Minnelli, Liza, 188
minstrel shows, 27, 28
Mitchell, Maj. John, 13
modern art, 130–8
Mondale, Walter, 105
Monroe, Marilyn, 134, 175
Montaigne, Michel Eyquem de, 237

Montana, Joe, 120
Moody, Dwight Lyman, 25
Moore, Mary Tyler, 166
Morris, Dick, 107
Moses, 173–4
Motion Picture Patents Company, 49
Motion Picture World, 47, 50
movies, 31, 46–52, 237–40
    acting style in, 218–19
    big-budget special effects, 17
    criminals and, 183–4
    fashion and, 207, 208
    newspapers and, 71–4, 79
    and modes of externalization, 195–7
    politics and, 110–14
    pornographic, 219–20
    self-created celebrities in, 161, 162
    shared experiences provided by, 57–8,
        168
    sports and, 118, 120
    star system in, 144–6
    see also specific films
Moyers, Bill, 87
MTV, 17
Mumford, Lewis, 211
Munsterberg, Hugo, 50
Murphy, Eddie, 168–9
Murray, Charles, 141
Murrow, Edward R., 152, 154
museums, 137–8
music
    nineteenth-century, 14, 17
    rock, 121, 175, 198
    tie-ins of books and, 129–30
Muslims, 127
myths, celebrity, 169–74

Nack, Augusta, 67
Napoleon, Emperor of France, 99
narcissism, 228
Nathan, George Jean, 39, 199
Nation, 69, 83
National Broadcasting Company
    (NBC), 82, 83, 118, 124, 152, 155,
    182
National Enquirer, 92, 116
National Hockey League, 118
nativism, 35
Navy Pier (Chicago), 212
Nazis, 6, 109n, 225n
    American, 139

Nesbit, Evelyn, 147
Network (film), 83–4
Neufeld, Peter, 158
New Grub Street (Gissing), 124
New Orleans, Battle of, 28
New Passages (Sheehy), 231
New York American, 76
New York Daily Graphic, 73n, 77–8
New York Daily Mirror, 72–3, 75, 76
New York Evening Post, 27
New York Herald, 61–4, 72, 217
New York Journal, 66–72
New York magazine, 104
New York Mirror, 32
New York Sun, 59, 62
New York Times, 54, 69–70, 72, 76, 79,
    84, 89–92, 117, 126, 153, 154, 158,
    183, 191, 200, 213
    Book Review, 149
    Magazine, 141
New York Tribune, 34, 35, 64, 72
New York World, 65–7, 69, 71, 72,
    74, 77
New Yorker, The, 102, 118, 121, 128, 141,
    156, 177, 186, 220
Newsday, 89
newsmagazines, television, 86–7
    celebrity interviews on, 154
newspapers, 5, 29, 34, 59–79
    celebrities and, 155
    criminals and, 182, 183
    early-nineteenth-century, 59–65
    photographs in, 54
    tabloid, *see* tabloids
    television and, 86, 88–93
    yellow, 65–72
    see also specific newspapers
newsreels, 80
Newsweek, 94, 181–2
Nichols, Mike, 161, 166
nickelodeons, 46, 48
Nietzsche, Friedrich, 219, 225n
Nike athletic shoe and apparel
    company, 174, 200
Nirvana (rock group), 175
Nixon, Richard, 102–3, 106, 108–10,
    166n, 181, 184
North, Oliver, 104–5
novels, 122–30
    nineteenth-century, 13, 14, 17, 42
    see also specific works

O'Brien, Geoffrey, 57, 58, 196
Obst, Lynda, 214–15
Ochs, Adolph, 69, 76, 92
O'Donnell, Robert, 191
O'Hair, Madalyn Murray, 139
Oklahoma City bombing, 5, 84, 181
Olivier, Laurence, 229
Olympic Games, 89, 118–19, 124
Onassis, Jacqueline Kennedy, 134, 180, 181
O'Neal, Shaquille, 120
O'Neill, Tip, 110
opera, 14, 29
Orlan, 210, 221
Ortega y Gasset, José, 21, 238
Oswald, Lee Harvey, 182
other-directed individuals, 224, 231
Our Hitler (film), 109
Out of Africa (film), 207
Outcault, R. F., 66n

Paglia, Camille, 140–1
Palmer, Michael, 128
Pan-American Exposition (1901), 71
paperback books, 122
Paramount Pictures, 68
Park, Robert E., 59, 65, 74
pastiche personality, 227
Patterson, Joseph Medill, 72
Pauley, Jane, 153
Payne, Philip, 72–3
Peachtree Center (Atlanta), 212
penny press, 5, 34, 59–65, 66n, 67, 69
People magazine, 142, 148–51, 159, 165, 169, 174, 184, 222
Person to Person (television show), 152, 154
Peters, Jon, 214–15
Philadelphia Public Ledger, 36–7
photographs, 44, 53–4
  of celebrities, 147, 151
  and sense of self, 195–6
  in tabloids, 72–5
Picasso, Pablo, 19, 132, 178
Pickford, Mary, 48, 144
Planet Hollywood, 216
plastic surgery, 210, 222
Plath, Sylvia, 128
Plato, 21
Playboy magazine, 158
Plutarch, 99

Poe, Edgar Allan, 19n, 64
poetry, 124, 128
politics, adoption of show business stratagems in, 99–117
Pollock, Jackson, 132
Pope, Alexander, 124
pornography, 219–20
  nineteenth-century, 13
positive illusions, 239
Postman, Neil, 54–6, 98, 123, 204, 242
postmodernism, 10
Power, Tyrone, 218
presidency
  campaigns of candidates for, 102–8
  media coverage of, 100–2, 108–17
President Reagan: The Role of a Lifetime (Cannon), 109
Presley, Elvis, 43, 134, 175, 219, 222
Presley, Gladys, 219
Presley, Lisa Marie, 222
Pretty Woman (film), 172
Price, Raymond, 103
Prime Time (television show), 154
Prince, 222
print media, *see* magazines; newspapers
Prinze, Freddie, 190
products, celebritized, 201–3
Progressivism, 49, 211
"protean self," 226–7
Protestantism, 38
  evangelical, 24–5, 120
Prozac, 243
Prozac Nation (Wurtzel), 130
Pryor, Richard, 221–2
pseudo-events, 96–7, 107, 136
Public Broadcasting System, 80
public relations, 96–7, 109, 135–6, 160
publishing industry, 122–31
Pulitzer, Joseph, 65–8, 71, 72, 74
Puritans, 23, 197
Pynchon, Thomas, 160

Quaker City, The (Lippard), 13, 14
Quayle, Dan, 105

radio, 76, 79–80, 151–2
ragtime, 42
Random House, 127
Rather, Dan, 84, 88, 182
"Raven, The" (Poe), 19n

Ray-Ban sunglasses, 202
Reagan, Nancy, 111
Reagan, Ronald, 7, 105, 109–16, 121,
    166n, 198
Rebel Without a Cause (film), 196
Redfield, James, 130
religion, 22–6, 120–2, 238
    celebrity and, 173–6
Remington Corporation, 156
Remnick, David, 88, 118
Renaissance, 23
Repin, Ilya, 19
Republican Party, 104, 105, 107, 113
Resnick, Faye, 84
restaurants, theme, 216
retailing, 199–205
Rich, Frank, 127, 154, 155
Riesman, David, 99–100, 103, 205,
    223–4
riots, nineteenth-century, 27–8, 33–7
RKO, 100
Roberts, Julia, 169, 172
Roberts, Oral, 120
Robertson, Pat, 120
Robinson, Richard P., 61–3, 75
rock music, 121, 175, 198
Rockefeller, John D., 156
Rockwell, George Lincoln, 139
Rockwell, Norman, 132, 209
Rodman, Dennis, 120
Rogin, Michael Paul, 241
Rolling Stone magazine, 87
Rollins, Ed, 107
Roman Catholic Church, 121–2
Roosevelt, Franklin Delano, 109
Roosevelt, Theodore, 99
Roscius, 99
Rosenbaum, Ron, 175
Rosenberg, Harold, 133, 136
Roth, Joe, 172
Roth, Philip, 3–5, 243
Rourke, Constance, 194
Rule of the Bone (Banks), 226
Ruscha, Ed, 135
Rushdie, Salman, 127–8

Saatchi, Charles, 177–8
sacralization, 38–9
Saddam Hussein, 113, 114
Saget, Bob, 233
Salinger, J. D., 160, 184

Salle, David, 136n
saloons, 37, 38, 42
Salvi, John C., III, 183
Sanders, Deion, 119–20
Sanders, George, 162, 218
Satanic Verses, The (Rushdie), 127
Saturated Self, The (Gergen), 227
Saturday Evening Post, 145, 148
Saturday Night Fever (film), 196
savings-and-loan scandals, 90
Sawyer, Diane, 153, 154, 182
scandals, political, 101
Schabowski, Günter, 90
Schapiro, Robert, 158
Scheck, Barry, 158
Schell, Jonathan, 108
Schiavone, Nicholas, 118–19
Schickel, Richard, 73, 100, 143, 144,
    174
Schnabel, Julian, 135, 136n, 178
Schudson, Michael, 60, 70
Schumpeter, Joseph, 9
Schwarzenegger, Arnold, 136
Scorsese, Martin, 188, 189
Scott, George C., 181
self, celebritized, 216–23
Selling of the President, The
    (McGinniss), 102
Senate, U.S., 104
Sennett, Mack, 48
Sennett, Richard, 42, 51, 99, 103, 193,
    206, 217, 228, 229
Serrano, Andres, 136
Sesame Street (television show), 138
Sessums, Kevin, 171, 172
700 Club (television show), 120
Sex (Madonna), 172
Shakespeare, William, 13, 29, 33,
    124
Shampoo (film), 196
Shaw, Knowles, 25
Sheehy, Gail, 231
shelter magazines, 215
Shepard, Sam, 220
Sherlock, Jr. (film), 237
Sherman, Cindy, 136n
shopping malls, 200–1, 213
Show Business Today (television show),
    98
Shultz, George, 110
Simmons, Richard, 159

Simon, John, 139
Simonson, Lee, 137
Simpson, O. J., 5, 76, 82, 84, 93, 95, 155, 158, 176, 186, 196, 220
Sinatra, Frank, 131
Sischy, Ingrid, 172
Skelton, Red, 131
Slotkin, Richard, 169, 217
Smith, Henry Nash, 15–16
Smith, William Kennedy, 91
Snyder, Mark, 241
Snyder, Ruth, 77
Sobek, Linda, 159
Sony Corporation, 201
Sotheby's auction house, 138n, 180
sound bites
    intellectual, 141
    political, 101
Sousa, John Philip, 14
South Street Seaport (New York), 212
Spanish-American War, 68, 71
Spenser, Edmund, 124
sports, 117–20
Spy magazine, 155
Stallone, Sylvester, 169, 171–2
Stanislavsky, Konstantin, 111, 229
Star (tabloid), 92
"Star Wars" antimissile system, 113
Starr, Kenneth, 94
Starr, Ringo, 166
stars, 7
    artists as, 135–6
    literary, 123–30
    ministers as (nineteenth century), 26
    movie, 144–6
    news anchors as, 84–5
    political, 100
    reporters as, 69, 83, 84
    sports, 119–21
    theatricality of lives of, 218
    see also celebrities
Steiner, Wendy, 242
Stewart, Martha, 8, 208–9
Stolley, Richard, 148–9
Stryker, Jeff, 219–21
suicides, celebrity, 190, 191
Sulloway, Frank, 141
Sun Also Rises, The (Hemingway), 197
supermarket tabloids, 92, 116
superstar, origin of term, 160
Susann, Jacqueline, 126, 187

Susman, Warren I., 51, 197, 223
Swaggart, Jimmy, 120
Swanberg, W. A., 67
Syberberg, Hans Jürgen, 109n

tabloids, 72–9
    convergence of respectable press and, 91–3
    politicians in, 116
    television and, 80–2
talk shows, television
    daytime exploitation, 189–90
    intellectuals on, 139
    politicians on, 116
Talma (actor), 99
Taylor, Elizabeth, 5, 6, 148, 150, 163–8, 181, 217, 19, 222
Taylor, Shelley E., 239–41
television, 17–18, 186
    advertising on, *see* commercials
    celebrity interviews on, 151–6
    and change in consciousness, 55–6
    criminals on, 182, 183
    news on, 80–95
    newspapers and, 88–92
    ordinary people on, 187–90, 233–4
    politics and, 99–107, 115–16
    presentation of ideas on, 139
    religion and, 120
    self-created celebrities on, 162
    sense of community provided by, 168
    show business news on, 98
    sports on, 118–20
term papers, customized, 198–9
Thackeray, William Makepeace, 151
Thaw, Harry K., 147
theater
    nineteenth-century, 13–14, 17, 27, 29, 32–9, 48
    politics and, 99
    religious prohibitions on, 22–4
theatricality
    architectural, 211–12
    social, 193–4
Theory of the Leisure Class, The (Veblen), 203
Thernstrom, Abigail, 141
Thernstrom, Stephan, 141
Thomas, Theodore, 17
Thompson, Gordon, III, 200
Thoreau, Henry David, 13

Time magazine, 148
To Die For (film), 188–9
Tobin, Colm, 121
Tocqueville, Alexis de, 17, 23, 26, 30, 59
Today show, 152
Todd, Michael, 164
Tonight Show, The, 120
Top Gun (film), 196
Townsend, Rosina, 61, 62
"traditional values," 111
transcendence, "easy," 168
transfiguration, 204
Travolta, John, 148
Treleaven, Harry, 102
Trevor-Roper, Hugh, 225n
Trollope, Frances, 11, 25, 32
trophy wives, 233
Trow, George W. S., 185–6
Truman Show (film), 85–6, 230
Trump, Donald, 157–8, 233
Trump, Ivana, 157–8
Trump, Ivanka, 158
Truth or Dare (film), 167
Turkle, Sherry, 235
Turner, Lana, 218
Turner, Ted, 156
Twain, Mark, 99
20/20 (television show), 86–7, 154
Tyson, Mike, 120

Unabomber, 183, 230–1
Uncle Tom's Cabin (Stowe), 14
universities, 139–42
    term papers in, 198–9
University of Virginia, 139
Updike, John, 12
Us magazine, 169
U.S. News & World Report, 104
USA Today, 88, 89

Valley of the Dolls (Susann), 126
Van Buren, Martin, 63
Vanity Fair magazine
    original, 56–7, 148, 149
    resurrected, 141, 146, 149–51, 153–6,
        158–9, 169, 171–2, 176, 203
vaudeville, 37, 38, 42, 46
Veblen, Thorstein, 203, 204
Verdi, Giuseppe, 33
Verdict, The (film), 196
Versace, Gianni, 180

Vidal, Gore, 139
video camera, 233–5
Vietnam war, 109, 113
Village Voice, 135
"virtual reality," 58
visual arts, 131–8
    nineteenth-century, 14, 29
Vogue magazine, 133
Vuarnet sunglasses, 202

Wag the Dog (film), 113
Wainwright, Col. Charles S., 64
Wallace, David Foster, 123, 243
Wallace, George, 181, 185
Wailer, Robert James, 129
Walters, Barbara, 152–5, 182, 183
War of 1812, 28
WarGames (film), 111
Warhol, Andy, 133–6, 141, 160, 180,
        182–3, 187, 212, 220–1, 223, 230
Warner, Susan, 13, 14, 62
Warner Bros., 130
Washington Post, 90, 91, 104, 183, 221
Watergate scandal, 101
Watkins, Paul, 129
Webster, Daniel, 27, 99
West, Cornel, 140
West Edmonton Mall (Alberta,
        Canada), 201
Where Love Goes (Maynard), 130
Whipple, Edwin Percy, 17
White, Capt. Joseph, 13
White, Stanford, 147, 211, 212, 213
Whitman, Walt, 13, 25, 32, 46, 124, 194
Wide, Wide World, The (Warner), 13, 14
Wilder, Billy, 80
Willis, Bruce, 170, 172, 173, 186
Willocks, Tim, 129
Wilson, Edmund, 125
Wilson, Robert, 138n
Winchell, Walter, 151, 152, 156
Windsors (British royal family), 130–1
Winfrey, Oprah, 5, 169
Wing and a Prayer, A (film), 111
Winner-Take-All Society, The (Cook and
        Frank), 179
Within the Context of No Context
        (Trow), 185–6
Wolf, Naomi, 141
Wolfe, Tom, 187, 206, 228n
Wood, Michael, 6

Wordsworth, William, 17
World Series, 117
World War I, 201
World War II, 111, 113, 114, 152
Wright, Stephen, 226
Wurtzel, Elizabeth, 130

Yeats, William Butler, 9
yellow press, 5, 65–72
Yeltsin, Boris, 115n

Zindler, Marvin, 85
Zukor, Adolph, 68

A Note About the Author

Neal Gabler is the author of *An Empire of Their Own: How the Jews Invented Hollywood,* for which he won the Los Angeles Times Book Prize for History, and *Winchell: Gossip, Power and the Culture of Celebrity,* which was a finalist for the National Book Critics Circle Award and was named the nonfiction book of the year by *Time* magazine. Mr. Gabler holds advanced degrees in film and American culture and has been a recipient of a Freedom Forum and a Guggenheim Foundation fellowship.

Mr. Gabler was born in Chicago and lives with his wife and two daughters in Amagansett, New York.

A Note on the Type

This book was set in Fairfield, the first typeface from the hand of the distinguished American artist and engraver Rudolph Ruzicka (1883–1978). In its structure Fairfield displays the sober and sane qualities of the master craftsman whose talent has long been dedicated to clarity. It is this trait that accounts for the trim grace and vigor, the spirited design and sensitive balance, of this original typeface.

Rudolph Ruzicka was born in Bohemia and came to America in 1894. He set up his own shop, devoted to wood engraving and printing, in New York in 1913 after a varied career working as a wood engraver, in photoengraving and banknote printing plants, and as an art director and free-lance artist. He designed and illustrated many books, and was the creator of a considerable list of individual prints: wood engravings, line engravings on copper, and aquatints.

Composed by Dix,
Syracuse, New York
Printed and bound by R. R. Donnelley & Sons,
Harrisonburg, Virginia
Designed by Cassandra J. Pappas